MARANATHA
OUR LORD, COME!

A Definitive Study
of the Rapture of the Church

MARANATHA OUR LORD, COME!

A Definitive Study
of the Rapture of the Church

Renald E. Showers

The Friends of Israel Gospel Ministry, Inc.
P. O. Box 908, Bellmawr, New Jersey 08099

MARANATHA
OUR LORD, COME!

Printed in the United States of America
Library of Congress Catalog Card Number 95-78233
ISBN 0-915540-22-3

The Friends of Israel Gospel Ministry, Inc.
P. O. Box 908, Bellmawr, NJ 08099

TABLE OF CONTENTS

Conclusion

Addendum

DEDICATION

This book is dedicated to the memory of John W. Cawood, Clair M. Hitz, Clarence E. Mason, Jr., and John F. McGahey—faithful men of God and His Word, whose consistent, exemplary lives, convictions, and commitment to ministry made an indelible impression upon me.

N ovel interpretations of Scripture and theories that are more confusing than clarifying are a fact of life for believers these days. This is particularly true of teaching about the Rapture of the church and the second advent. It has come to the point that some seem to be persuaded that no one really knows what the Bible teaches about the timing, circumstances, and order of events associated with the Lord's return. With over one-third of the Bible devoted to the subject of prophecy, the essence of which is the Lord's return, we can ill afford to be uninformed or confused about a hope so basic to our lives.

Renald Showers has dedicated years of his life to produce this definitive study of the Rapture question. And while this book provides a splendid source for serious students, it will also inform and challenge those who have limited backgrounds in the study of prophecy.

Indispensable to any comprehensive work on the Lord's coming is an examination of the question of imminency—the "any moment" return of Christ. On this subject Dr. Showers has excelled. Theologian Thomas Ice says, "His section on 'imminency' is a classic, demonstrating that it was taught throughout the New Testament. . . . " I could not agree more. Reading this chapter alone will, I'm convinced, answer the most important questions related to the all-important issue of the timing of the Lord's return for His church.

Maranatha: Our Lord Come! will enrich your knowledge of the Word and enliven your expectancy for the Lord's return.

Elwood McQuaid
Executive Director
THE FRIENDS OF ISRAEL
GOSPEL MINISTRY, INC.

THE FOCUS OF THIS BOOK

The Scriptures present six raptures. Four have already taken place. Two are still to come.

This book will examine one of those raptures: a major future event foretold in the Bible, namely, the coming of Christ to take His bride, the church. Most theologians call this "the Rapture"—from the Latin verb *rapto*, which means *to seize and carry off*[1]—because 1 Thessalonians 4:17 states that the church will be "caught up" to meet the Lord in the air. Other theologians have called this event "the Translation," taking that name from the Latin word *translatio* (*transporting, transferring*[2]) because Christ will transport the church from one location to another at that time.

The four raptures that have taken place include when both Enoch and Elijah were taken up from earth to heaven without experiencing death (Gen. 5:24; Heb. 11:5; 2 Ki. 2:1, 11), when the Lord Jesus ascended to heaven after His death and resurrection (Mk. 16:19; Acts 1:9-11; Rev. 12:5), and when Paul referred to the rapture of a man (probably Paul himself) to the third heaven (2 Cor. 12:2-4). Paul used the same verb there, translated *caught up*, as is used in Revelation 12:5 for the Lord's ascension and in 1 Thessalonians 4:17 for the church's Rapture.

The other future rapture will occur when the two witnesses of the future Tribulation period ascend to heaven after God has resurrected them from death (Rev. 11:3, 11-12).

A DESCRIPTION OF THE RAPTURE OF THE CHURCH

Three key New Testament passages deal with the Rapture of the church: John 14:1-3; 1 Corinthians 15:51-53; and 1 Thessalonians 4:13-18. When taken together, the three present the following description:

1. Christ will descend with a shout and blast of a trumpet from the Father's house in heaven to the air above the earth (Jn. 14:3; 1 Th. 4:16-17).

2. The souls of dead church saints will descend from heaven with Christ at this coming (1 Th. 4:14). When these church saints died, their souls left their bodies and went to be with the Lord in heaven (2 Cor. 5:6-8; Phil. 1:21-23).

3. The bodies of dead church saints will be raised as immortal, incorruptible bodies and will be reunited with their returning souls (1 Cor. 15:42-44, 52-53; 1 Th. 4:14-16).

4. The bodies of church saints who have not died before this coming of Christ will be changed instantly into immortal, incorruptible bodies (1 Cor. 15:51-53).

5. Both the resurrected and changed church saints will be caught up together to meet Christ in the air (1 Th. 4:17; Jn. 14:3).

6. The church saints will return with Christ to His Father's house in heaven to dwell with Him in living accommodations He has prepared there for them (Jn. 14:2-3).

The Scriptures indicate the Rapture of the church will take place suddenly, not as a process stretched out over an extended period of time. As mentioned, "caught up" in 1 Thessalonians 4:17 means to "snatch, seize, i.e., take suddenly."[3] At that time the bodies of church saints will be changed "in a moment" (an amount of time so brief it cannot be cut or divided)[4], "in the twinkling of an eye" (the extremely short time it takes to cast a glance with the eyes)[5] [1 Cor. 15:51-52].

At the end of 1 Thessalonians 4:17, Paul presented a significant result of the church's being raptured from the earth. Not only will we resurrected and changed church saints be caught up together to meet the Lord in the air, but "so shall we ever be with the Lord." We will never be separated from Him again. Wherever Christ goes, we will go. We will be with Him always, at all times. The word translated "ever" in Paul's declaration indicates this.[6]

This result of the Rapture corresponds with the Lord's declared purpose for coming again to receive church saints to Himself: "that where I am, there ye may be also" (Jn. 14:3; cp. 1 Th. 5:10).

THE TIME OF THE RAPTURE OF THE CHURCH

The most controversial issue related to the Rapture of the church concerns its time. When will the church be caught up from the earth to meet Christ in the air?

Sincere Christians hold different views. Some claim Christ will rapture the church before the Tribulation or 70th week of Daniel 9, that last seven-year period before His coming to earth in judgment with His holy angels. The church will not enter or go through any part of the seven-year

Tribulation period. Instead, when Christ raptures the church from the earth, He will take it to heaven to live with Himself in His Father's house for those seven years. After the Tribulation period, at the time of His coming with His angels, He will bring the church with Him from heaven to remain with Him on the earth throughout the Millennium. We call this the Pretribulation Rapture view.

Others hold the Midtribulation Rapture view that the church will be raptured in the middle of the seven-year Tribulation period or 70th week.

The advocates of a third view teach that the church will remain on earth throughout the entire seven-year Tribulation period but then will be raptured to meet Christ in the air immediately *after* that period, when He returns in His glorious Second Coming. This is the Posttribulation Rapture view.

Those Posttribulationists who are also premillennial believe that after the church meets Christ in the air, it will return immediately to earth with Him as He continues His descent from heaven and will remain with Him on the earth throughout the Millennium.

Posttribulationists who are not premillennial believe that after the church meets Christ in the air, it will be taken by Him to heaven for eternity.

Of course, as we would expect, there are a series of derivative views that reflect these basic positions in some way. One of them is the recently proposed Pre-Wrath Rapture, which is a variation of the Midtribulation Rapture and therefore is not actually new but a revised version of an already existing position. Advocates of this view assert that the church will be raptured between the middle and end of the 70th week of Daniel 9 (perhaps about three-fourths of the way through the seven-year 70th week). According to this position, the church will go through the first half and a significant part of the second half of the 70th week before being removed from the earth.

The Pretribulation, Midtribulation, and Posttribulation Rapture views have been widely recognized by sincere Christians as established views for many years, and, as mentioned above, various derivative forms of those views have surfaced from time to time. Why then do Christians come to different conclusions regarding the time of the Rapture of the church? The Scriptures do not give a specific statement concerning the time of this event. As a result, every person who studies the subject of the Rapture is forced to look for inferences of its time from different details presented in the Bible.

AN OVERVIEW OF THIS BOOK

This author believes that biblical inferences concerning the time of the Rapture of the church favor the Pretribulation Rapture view. The church will not enter or go through any part of the Tribulation period.

He wants to present significant biblical inferences that he believes favor the Pretribulation Rapture view. The book will have two major divisions. Part I will contain preliminary considerations. Part II will present the significant inferences, some of which are based on those considerations. A conclusion and an addendum will follow.

The preliminary considerations (Part I) will deal with the following items:

Chapter 1: The concept of birth pangs in the Bible and Judaism; the relationship of birth pangs to the 70th week of Daniel 9, the Day of the Lord, and the Messianic Age.

Chapter 2: The Day of the Lord—its significance and relationship to human instruments; its twofold nature and double sense in the future; the implications of its double sense; the coming of Elijah before the great and terrible Day of the Lord.

Chapter 3: The relationship of the Day of the Lord, the Time of Jacob's Trouble, and the Great Tribulation; the beginning and length of the Great Tribulation; and what Jesus meant by the shortening of the days of the Great Tribulation.

Chapter 4: The beginning and end of the beginning judgment phase of the Day of the Lord; the significance of the 30 and 75 days beyond the end of the 70th week of Daniel 9; the relationship of the Rapture to the Day of the Lord; the relationship of 1 Thessalonians 5, 2 Thessalonians 2, and cosmic disturbances to the beginning of the Day of the Lord.

Chapter 5: The importance and identification of the sealed scroll of Revelation 5 and the significance of Christ's taking the sealed scroll, breaking its seals, opening it, and looking at its contents.

Chapter 6: The relationship of these seals to security; the significance of all seven seals belonging to the same scroll; the significance of Christ alone breaking the seals; the identification of the one who turns the Antichrist loose with the breaking of the first seal; the identification of the restrainer of 2 Thessalonians 2; the relationship of the breaking of the fifth seal to the martyrdom of saints; the relationship of the seven seals to the Day of the Lord wrath.

The biblical inferences for the Pretribulation Rapture of the church (Part II) will address the following matters:

Chapter 7: The meaning of "imminent"; the concept of the imminent coming of Christ; the New Testament and the imminent coming of Christ; significant individuals and groups in different periods of church history who believed in the imminent coming of Christ; the practical effect of imminency; the implication of imminency for the different Rapture views.

Chapter 8: The significance of Jesus' promise in John 14:3; a critique of the different views of the John 14:3 coming; the relationship of John 14:2-3 to 1 Thessalonians 4:13-18 and the Jewish marriage analogy; the implication of John 14:2-3 for the different Rapture views.

Chapter 9: Evidences to the effect that the Rapture of the church and the coming of Christ with His holy angels will be two separate events; the relationship of Matthew 24:37-41 to the Rapture of the church and the coming of Christ; the significance of the Lord's using two different verbs for "taken" in verses 39-41; the identification of His "elect" in verse 31; the relationship of Matthew 24:37-41 to Luke 17:26-37 and Matthew 25:31-46; the Rapture of the church and the fulfillment of certain prophecies; the implications for the different views of the Rapture of the church and the coming of Christ being two separate events.

Chapter 10: The relationship of church saints to the wrath of God; the significance of 1 Thessalonians 1:10; 4:13-18; 5:9; and Revelation 3:10; the implication of the relationship of church saints to the wrath of God for the time of the Rapture of the church.

Chapter 11: Paul's request in 2 Thessalonians 2:1-2 and its implication; the issue at stake with the Thessalonians.

Chapter 12: The distinction between Israel and the church; the time that the church began; the 70-weeks prophecy of Daniel 9 and its implication for the time of the Rapture of the church.

Chapter 13: The references to the church and Israel in the Book of the Revelation; the implication of these references for the time of the Rapture of the church; the identification of the saints on earth during the 70th week or Tribulation period; the identification of the great multitude of Revelation 7.

The conclusion (Chapter 14) will deal with the practical implications of the time of the Rapture of the church for individual Christians and the church as a whole.

An addendum (Chapter 15) will address the issue of the identification of "the last trump" (1 Cor. 15:52).

THE USE OF TERMS

Regarding the use of terms in this volume, historically many theologians have used the terms *Tribulation* or *Tribulation period* for the seven-year 70th week of Daniel 9, thereby indicating their belief that the Tribulation and the 70th week are equatable. On occasion in this book the author will do the same because, for four reasons, he is convinced that the equation of the Tribulation with the entire seven years of the 70th week is legitimate.

First, the Lord Jesus used the terms "Great Tribulation" and "tribulation" for a specific period of time (Mt. 24:21, 29). This book will give evidence showing that that time period will begin in the middle of the seven-year 70th week and will continue to its end. Thus, the entire second half of the 70th week will be characterized by tribulation.

Second, the Hebrew words for "tribulation" in the Hebrew Old Testament and the Greek word for "tribulation" in the Septuagint (the Greek translation of the Hebrew Old Testament, which Jesus and the apostles sometimes quoted and based some teaching upon) were used to indicate that the latter-days Tribulation will last until Israel turns to God and is rescued by Him (Dt. 4:30; Ps. 50:7, 15; Hos. 5:15). Later it will be demonstrated that these actions by Israel and God will not happen until the end of the 70th week and that tribulation will therefore continue until the end of the 70th week.

Third, the Hebrew words for "tribulation" in the Hebrew Old Testament and the Greek word for "tribulation" in the Septuagint and Greek New Testament associate the concept of tribulation with the following things:

1. Birth pangs (2 Ki. 19:3; Jer. 6:24; Jn. 16:21).

2. Sword, famine, and pestilence (2 Chr. 20:9; Job 15:20-23; Acts 7:11).

3. Removal of peace and nations warring against nations (2 Chr. 15:5-6).

4. Persecution of saints during that part of the 70th week that will precede the abomination of desolation of the middle of that week (Mt. 24:9; cp. Dan. 9:27).

The Bible thereby associates the concept of tribulation with the same kinds of things included in "the beginning of birth pangs" (literal translation) of Matthew 24:4-9 and the first four seals of Revelation 6:1-8. This book will demonstrate that the beginning of birth pangs and the first four seals are the same and that they will take place during the first half of the 70th week. Thus, the kinds of things associated with tribulation will take place during the first half of the 70th week. It is appropriate therefore to apply the term "Tribulation" even to the first half of that week.

Fourth, these Hebrew and Greek words for "tribulation" in the Bible associate it with the outpouring of God's wrath, even His Day of the Lord wrath or anger (Dt. 31:17, 21; Ps. 66:11; Zeph. 1:14-15; Rom. 2:5, 8-9). Evidence will be given to the effect that God's Day of the Lord wrath will be poured out throughout the entire 70th week, even during its first half. Thus, another detail associated with tribulation will be characteristic of the entire 70th week, including its first half.

These four things concerning the concept of tribulation in the Bible prompt the conclusion that it is proper to apply the terms "Tribulation" and "Tribulation period" to the entire seven-year 70th week of Daniel 9.

Although the Hebrew and Greek words for "tribulation" appear in the passages cited in these four observations, the various English translations do not consistently use the word "tribulation" for their translation.

THE AUTHOR'S HOPE

Believers in the early church held vigorously to belief in the imminent coming of Jesus Christ, and that belief powerfully motivated them to holy living. May the Lord use this book to help revive that belief just as vigorously in His present-day believers with the same practical result.

MARANATHA—OUR LORD, COME!

ENDNOTES

1. D. A. Kidd, *Collins Latin Gem Dictionary*, ed. by G. F. Maine (London: Collins, 1957), p. 278.

2. *Ibid.*, p. 340.

3. William F. Arndt and F. Wilbur Gingrich, *A Greek-English Lexicon of the New Testament*, 4th rev. ed. (Chicago: The University of Chicago Press, 1957), p. 108.

4. *Ibid.*, p. 120.

5. *Ibid.*, p. 743.

6. *Ibid.*, p. 614.

PART I

PRELIMINARY CONSIDERATIONS

CHAPTER ONE

THE BIRTH PANGS OF THE MESSIAH

A SIGNIFICANT CONCEPT

The concept of birth pangs has played a significant role in ancient Judaism and the Bible.

BIRTH PANGS IN JUDAISM

Ancient Judaism taught that a seven-year period of time will immediately precede the Messiah's coming to rule the world.

The Babylonian Talmud states, "Our Rabbis taught: In the seven-year cycle at the end of which the son of David will come . . . at the conclusion of the septennate the son of David will come."[1]

Raphael Patai, writing on the Messianic texts, said, "The idea became entrenched that the coming of the Messiah will be preceded by greatly increased suffering . . . This will last seven years. And then, unexpectedly, the Messiah will come."[2]

According to *The Babylonian Talmud*, "The advent of the Messiah was pictured as being preceded by years of great distress."[3]

The Dead Sea Scrolls and other literature called the severe troubles of the seven years before the Messiah's coming "the birth pangs of the Messiah."

Millar Burrows pointed this out in his book on the Scrolls: "A prominent feature of Jewish eschatology, as represented especially by the rabbinic literature, was the time of trouble preceding Messiah's coming. It was called 'the birth pangs of the Messiah,' sometimes more briefly translated as 'the Messianic woes.' "[4]

Why call these future troubles "the birth pangs of the Messiah"? Because travail precedes birth, and this travail "precedes the birth of a new era"[5]— the Messianic Age. Just as a woman must go through a period of agony before her child is born into the world, so the world will go through birth pangs before the Messianic Age is born into the world.

Martin Buber wrote in *Gog and Magog* that "the world-body must be in labor, must suffer great pain, must come to the brink of death, before

Redemption can be born. For its sake God permits the earthly powers to rise up against Him more and more . . . until the struggle be intensified into the pangs of the Messiah."[6]

Those birth pangs, according to the *Apocalypse of Abraham* (p. 82), will involve such things as the sword (war), famine, pestilence, and wild beasts.[7] In addition,

> The pangs of the Messianic times are imagined as having heavenly as well as earthly sources and expressions. From Above, awesome cosmic cataclysms will be visited upon the earth: conflagrations, pestilence, famine, earthquakes, hail and snow, thunder and lightning. These will be paralleled by evils brought by men upon themselves: insolence, robbery, heresy, harlotry, corruption, oppression, cruel edicts, lack of truth, and no fear of sin. All this will lead to internal decay, demoralization, and even apostasy. Things will come to such a head that people will despair of Redemption. This will last seven years. And then, unexpectedly, the Messiah will come.[8]

Some rabbis have taught that the Messiah will not come until the birth pangs become so severe that the Jews will "despair of the Redemption . . . when, as it were, Israel will have neither supporter nor helper."[9]

RABBINIC RESPONSE TO THE BIRTH PANGS OF THE MESSIAH

In light of Judaism's teaching concerning the severity of the birth pangs to precede the Messiah's coming, some rabbis have expressed the wish not to be alive when the Messiah comes. One said, "Let him come, but let me not see him."[10]

In response to this statement, which startled its hearers,

> Abaye enquired of Rabbah: "What is your reason [for not wishing to see him]? Shall we say, because of the birth pangs of the Messiah? But it has been taught, R. Eleazar's disciples asked of him: 'What must a man do to be spared the pangs of the Messiah?' [He answered,] 'Let him engage in study and benevolence.' "[11]

Rabbi Simeon b. Pazzi said, "He who observes [the practice of] three meals on the Sabbath is saved from three evils: the travails of the Messiah, the retribution of Gehinnom, and the wars of Gog and Magog."[12]

Raphael Patai wrote, "The teaching which gained general acceptance was that by occupying oneself with Tora study and deeds of charity, one can escape the Messianic sufferings."[13] Thus, ancient Judaism had the hope of escaping the birth pangs of the Messiah of the last seven years prior to His coming to rule the world.

BIRTH PANGS IN THE BIBLE

The concept of birth pangs has played a significant role in the content of Scripture as well. The birth pangs (as described in these succeeding quotes from the *Theological Dictionary of the Old Testament*) are "recurring spasms of pain which are not subject to conscious control, during which the woman in labor writhes—a process that can be accompanied by a sense of fear or anxiety, screams, and groans."[14]

The Scriptures have used this concept to refer to other situations that involve painful experiences comparable to the pains of childbirth. In this usage " 'birth pangs' are a favorite metaphor for the tribulations God's judgment brings upon man."[15]

The Bible includes several samples of this metaphoric use. Job declared, "God distributeth sorrows [a translation of a Hebrew word for birth pangs] in his anger" (Job 21:17). The wicked peoples of Israel and Jerusalem (Isa. 26:17-18; Jer. 4:31; 6:24; 13:21; Hos. 13:12-13; Mic. 4:9-10), Babylon (Isa. 13:8; Jer. 50:43), Damascus (Jer. 49:24), Moab (Jer. 48:41), Edom (Jer. 49:22), and Nineveh (Nah. 2:10) all experienced birth pangs. (Some Hebrew words for birth pangs have been translated with the English words "distress" and "sorrows.") The contexts of these passages indicate that these birth pangs were associated with God's purposed judgment, wrath, and fierce anger on these peoples frequently through other nations warring against them.

The Scriptures describe the physical effects of being seized by birth pangs—the loins are filled with pain, the heart faints, the knees tremble, the face flushes with anxiety (Isa. 13:7-8; Nah 2:10), the hands become helpless (Jer. 6:24), and the voice groans and cries (Isa. 26:17; Jer. 4:31; Mic. 4:9). Thus, birth pangs involve a state of "involuntary and uncontrolled spasmodic movement, to which the body is surrendered, accompanied by a sense of weakness and heat."[16]

"Such a state can occur in the face of battle, in times of judgment, on the 'day of Yahweh.' "[17]

Not only for the judgment of events now past, but also for judgment in the future, the Bible makes metaphoric use of birth pangs. In the Old Testament they are associated with the future Time of Jacob's Trouble (Jer. 30:6-7).

The Time Period of the Time of Jacob's Trouble. To discern what future period will be covered by the Time of Jacob's Trouble, we must examine what the Scriptures say concerning the Great Tribulation. Both the Time of Jacob's Trouble (Jer. 30:6-7) and the Great Tribulation (Mt. 24:21) are described as the unparalleled time of trouble. Since there can be only one such time, both will cover the same time period.

The Great Tribulation will begin in the middle of the seven-year 70th week. We know this because Jesus indicated that the Great Tribulation will begin with the abomination of desolation (Mt. 24:15-21), which will take place in the middle of the 70th week (Dan. 9:27).

A later chapter will demonstrate that the Great Tribulation will last for the entire second half of the 70th week, terminating at the end of that seven-year period. Jesus declared that His glorious coming with His angels will take place "immediately after" the Great Tribulation (Mt. 24:29-31), thus, immediately after the end of the seven-year 70th week. From this and what we noted earlier, we see that both the Bible and ancient Judaism teach that a seven-year period will precede the Messiah's coming to rule the world.

Since the Great Tribulation will begin in the middle and terminate at the end of the 70th week and will cover the same time period as the Time of Jacob's Trouble, the Time of Jacob's Trouble will also cover the entire second half of the 70th week.

Since the Time of Jacob's Trouble will have birth pangs associated with it and will, together with the Great Tribulation, cover the second half of the 70th week, the Great Tribulation will also have birth pangs associated with it. On the basis of this, we can conclude that the entire second half of the 70th week will be characterized by birth pangs.

Since the Time of Jacob's Trouble and the Great Tribulation will be the unparalleled time of trouble, it is apparent that the birth pangs of the second half of the 70th week will be the later, most severe birth pangs of hard labor, parallel to the later, most severe birth pangs of a woman's hard labor.

The Beginning of Birth Pangs. Christ referred to "the beginning of sorrows" (lit., "the beginning of birth pangs," Mt. 24:8). The fact that He called these "the *beginning* of birth pangs" indicates that more birth pangs would follow them. It seems apparent that by this expression He had in mind the earlier, less severe birth pangs that precede the later, most severe birth pangs of hard labor. Concerning the deceptive false messiahs, wars and rumors of wars, famines, pestilences, and earthquakes in many places that Christ said will make up the beginning of birth pangs, George Bertram said they "are the woes with which the end-time is ushered in, or the beginning of sorrows which will be followed by others that are even more severe."[18]

Two things indicate that the beginning of birth pangs will occur during the first half of the 70th week. First, it is obvious that Jesus was drawing an analogy with a woman's birth-pang experience. Just as a woman's beginning, less severe birth pangs precede her later, most severe pangs of hard labor, so the beginning, less severe pangs of the world's future time of trouble must precede its later, most severe pangs of hard labor. Since those later hard labor pangs will occur during the second half of the 70th week, the beginning of birth pangs must take place during the first half of those seven years.

Second, Christ introduced and discussed the *beginning* of birth pangs (Mt. 24:4-8) *before* He introduced the abomination of desolation and the Great Tribulation (Mt. 24:15-21), and it appears that He introduced and discussed events in chronological order in this section of Matthew 24. This implies that the beginning of birth pangs will precede the abomination of desolation (of the middle of the 70th week) and the Great Tribulation (of the second half of the 70th week) and therefore will occur during the first half of that seven-year period.

The Two Divisions of Future Birth Pangs. In light of what has been seen, we can conclude that the birth pangs of the future period of world trouble will have two divisions parallel to the two divisions of the seven-year 70th week before the Messiah comes to rule the world. The beginning, less severe birth pangs will be in the first half of the 70th week; the later, most severe pangs will occur in the second half (see the diagram at the end of this chapter).

THE BEGINNING OF BIRTH PANGS AND THE FIRST FOUR SEALS

A comparison of Christ's description of the beginning of birth pangs in Matthew 24:5-7 with the first four seals of Revelation 6:1-8 indicates that the beginning of birth pangs and the first four seals are the same thing.

Beginning of birth pangs (Mt. 24)	First Four seals (Rev. 6)
1. False messiahs who will mislead many (v. 5)	1. First seal: Rider on white horse, a false messiah (v. 2)
2. Wars, rumors of wars, nation rising against nation (vv. 6-7)	2. Second seal: Rider on red horse takes away peace from earth (vv. 3-4)
3. Famines (v. 7)	3. Third Seal: Rider on black horse holds balances, represents famine (vv. 5-6)
4. Death through famines, pestilences, and earthquakes (v. 7)	4. Fourth seal: Rider on pale horse, represents death through famine, pestilence, and wild beasts (vv. 7-8)

In addition, immediately after His description of the beginning of birth pangs, Christ referred to the killing of those associated with Him (Mt. 24:9). Parallel to this, the fifth seal refers to people killed because of their testimony (Rev. 6:9-11).

Since the beginning of birth pangs that will occur during the first half of the 70th week are the same as the first four seals, we can conclude that the first four seals of Revelation 6 will take place during the first half of Daniel's 70th week.

Earlier we noted that ancient Judaism taught that the birth pangs of the Messiah will involve such things as war, famine, pestilence, and wild beasts as expressions of divine wrath upon the world. It is interesting to see how this concept corresponds with the beginning of birth pangs and the first four seals.

Birth Pangs and the Messianic Age. Immediately after referring to the severe birth pangs of the Time of Jacob's Trouble (Jer. 30:6-7), Jeremiah introduced the subject of the blessings of the future Messianic Age (Jer. 30:8-11, 17-22). Also, after discussing the beginning of birth pangs and the Great Tribulation, which will involve the hard-labor birth pangs, Jesus declared that immediately after the Great Tribulation He will come (Mt. 24:29-31), sit on His throne to rule (Mt. 25:31), and send the righteous into the kingdom of the Messianic Age (Mt. 25:34). Thus, the Bible teaches, just as did ancient Judaism, that the Messianic Age will be preceded by the seven years of birth pangs.

In Matthew 19:28 Jesus said that when He sits on His throne to rule the world, the earth will be regenerated. The curse of mankind's sin, which was placed on nature as the result of Adam's original sin (Gen. 3:17; 5:29), will be removed when the Messianic Age comes. As a result, nature will be restored to the original condition it enjoyed before the fall of mankind.

For this reason Peter, when referring to the future Messianic Age when Christ will be present again in the world, called it "the times of refreshing" and "the times of restitution of all things" (Acts 3:19-21).

Paul indicated that creation, which was subjected to vanity and groans and travails in pain, eagerly awaits its future redemption from the curse when it is delivered from the bondage of corruption (Rom. 8:19-22). The miracles Christ performed during His first coming demonstrated that He possesses the powers necessary to transform the earth in the future Messianic Age.[19] Thus, the Bible calls His miracles "the powers of the age to come" (Heb. 6:5; the word translated "world" literally means "age").

The Scriptures also teach that since Adam's original sin, the world system has been bound or ruled by Satan and rebellious mankind (Lk. 4:5-6; Jn. 14:30; 1 Cor. 2:8; 1 Jn. 5:19). Both are totally opposed to the future Messianic Age for two reasons. First, in that age the world system will be ruled by Christ and the righteous, and, second, before the Messianic Age, Satan, rebellious mankind, and their rule of the world system must be removed from the earth (Dan. 7:9-11, 13-14, 18, 21-22, 24-27; Mt. 13:36-43, 47-50; 25:31-41; 2 Tim. 2:12; Rev. 19:11–20:6).

Because Satan and rebellious mankind are totally opposed to the future Messianic Age, they will do everything possible to hinder its coming into the world (Ps. 2; Dan. 7:21-22, 24-27; Joel 3:9-14; Zech. 12:1-9; 14:1-9; Rev. 11:3-11; 16:12-16; 19:11-19).

To repeat, just as a woman must endure birth pangs to overcome that which hinders her baby from coming into the world, so the world will have to endure birth pangs to overcome that which will hinder its future Messianic Age from coming into being. Thus, the birth pangs of the seven years (the 70th week of Daniel 9) before the Messiah's coming to reign are absolutely necessary to remove Satan and rebellious mankind and their rule of the world system from the earth so that the Messianic Age can be born. H. J. Fabry said, "They are the necessary transition to a new age of salvation."[20]

Birth Pangs and the Day of the Lord. The Scriptures indicate that birth pangs will also characterize the Day of the Lord. More specifically, Isaiah 13:6-13 and Zephaniah 1:14-18 associate birth pangs with the divine wrath and fierce anger of the Day of the Lord. (The word translated "distress" in Zephaniah 1:17 is one of the Hebrew words for birth pangs.) First Thessalonians 5:2-3 also associates the birth-pang concept with the Day of the Lord. (The word translated "travail" in v. 3 is the Greek word for birth pang.) The emphasis in that passage is on the suddenness with which the Day of the Lord will begin with its destruction.[21]

The significance of birth pangs being characteristic of the Day of the Lord will be dealt with more fully in another chapter.

CONCLUSIONS

This study of the concept of birth pangs in the Scriptures and ancient Judaism has produced several conclusions.

1. In the Bible, birth pangs are associated with God's purposed judgment, wrath, and fierce anger against the wicked.

2. The divine judgment, wrath, and fierce anger associated with birth pangs frequently come through human instruments.

3. Both the Bible and ancient Judaism teach that the last seven years before the Messiah comes to reign over the earth will be characterized by severe birth pangs. Judaism called these the birth pangs of the Messiah. The Bible indicates these seven years are the 70th week of Daniel 9.

4. The Bible indicates that the Great Tribulation and the Time of Jacob's Trouble cover the same time period—the second half of the seven years before the Messiah comes to reign.

5. The Bible reveals the time period covered by the Great Tribulation and the Time of Jacob's Trouble will be characterized by birth pangs—specifically, the later, more severe birth pangs of hard labor.

6. The Bible indicates that the seven years before the Messiah comes to reign will be divided into two divisions of birth pangs. The first division will cover the first half of the time period and will contain the less severe beginning of birth pangs. The second division will cover the second half and will contain the later, more severe, hard-labor birth pangs.

7. The Bible demonstrates that the beginning of birth pangs and the first four seals are the same thing. Thus, the first four seals will be present during the first half of the seven years.

8. Both the Bible and ancient Judaism teach that the world must go through the seven years of birth pangs in order for the Messianic Age to be born into the world. The Bible indicates that these birth pangs are absolutely necessary to remove Satan, rebellious mankind, and their rule of the world system from the earth so that the Messianic Age can come.

9. The Bible teaches that birth pangs are characteristic of the Day of the Lord. It associates birth pangs with the divine wrath, fierce anger, and destruction of that day.

10. Ancient Judaism had the hope of escaping the birth pangs of the Messiah of the last seven years before His coming to reign on earth.

Diagram of Two Divisions of Birth Pangs

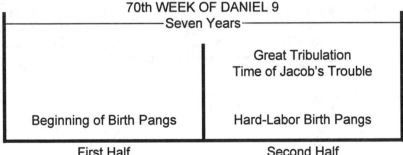

70th WEEK OF DANIEL 9
Seven Years

Beginning of Birth Pangs	Great Tribulation Time of Jacob's Trouble
	Hard-Labor Birth Pangs
First Half	Second Half

ENDNOTES

1. *Sanhedrin*, 97a, in *The Babylonian Talmud* (London: Soncino Press, 1935), p. 654.

2. Raphael Patai, *The Messianic Texts* (Detroit: Wayne State University Press, 1979), pp. 95-96.

3. *Shabbath*, 118a, in *The Babylonian Talmud* (London: Soncino Press, 1938), footnote on "travails of the Messiah," p. 580.

4. Millar Burrows, *More Light on the Dead Sea Scrolls*, in *Burrows on the Dead Sea Scrolls* (Grand Rapids: Baker Book House, 1978), pp. 343-44.

5. *Sanhedrin*, 98b, footnote on "birth pangs of the Messiah," p. 665.

6. Martin Buber, *Gog and Magog*, pp. 84-85, quoted in Patai, *The Messianic Texts*, pp. 280-81.

7. Patai, *The Messianic Texts*, p. 96.

8. *Ibid.*, pp. 95-96.

9. *Ibid.*, p. 98.

10. *Sanhedrin*, 98b, p. 665.

11. *Ibid.*

12. *Shabbath*, 118a, p. 580.

13. Patai, *The Messianic Texts*, p. 95.

14. A. Bauman, "Chil," *Theological Dictionary of the Old Testament*, Vol. IV, ed. by G. Johannes Botterweck and Helmer Ringgren, trans. by David E. Green (Grand Rapids: William B. Eerdmans Publishing Company, 1980), p. 345.

15. H. J. Fabry, "Chebel," *Theological Dictionary of the Old Testament*, Vol. IV, ed. by G. Johannes Botterweck and Helmer Ringgren, trans. by David E. Green (Grand Rapids: William B. Eerdmans Publishing Company, 1980), p. 191.

16. Bauman, "Chil," p. 346.

17. *Ibid.*

18. George Bertram, "odin," *Theological Dictionary of the New Testament*, Vol. IX, ed. by Gerhard Friedrich, trans. and ed. by Geoffrey W. Bromiley (Grand Rapids: William B. Eerdmans Publishing Company, 1974), p. 672.

19. For a study of this significance of Jesus' miracles, see the article "The Purpose of Jesus' Miracles" by Renald E. Showers in the Dec./Jan., 1975-76 issue of *Israel My Glory* magazine.

20. Fabry, "Chebel," p. 192.

21. Bertram, "odin," p. 672.

CHAPTER TWO

THE BIBLICAL CONCEPT OF THE DAY OF THE LORD

THE SIGNIFICANCE OF THE DAY OF THE LORD

The Scriptures teach that God created the universe for His own sovereign purposes (Rev. 4:11). As a result, the heavenly and earthly realms are owned and ruled by God (1 Chr. 29:11-12; 2 Chr. 20:6; Ps. 47:2; 103:19; 135:6; Isa. 40:12-26; Jer. 10:7, 10; Dan. 4:17, 34-35, 37; Acts 17:24; 1 Tim. 1:17; Rev. 5:13). As the owner and ruler of the earth, God has His own sovereign purpose for world history and, therefore, for specific events within that history (Isa. 14:24-27; 19:12; 23:9; 46:8-11; Jer. 4:28; 23:20; 26:3; 30:24; 36:3; 49:20; 50:45; 51:29; Lam. 2:8; Rom. 8:28; 9:11, 17; Eph. 1:9-11; 3:10-11; 2 Tim. 1:9; 1 Jn. 3:8).

In the Scriptures the expression "the Day of the Lord" (together with other synonymous expressions, such as "that day," "the day of God," etc.) is strongly related to God's rule of the earth and, therefore, to His sovereign purpose for world history and specific events within that history. The Day of the Lord refers to God's special interventions into the course of world events to judge His enemies, accomplish His purpose for history, and thereby demonstrate who He is—the sovereign God of the universe (Isa. 2:10-22; Ezek. 13:5, 9, 14, 21, 23; 30:3, 8, 19, 25-26).

This significance of the Day of the Lord has been recognized by several scholars. For example, John A. T. Robinson stated, "In itself, 'the Day of the Lord' is a general and comprehensive expression for the consummation of God's purpose, alike in victory and in judgment."[1]

A. B. Davidson wrote, "It is a day that is a special time; and it is the Day of the Lord, belongs to Him, is His time for working, for manifesting Himself, for displaying His character, for performing His work—His strange work upon the earth."[2] Again he said, "It is a manifestation of God—of God as what He is truly, and in the whole round of His being. Hence it displays His whole character, and sees His whole purpose effected."[3]

J. Barton Payne declared, "The comprehensive phrase, by which the Old Testament describes God's intervention in human history for the accomplishment of His testament is *yom Yahwe*, 'the day of Yahweh.' "[4] And again he stated, "The 'day' is thus characterized by an observable accomplishment of the general aims of divine providence. It refers to that point in history at which the sovereign God lays bare His holy arm on the behalf of His testament and of its heirs, whether in a way that is specifically miraculous, or not."[5]

Evidence for this significance of the Day of the Lord is found in past Days of the Lord referred to in the Scriptures. The Bible indicates that there have been several Days of the Lord in the past in which God demonstrated His sovereign rule by raising up several nations to execute His judgment on other nations. He raised up Assyria to judge the northern kingdom of Israel during the 700s B.C. (Amos 5:18, 20), Babylon to judge the southern kingdom of Judah during the 600s and 500s B.C. (Lam. 1:12; 2:1, 21-22; Ezek. 7:19; 13:5; Zeph. 2:2-3), Babylon to judge Egypt and its allies during the 500s B.C. (Jer. 46:10; Ezek. 30:3), and Medo-Persia to judge Babylon during the 500s B.C. (Isa. 13:6, 9).

THE DAY OF THE LORD AND HUMAN INSTRUMENTS

In these past Days of the Lord, God used human instruments and activity through war to execute His sovereign purpose against His enemies.

Several scholars have recognized this biblical indication. For example, Gerhard Von Rad wrote, "The prophets expect the day of Jahweh to bring war in its train."[6]

With reference to the judgments associated with the Day of the Lord, A. B. Davidson stated, "Judgment always took place in an external manner, in the form of chastisement at God's hands through His instruments—often in war."[7]

After indicating that sometimes the Day of the Lord involves a direct, miraculous intervention of God, A. B. Davidson declared, "But at other times, besides the supernatural gloom and terrors that surround Him when He appears, He is represented as using some fierce, distant nation as the instrument by which He executes His judgment (Is 13, Zeph)."[8]

THE DAY OF THE LORD IN THE FUTURE

Timing. The Scriptures indicate that the concept of the Day of the Lord is applicable, not only to the past interventions of God in history, but also to the future. Several things in the Bible make this very obvious. First, Isaiah 2:10-22 describes a Day of the Lord that will involve the sixth seal described by the Apostle John in Revelation 6:12-17. Because this sixth seal will take place during the 70th week of Daniel 9, the Day of the Lord that will involve that seal must also take place during that future time period.

Second, Isaiah 34:1-8 and Obadiah 15 describe a Day of the Lord when God will judge all nations or Gentiles of the world. None of the past Days of the Lord involved divine judgment of all the nations. Up to this point in history, there has not been a judgment of all nations during the same time period. In light of this, we can conclude that the Day of the Lord of Isaiah 34 and Obadiah must be future.

Third, Joel 3:1-16 and Zechariah 14:1-3, 12-15 refer to a Day of the Lord that will involve God's judgment of the armies of all the nations of the world, when those armies gather in Israel to wage war against that nation and the city of Jerusalem and when the Messiah comes to war against them. According to Revelation 16:12-16, those armies will not begin to gather until the sixth bowl is poured out during the 70th week of Daniel 9. In addition, Revelation 19:11-21 indicates that Christ will wage war against them when He comes from heaven to earth. This, too, forces the conclusion that the Day of the Lord of Joel 3 and Zechariah 14 is future.

Fourth, in 1 Thessalonians 5:1-11 the Apostle Paul referred to a Day of the Lord that was future beyond the time when he wrote his epistle and that would bring sudden, inescapable destruction upon the unsaved of the world. That Day of the Lord had not taken place before Paul wrote his Thessalonian epistle, and it seems evident that nothing of its nature has transpired since. Thus, the Day of the Lord of 1 Thessalonians 5 is also future.

THE TWOFOLD NATURE OF THE DAY OF THE LORD IN THE FUTURE

The Scriptures indicate that the future Day of the Lord will have at least a twofold nature. First, it will be characterized by darkness and a tremendous outpouring of divine wrath upon the world (Joel 2:1-2; Amos 5:18-20; Zeph. 1:14-15; 1 Th. 5:1-11). Amos 5:18-20 emphasizes that this will be the total nature of the Day of the Lord for God's enemies. It will bring no divine light or blessing to them. This will be the nature of the Day of the Lord during the 70th week of Daniel.

Second, the Day of the Lord will also be characterized by light, an outpouring of divine blessing, and the administration of God's rule. The Prophet Joel, after talking about the darkening of the sun, moon, and stars and God's Day of the Lord judgment of the armies of the nations gathered in Israel (3:9-16), foretold great divine blessing "in that day" (vv. 17-21).

In addition, the Prophet Zechariah, after discussing the future Day of the Lord, when all nations will war against Jerusalem and the Messiah will come to the earth to fight against the nations (14:1-5), indicated that although the earlier part of "that day" will be characterized by darkness, the latter part will be characterized by light (vv. 6-7), great blessing (v. 8), and God's rule over all the earth (v. 9). This will be the nature of the Day of the Lord during the Millennium.

This twofold nature of the Day of the Lord in the future has been recognized by numerous scholars. For example, A. B. Davidson wrote,

> Hence the 'Day of the Lord' acquires a double-sided character. It is a day of salvation and judgment, or a day of salvation through judgment . . . a day of salvation behind this. Sometimes one side is prominent and sometimes another . . . Sometimes both sides of the Divine manifestation are brought forward, as in Joel.[9]

J. Barton Payne stated that the Day of the Lord involves a twofold pattern of judgment and restoration.[10]

On the one hand, H. H. Rowley asserted, "This element of judgement [sic] belongs essentially to the thought of the Day of the Lord."[11] On the other hand, he declared,

> From this it follows that in biblical thought the Golden Age has a fundamentally religious basis. It is essentially the Day of the Lord, and what is of importance is that there shall not only be unity of rule, but that all shall be permeated by the spirit of God, so that all life shall reflect his will. It was never conceived in merely economic or political terms, but always in moral and spiritual terms, so that it is appropriately thought of as the Kingdom of God, whether the term is found or not. It was the age when peace and justice should be universal amongst men. . . . [12]

> In all this we should not forget that the Golden Age was always conceived of as the Day of the Lord . . . All the passages in the Old Testament which present in various ways the vision of the Golden Age, or of the Day of the Lord, are commonly referred to as messianic. . . . [13]

> It will be seen that all of the elements of the description of the Day of the Lord are to be found here—the universality and permanence of peace, judgement and deliverance, economic bliss, righteous and world-wide dominion.[14]

Thus, the Day of the Lord in the future will be at least twofold in nature. Just as each day of creation and the Jewish day consisted of two phases—a time of darkness ("evening") followed by a time of light ("day") [Gen. 1:4-6]—so the future Day of the Lord will consist of two phases, a period of darkness (judgment) followed by a period of light (divine rule and blessing).

Since, as noted earlier, the Day of the Lord will demonstrate who God is, it would seem strange for the God who is light and in whom there is no darkness at all (1 Jn. 1:5) to have His day consist totally of darkness with no period of light, especially since the present day of Satan and rebellious mankind is characterized by a rule of darkness (Eph. 6:12; Col. 1:13).

In addition, since, as shall be seen later, the present day of Satan and rebellious mankind involves their rule of the world system, the future Day of the Lord would not truly be *His* day if it did not involve His rule of the world system during the Millennium. How could the Day of the Lord fully demonstrate who He is—the sovereign God of the universe—without the sovereign exercise of His rule in visible form over the entire world?

THE BACKGROUND OF THE DAY OF THE LORD IN THE FUTURE

Why has the Holy Spirit chosen to use the expression "the Day of the Lord" for God's divine interventions into the course of world events to judge His enemies, accomplish His purpose for world history, and demonstrate who He is—the sovereign God of the universe? Some background is necessary to understand the reason.

After God created mankind, He gave them dominion over everything on planet earth (Gen. 1:26, 28; Ps. 8:3-9). This indicates that God intended mankind to serve as His representative, administering His rule over the earthly province of His universal domain. In other words, God designed the government of the earth to be a theocracy, a form of government in which He is the sovereign ruler of the earth; but His rule is administered through an Adam, a human representative.

As a result of Satan's convincing the first Adam to rebel against God and His rule, God's theocratic kingdom rule over the world system was lost (Gen. 3). Through Adam's rebellion, Satan usurped the rule of the world system away from God (Lk. 4:5-6; Jn. 14:30; 1 Jn. 5:19). Since that time, Satan and rebellious mankind have been dominating the world system according to their own thoughts and ways (Isa. 55:7-9). They have been having their day in the world, during which they try to establish and assert their own sovereignty and deity.

In light of what has happened, God's purpose for world history is to glorify Himself by demonstrating that He alone is the sovereign God. To accomplish this purpose, He has determined to have His day in the end times of world history (Isa. 2:10-22).

Several times in the past, God has broken into the day of Satan and mankind with the interventions or Days of the Lord that were noted earlier. He did this to accomplish an immediate divine purpose (namely, the disruption, frustration, or destruction of some plan, purpose, or accomplishment of Satan and rebellious mankind), to graphically remind them that God is still the ultimate sovereign over the earth and universe, and to give them a foretaste or forewarning of the ultimate Day of the Lord that will come at the end of world history.

The future Day of the Lord will be far more significant than those days of the past. Its first phase will be a period of unprecedented, concentrated judgment involving the 70th week of Daniel and the coming of Christ after that week. In this phase God, who throughout most of history has permitted Satan and rebellious mankind to have their day, will suddenly intervene to destroy their rule over the world system, evict them from the earth, and thereby end their day in the world (Isa. 42:13-14; Rev. 6-19). This phase will be characterized by darkness and an intense outpouring of God's wrath.

The second phase will be a period of divine dominion over the world system. God will intervene to restore and exercise His theocratic-kingdom rule over the world through the last Adam, Jesus Christ (Zech. 14:1-9; 1 Cor. 15:45, 47; Rev. 20:1-6). This phase will be characterized by light and an outpouring of God's blessing.

THE DOUBLE SENSE OF THE DAY OF THE LORD

The Broad and Narrow Sense. We have seen that the Day of the Lord will have a twofold nature and, therefore, two phases. In addition, we should note that the biblical expression "the Day of the Lord" has a double sense (broad and narrow) in relationship to the future. The broad sense refers to an extended period of time involving divine interventions related at least to the 70th week of Daniel and the thousand-year Millennium. Evidence for this has been seen already. Concerning this broad sense, A. B. Davidson wrote, "Though the 'Day of the Lord,' as the expression implies, was at first conceived as a definite and brief period of time, being an era of judgment and salvation, it many times broadened out to be an extended period. From being a day it became an epoch."[15]

The narrow sense refers to one specific day—the day on which Christ will return to the earth from heaven with His angels.

Just as the word "day" in Genesis 1:5 has both a broad sense (a 24-hour day—"And the evening and the morning were the first day") and a narrow sense (the light part of a 24-hour day in contrast with the darkness part—"And God called the light Day, and the darkness he called Night")—so the expression "the Day of the Lord" has both a broad and a narrow sense in relationship to the future.

Diagram of Twofold Nature and Two Phases
of the Future Day of the Lord

THE DAY OF THE LORD	
70th WEEK darkness, divine wrath	MILLENNIUM light, divine blessing, administration of God's rule
7 years	1000 years

Evidence for the Narrow Sense. The fact that the Scriptures present a future Day of the Lord that will be narrowed or limited to one specific day is evident from the following combination of facts.

First, Revelation 16:12-16 indicates that the armies of all the nations of the world will not begin to gather in Israel for Armageddon until the sixth bowl is poured out. We should note that the pouring out of the sixth bowl and the resultant gathering of the armies will take place after a significant part of the broad Day of the Lord has already run its course.

Second, both Joel 3:9-16 and Zechariah 14:1-5 indicate that after the armies of the nations have gathered in Israel, "the day of the LORD cometh" and is "near." It is obvious from the language that this Day of the Lord will not take place until after the armies have gathered in Israel.

Since this Day of the Lord of Joel 3 and Zechariah 14 will not take place until after the armies have gathered in Israel, and since the armies will not begin to gather until after a significant part of the broad Day has run its course, another Day of the Lord will be yet to come.

This other Day will be one part of the broad Day of the Lord, but there is a genuine sense in which it will be a complete Day of the Lord on its own, different from the broad Day of the Lord. One difference will be its duration. As noted earlier, the broad Day will cover an extended period of time. By contrast, the Joel 3 and Zechariah 14 Day will be narrow or limited in time. Thus, there will be two future Days of the Lord.

Third, both Joel 3 and Zechariah 14 indicate that their Day of the Lord will be the specific time when the Messiah comes to fight against and destroy the armies gathered in Israel. Revelation 19:11-21 says that time will be when Christ comes from heaven to the earth. Thus, the narrow Day of Joel 3 and Zechariah 14 will be the day on which Christ comes to the earth.

The Great and Terrible Day of the Lord. We should note that Joel 3:14-15 indicates that the sun, moon, and stars will be darkened when the narrow Day of the Lord is near. Those heavenly bodies will be darkened before the narrow Day comes. Joel 2:31 declares that the heavenly bodies will be darkened before "the great and terrible day of the LORD come." It is obvious from this that Joel 3 and 2 are referring to the same Day of the Lord. We can conclude, then, that the narrow Day of Joel 3 and Zechariah 14 is to be identified with the great and terrible Day of the Lord—the day on which Christ will come to the earth.

The Babylonian Talmud made the following statement concerning the great and terrible Day of the Lord: "This is understood to refer to the advent of the Messiah."[16]

In light of what we have seen, we should note that the Scriptures apply the expression "the great and terrible day of the LORD" to the narrow Day, not the broad Day. The implication is that the narrow Day will differ from the rest of the broad Day, not only in duration, but also in significance.

Although the earlier part of the judgment phase of the broad Day will involve a great outpouring of divine wrath upon the domain of Satan and mankind, the narrow Day will be the grand climax of that judgment phase. Thus, E. W. Bullinger, when referring to the Day of the Lord of Joel 2:31, said, "It is called 'the great and terrible day of the LORD,' as though it were the climax of the whole period known as 'the day of the LORD.' "[17]

Along similar lines, C. F. Keil, when referring to the judgment of the narrow Day of Joel 3, declared, "It is the last decisive judgment, in which all the single judgments find their end."[18]

The narrow Day will be the great and terrible Day of the Lord because, in contrast with the earlier part of the judgment phase of the broad Day, the narrow Day will involve the coming of Christ from heaven to the earth. It therefore will do several things. It will expose God's enemies to the actual presence of Christ and the fullness of His divine power and glory, judgment and warfare (Mt. 24:29-30; 25:31; Rev. 19:11-12, 15). It will bring the angelic armies of heaven against these enemies (Mt. 13:40-42, 49-50; 25:31; Rev. 19:14). It will end the rule of Satan and rebellious mankind over the world system and evict them from the earth (Mt. 13:40-42, 49-50; 25:41, 46; Lk. 17:26-37; Rev. 19:17–20:3), thus ending their day on earth forever.

Because the narrow Day of the Lord will bring such a decisive, permanent change to the world, the Prophet Joel called the place where the grand climax of God's judgment will fall on Satan and rebellious mankind "the valley of decision" (3:14). Concerning this designation, C. F. Keil called it the "valley of the deciding judgment, from *charats*, to decide, to determine irrevocably."[19]

Double Sense of the Future Day of the Lord

	BROAD DAY OF THE LORD	
70th WEEK	The Coming of Christ with His Angels / Narrow Day of the Lord (Great and Terrible)	**MILLENNIUM**
divine wrath		
7 years		1000 years

IMPLICATIONS OF THE DOUBLE SENSE
OF THE DAY OF THE LORD

There are at least two significant implications of the fact that there will be both a broad Day of the Lord and a narrow Day of the Lord.

Since, as noted earlier, the narrow Day of Joel 3 and Zechariah 14 will take place *after* a significant part of the broad Day has already run its course, and since that narrow Day will be the day on which Christ comes to the earth, we can conclude that Christ will come to the earth after a significant part of the broad Day has already run its course, after a major part of God's wrath has been poured out upon the world. It will not take place before or at the beginning of the outpouring of God's wrath upon the world.

Second, we demonstrated earlier that the expression "the great and terrible day of the LORD" of Joel 2:31 refers to the narrow Day when Christ will come to the earth. It does not refer to the broad Day.

The Prophet Malachi (4:5) referred to the same great and terrible Day of the Lord as Joel (Malachi used identically the same Hebrew words and constructions that Joel used for the great and terrible Day of the Lord in 2:31). In its comments on Joel 2:31, *The International Critical Commentary* states, "The clause *before the great and terrible day of Yahweh comes* is the same as in Mal. 3:25 [Engl. 4:5])."[20]

Since Joel and Malachi were both referring to the same great and terrible Day of the Lord, and since Joel was referring to the narrow Day, we can conclude that Malachi's great and terrible Day of the Lord is also the narrow Day, the day on which Christ will come after the 70th week.

Malachi declared that God will send Elijah the prophet before the coming of the great and terrible Day of the Lord (4:5).

Since Malachi was referring to the narrow Day, we can conclude that he was indicating that God will send Elijah before the narrow Day, not before the broad Day when God begins to pour out His wrath upon the world. In light of the meaning of the great and terrible Day of the Lord, Malachi's declaration leaves room for Elijah to come and minister after the broad Day has begun and, therefore, while the wrath of God is being poured out upon the world.

CONCLUSION

This chapter on the biblical concept of the Day of the Lord has produced several conclusions.

1. The Day of the Lord refers to God's special interventions into the course of world events to judge His enemies, accomplish His purpose for history, and thereby demonstrate who He is—the sovereign God of the universe.

2. The Scriptures indicate that God's Day of the Lord interventions into the course of world events sometimes involve human instruments and activity, not just His direct, miraculous works.

3. The Scriptures indicate that the concept of the Day of the Lord is applicable, not only to past interventions of God into history, but also to the future.

4. The Scriptures indicate that the Day of the Lord in the future will be at least twofold in nature and thus will have two phases. First, during the 70th week of Daniel it will be characterized by darkness and a tremendous outpouring of divine wrath upon the world. Second, during the Millennium it will be characterized by light, an outpouring of divine blessing, and the administration of God's rule over the whole world.

5. The background of the Day of the Lord in the future involves the original establishment of the theocratic kingdom rule of God on earth. It also includes the loss of that rule and the usurping of the rule of the world system by Satan and rebellious mankind through the first Adam's rebellion against God. It includes both the function of the day of Satan and mankind through much of history and also the future intervention of God into world events to judge His enemies, end their rule over the world system, evict them from the earth, end their day in the world, and restore His theocratic kingdom rule on the earth through the last Adam, Jesus Christ.

6. The expression "the Day of the Lord" has a double sense in relationship to the future. First, in the broad sense it refers to an extended period of time involving divine interventions related to the 70th week of Daniel 9 plus the thousand-year Millennium. Second, in the narrow sense it refers to one specific day—the day on which Christ will return to the earth from heaven with His angels.

7. There is a genuine sense in which the narrow Day of the Lord will be a complete Day of the Lord on its own. It will be different from the broad Day of the Lord and will take place after a significant part of the broad Day has run its course. Thus, there will be two Days of the Lord.

8. Since the narrow Day is the day of Christ's coming to the earth, and since it will take place after a significant part of the broad Day has run its course, the coming of Christ to the earth will also take place after a significant part of the broad Day has run its course.

9. The great and terrible Day of the Lord is the narrow Day, the day of Christ's coming to the earth.

10. The narrow Day will be the grand climax of the judgment phase of the broad Day.

11. The narrow Day will be the great and terrible Day of the Lord because, in contrast with the earlier part of the judgment phase of the broad Day, the narrow Day will involve the coming of Christ from heaven to the earth. It therefore will expose God's enemies to the presence of Christ and

the fullness of His divine power and glory, judgment and warfare; and it will mark the end of the day of Satan and rebellious mankind on the earth.

12. Christ's coming to the earth will take place after a major part of God's wrath has been poured out upon the world in His broad Day of the Lord judgment. It will not take place before or at the beginning of the outpouring of God's wrath.

13. Malachi's great and terrible Day of the Lord is the narrow Day, not the broad Day.

14. Malachi indicated that God will send Elijah before the narrow Day (4:5), not before the broad Day (before God begins to pour out His wrath upon the world).

ENDNOTES

1. John A. T. Robinson, *Jesus and His Coming* (Philadelphia: The Westminster Press, 1979), p. 19.

2. A. B. Davidson, *The Theology of the Old Testament* in *International Theological Library* (New York: Charles Scribner's Sons, 1936), pp. 374-75.

3. *Ibid.*, pp. 378-79.

4. J. Barton Payne, *The Theology of the Older Testament* (Grand Rapids: Zondervan Publishing House, 1962), p. 464.

5. *Ibid.*, p. 465.

6. Gerhard Von Rad, *Old Testament Theology*, Vol. II, Trans. by D. M. G. Stalker (New York: Harper & Row, Publishers, 1965), p. 123.

7. Davidson, *Theology of the Old Testament*, p. 374.

8. A. B. Davidson, "Eschatology," *A Dictionary of the Bible*, James Hastings, ed., Vol. 1 (Peabody, MA: Hendrickson Publishers, 1988), p. 736.

9. Davidson, *Theology of the Old Testament*, pp. 377-78.

10. Payne, *Theology of the Older Testament*, p. 464.

11. H. H. Rowley, "The Day of the Lord," *The Faith of Israel* (Philadelphia: The Westminster Press, 1957), p. 178.

12. *Ibid.*, p. 181.

13. *Ibid.*, p. 187.

14. *Ibid.*, p. 191.

15. Davidson, *Theology of the Old Testament*, p. 381.

16. *Shabbath*, 118a, in *The Babylonian Talmud* (London: Soncino Press, 1938), footnote, p. 580.

17. E. W. Bullinger, *The Apocalypse Or "The Day of the Lord"* (London: Eyre and Spottiswoode, 1935), p. 248.

18. C. F. Keil, *The Twelve Minor Prophets*, Vol. I, in *Biblical Commentary on the Old Testament*, trans. by James Martin (Grand Rapids: Wm. B. Eerdmans Publishing Company, 1954), p. 226.

19. *Ibid.*, p. 228.

20. John Merlin Powis Smith, William Hayes Ward, and Julius A. Bewer, *A Critical and Exegetical Commentary on Micah, Zephaniah, Nahum, Habakkuk, Obadiah and Joel*, in *The International Critical Commentary* (Edinburgh: T. & T. Clark, 1911), p. 124.

CHAPTER THREE

THE DAY OF THE LORD, THE TIME OF JACOB'S TROUBLE, AND THE GREAT TRIBULATION

N ow that we have presented evidence to the effect that the future broad Day of the Lord will begin with a phase of divine judgment, we must ask a significant question: How long will the beginning judgment phase of the Day of the Lord last? To obtain an answer, we must look at several things, one being the relationship of the Day of the Lord to the Time of Jacob's Trouble and the Great Tribulation. (Note: In our effort to study these features thoroughly, we will have to repeat some things we have already examined. We are building a case as an attorney would fashion a brief. One point builds upon the next and the two on a third, etc.)

A COMPARISON OF THE DAY OF THE LORD, THE TIME OF JACOB'S TROUBLE, AND THE GREAT TRIBULATION

The Scriptures indicate that the Day of the Lord, the Time of Jacob's Trouble, and the Great Tribulation have several things in common.

First, the concept of trouble or tribulation is associated with all three (the Day of the Lord in Zeph. 1:14-17, the Time of Jacob's Trouble in Jer. 30:7, and the Great Tribulation in Dan. 12:1 [Jesus' Great Tribulation statements in Mt. 24:21, 29 were a reference to Daniel 12:1, indicating that Daniel is referring to the Great Tribulation]). All three of these Old Testament passages use the same Hebrew word for trouble. The Hebrew scholars who produced the Septuagint used the Greek word for tribulation to translate this Hebrew word for trouble in Zephaniah 1:15 and Daniel 12:1, showing they understood that both the Day of the Lord and the Great Tribulation will be characterized by tribulation.

Since the Day of the Lord will be "a day of wrath" (Zeph. 1:14-15) and will not be characterized by tribulation, it is evident that the Bible associates tribulation, not only with the persecution of believers by Satan and his human agents (Rev. 1:9; 2:9-10; Mt. 24:9 [where the words translated "they deliver you up to be afflicted" literally mean "they deliver you unto tribulation"]), but also with the outpouring of God's wrath.

Along similar lines, Romans 2:5-9 associates tribulation with the outpouring of God's wrath upon the unsaved in "the day of wrath and revelation of the righteous judgment of God." Second Thessalonians 1:6-10 also links tribulation with the judgment God will administer at Christ's Second Coming, not only upon those who persecute believers, but also upon all unbelievers.

Second, the concept of an unparalleled time of trouble is identified with all three (the Day of the Lord in Joel 2:1-2, the Time of Jacob's Trouble in Jer. 30:7, and the Great Tribulation in Dan. 12:1 and Mt. 24:21).

Since there can be only one unparalleled time of trouble, and since that unparalleled time is identified with all three, we can conclude that the Time of Jacob's Trouble and the Great Tribulation will be included within the Day of the Lord.

Third, the term "great" is used for all three (the Day of the Lord in Zeph. 1:14, the Time of Jacob's Trouble in Jer. 30:7, and the Great Tribulation in Mt. 24:21 and Rev. 7:14).

Fourth, the concept of birth pangs is associated with all three (the Day of the Lord in Isa. 13:6-9 and 1 Th. 5:2-3, and the Time of Jacob's Trouble in Jer. 30:6-7). An earlier chapter demonstrated that the Time of Jacob's Trouble and the Great Tribulation are equal to the same time period and that since birth pangs are associated with the Time of Jacob's Trouble, birth pangs must also be associated with the time period of the Great Tribulation.

Fifth, the expression "that day" is used for all three (the Day of the Lord in Isa. 2:12, 17, 19-21 and Zeph. 1:7, 9-10, 14-15, and the Time of Jacob's Trouble in Jer. 30:7). It is interesting to note that, with reference to the Great Tribulation, the Septuagint translates "a time of trouble" in Dan. 12:1 as "that day of tribulation."

Sixth, Israel's future repentance or spiritual restoration to God is associated with all three (the Day of the Lord in Zech. 12:2-3, 9-14; 13:1-2; 14:1-3, the Time of Jacob's Trouble in Jer. 30:7-9, 22, and the latter day Tribulation in Dt. 4:27-30; 30:1-3).

These comparisons demonstrate that several of the same concepts and terms are associated with the Day of the Lord, the Time of Jacob's Trouble, and the Great Tribulation in the Scriptures. These consistent associations indicate that the broad Day of the Lord will not be totally separate or distinct from the Time of Jacob's Trouble or the Great Tribulation. Indeed, they indicate that the Day of the Lord will cover or at least include the same time period as the Time of Jacob's Trouble and the Great Tribulation. This is especially demonstrated by the fact that all three are identified with the unparalleled time of trouble.

Since the Day of the Lord will cover or include the Great Tribulation, we must determine how long the Great Tribulation will last if we want to learn the duration of the judgment phase of the Day of the Lord.

THE BEGINNING OF THE GREAT TRIBULATION

The Great Tribulation will begin in the middle of the seven-year period known as the 70th week of Daniel. This is evidenced in Daniel 9:27, which states that in the middle of the 70th week the Antichrist will put a stop to the Jewish sacrifices and grain offerings. This teaching implies that before the middle of the 70th week there will be a restoration of the nation of Israel to its homeland, that Israel will have a new Temple, and that the nation's sacrificial system will have been reinstituted.

The Antichrist will put a stop to the Jewish sacrifices because of his desire to be worshiped as God. By the middle of the 70th week, he will turn against every form of established worship to clear the way for the worship of himself. He will magnify himself to the level of deity, take his seat in the new Temple, announce that he is God, demand that his subjects worship him, wage war against the saints of that time, and set up some detestable thing (probably an image of himself) in the Temple (Dan. 7:8, 11, 20, 25; 11:36-37; 2 Th. 2:3-4; Rev. 13:4-8, 11-17; 19:20; 20:4). Daniel 9:27 called this detestable activity of the Antichrist "the overspreading of abominations."

It is interesting to note that the Antichrist will make the Temple, in which the Jews will offer sacrifices, the center of the worship of himself. The fact that he will stop the Jewish sacrifices there in order to clear the way for the worship of himself, together with the fact that he will do this in the middle of the 70th week, prompts the conclusion that he will enact the overspreading of abominations in the middle of the 70th week.

Jesus referred to this Daniel 9:27 "overspreading of abominations" in Matthew 24:15. Then He said, "then shall be Great Tribulation, such as was not since the beginning of the world to this time, no, nor ever shall be" (Mt. 24:21), thereby indicating that the Great Tribulation will begin when the overspreading of abominations of Daniel 9:27 occurs.

Since the Great Tribulation will begin when the overspreading of abominations occurs in the middle of the 70th week, we can conclude that the Great Tribulation will begin in the middle of the 70th week of Daniel, or after the first three and one-half years of that seven-year period have transpired.

THE LENGTH OF THE GREAT TRIBULATION

The Great Tribulation will last throughout the entire second half (second three and one-half years) of the 70th week of Daniel. Several things indicate this.

The First Indicator. In Matthew 24:15-21 Jesus issued a forewarning to the Jews who will be living in their homeland during the 70th week. He warned that when the Antichrist enacts the abomination of desolation (a reference to the overspreading of abominations of Dan. 9:27) in the middle of the 70th week, the Jews who will be in Judea at that time should flee to the wilderness of the mountains, because his enactment of the abomination of desolation will begin the unparalleled time of trouble known as the Great Tribulation.

This forewarning to the Jews indicates two things. First, the enactment of the abomination of desolation in the middle of the 70th week will begin a time of terrible persecution of the Jews, which is why they should flee to the wilderness. Second, two of the characteristics of the Great Tribulation will be severe persecution of the Jews and their hiding in the wilderness. Consequently, any biblical indication of the length of this persecution and hiding will also indicate the length of the Great Tribulation.

In Revelation 12 the Apostle John recorded two divinely revealed signs that God used to disclose some significant events of the 70th week. One was a great red dragon (v. 3). John clearly stated that the dragon represented the Devil or Satan (v. 9). The other sign was a woman who was clothed with the sun, stood on the moon, had a crown of 12 stars on her head, and gave birth to a son who was caught up to God in heaven and would eventually rule all the nations with a rod of iron (vv. 1-2, 4-5).

The sign of the woman is based on imagery found in the Old Testament. In Isaiah 54:5-6 and Ezekiel 16:7-14, Israel is portrayed as a woman. In Genesis 37:9-10, Jacob (whom God renamed Israel) is portrayed as the sun; Rachel, his wife, is portrayed as the moon; and his sons, the heads of the 12 tribes of Israel, are portrayed as stars. This imagery indicates that the woman in Revelation 12 represents the nation of Israel through which the Messiah was born into the world. The Scriptures clearly present the Messiah as the one who will rule the nations with a rod of iron (Ps. 2:7-9; Rev. 19:15).

Revelation 12 teaches that the dragon (Satan) will persecute the woman (Israel) during the 70th week of Daniel (v. 13). It also indicates that Israel will flee to a wilderness area to escape this persecution (vv. 6, 14) and that Satan will try to destroy Israel (vv. 15-17).

Revelation 12 states the length of time this persecution and hiding of the Jews in the wilderness will last and expresses it in two different ways.

First, it will last for 1,260 days (v. 6). The ancient world followed a lunar rather than a solar calendar system and therefore reckoned a year to consist of 360 days.[1] The Bible follows that ancient system (for example, Gen. 7:11, 24; 8:4—the five months contained 150 days; thus, each month consisted of 30 days, and 12 months consisted of 360 days). The 1,260 days of Revelation 12:6 divided by the 360 days of the ancient lunar year equal three and one-half years, exactly one-half of the seven-year 70th week.

Second, Revelation 12:14 states that Israel will hide in the wilderness from Satan for "a time, and times, and half a time." Daniel 7:25 uses this identical time designation for the length of time that the Antichrist will persecute the saints of the 70th week. There the original language indicates that this designation refers to one time plus two times plus one-half time, for a total of three and one-half times.

How long will three and one-half times be? Revelation 13:5-7, when referring to this same persecution of 70th-week saints by the Antichrist, declares that it will last for 42 months, which equal three and one-half years. It is obvious from this that the three and one-half times of Daniel 7:25 equal three and one-half years. Therefore, since Daniel 7:25 uses the identical time designation as Revelation 12:14, we can conclude that the "time, and times, and half a time" also equal three and one-half years.

Thus, the time expressions in Revelation 12:6 and 14 indicate the same thing: The Jews will be persecuted and will hide in a wilderness area for three and one-half years, exactly one-half of the seven-year 70th week.

This leads to two conclusions. First, since, as noted earlier, this persecution and hiding will begin in the middle of the 70th week, we can conclude that this three and one-half years will cover the second half of the 70th week. Second, since, as noted earlier, this persecution and hiding of the Jews will characterize the Great Tribulation, and since they will last for the three and one-half years of the second half of the 70th week, we can conclude that the Great Tribulation will last for the three and one-half years of the second half of the 70th week.

The Second Indicator. Daniel 12 also indicates that the Great Tribulation will last throughout the three and one-half years of the second half of the 70th week. In Daniel 12:1, Daniel was told about a future "time of trouble, such as never was since there was a nation even to that same time." As noted earlier, Jesus referred to Daniel 12:1 in Matthew 24:21-22, calling it "Great Tribulation." Thus, Daniel 12:1 is referring to the Great Tribulation, which, as has already been demonstrated, will begin in the middle of the 70th week.

In Daniel 12:6 an angel asked, "How long the end of the wonders?" (literal translation). Hebrew scholar C. F. Keil indicated that the angel was not asking how long all the wondrous things of the latter part of Daniel 11 and early part of Daniel 12 will continue. Instead, he was asking how long *the end* of those wondrous things will continue.[2] Since the language of Daniel 12:1 indicates that the Great Tribulation will begin after the other wondrous things described in the latter part of Daniel 11 have taken place, we can conclude that the Great Tribulation will be the end of those wondrous things. Thus, the angel was asking how long the Great Tribulation will last.

The angel was given two answers to his question in Daniel 12:7. First, he was told that the Great Tribulation will last for "a time, times, and an half." Earlier it was demonstrated that this time designation equals three and one-half years. Thus, the angel was told that the Great Tribulation will last for three and one-half years. Since the Great Tribulation will begin in the middle of the 70th week, this means that it will last throughout the entire second half of the seven-year 70th week.

The Third Indicator. The second answer to the angel's question provides the third indication of how long the Great Tribulation will last. This answer indicates that all the events of the Great Tribulation will be finished "when he shall have accomplished to scatter the power of the holy people" (v. 7). The primary meaning of the word translated "to scatter" is "to beat to pieces, to shatter."[3]

The word translated "power" is literally the word for "hand." "The primary meaning of this noun is 'the terminal part of the arm used to perform functions of man's will.' "[4] Thus, the word is related to the function of the human will. In line with this, sometimes the word is used to express "submission" and "obstinate rebellion."[5]

The expression "the holy people" is a reference to the people of Israel. The root term for the word "holy" means "to divide"[6]—to be divided from other people or things, to be different or distinct from them. Sometimes it goes so far as to mean unique. The Old Testament Scriptures teach that the nation of Israel is holy or unique because God divided it from other nations. He made Israel different by entering into a unique relationship with it and by doing certain things uniquely for it.

In Deuteronomy 7:6 Moses declared to Israel, "For thou art an holy people unto the LORD thy God; the LORD thy God hath chosen thee to be a special people unto himself, above all people who are upon the face of the earth" (cp. Ex. 11:7; 19:5-6; Dt. 4:6-8, 32-34; 10:15; 14:2; 26:18-19; Jer. 2:2-3; Amos 3:1-2). God locked Israel into this unique relationship forever (2 Sam. 7:23-24).

Taken together, these meanings of the expressions "to scatter," "power," and "the holy people" indicate that the second answer to the angel's question means that the Great Tribulation will be finished when God has completely shattered the obstinate rebellion of the nation of Israel against Him. In other words, the Great Tribulation will end when Israel's rebellion against God's rule ends. In light of this, any biblical indication of when Israel's rebellion will end will also indicate when the Great Tribulation will end.

The Scriptures teach that Israel has been repeatedly and stubbornly rebellious against God throughout most of its history and that this rebellion causes God's wrathful judgment to come against His unique nation (Dt. 9:7, 23-24; 28:15-68; 30; Neh. 9:16-17, 26-30; Ps. 89:32; Isa. 1:2-5; 30:1, 9-15; 63:7-10; Ezek. 2:3-8; Acts 7:51-52).

In light of Israel's persistent rebellion, God revealed to Daniel an extended future program that He has determined specifically for Israel and its holy city, Jerusalem (Dan. 9:24-27). God indicated that this program would involve 70 "weeks" (lit., 70 "sevens") of time (v. 24).

God also revealed that He would use the 70 weeks of this program to accomplish several things with regard to Israel and Jerusalem. The first is "to finish the transgression" (v. 24). The word translated "transgression" has the root meaning "to rebel."[7] With the word "the" in this context, the word refers to Israel's specific sin of rebellion against God's rule, which was the root sin that prompted all of Israel's other sins. God was revealing that Israel will not stop its rebellion against His rule until all 70 weeks of His extended program for Israel have run their course. Thus, Israel's rebellion will be shattered or ended when the 70th week of Daniel ends.[8]

Another prophetic revelation demonstrates the validity of this conclusion. Zechariah 12 indicates that Israel will repent of its rebellion and receive Jesus Christ as its Messiah-Savior when it sees Him at His Second Coming (vv. 10-14) when the armies of all the nations are gathered in its land and are warring against it (vv. 1-9; cp. Joel 3:9-17; Zech. 14:1-5; Rom. 11:25-27; Rev. 19:11-21).

Revelation 16:12-16 says the armies of the nations will not even begin to gather in Israel for Armageddon until the sixth bowl is poured out—after the seven seals, the seven trumpets, and the first five bowls of the 70th week have already taken place (Rev. 6:1–16:11) and there will be only one more judgment (the seventh bowl, Rev. 16:17–18:24) left before the end of the 70th week and the Second Coming of Christ (Rev. 19:11-21). This indicates that the armies of the nations will not gather in Israel until nearly the end of the 70th week.

Since Israel will repent of its rebellion and receive Jesus Christ as its Messiah-Savior when it sees Him at His Second Coming, as the armies of all the nations are gathered in its land and are warring against it, and since the armies of the nations will not gather in Israel until nearly the end of the 70th week, we can conclude again that Israel's rebellion will be shattered or ended when the 70th week ends.

Since, as noted earlier, the Great Tribulation will end when Israel's rebellion against God's rule ends, and since that will occur at the end of the 70th week, we can conclude that the Great Tribulation will end when the 70th week ends. Thus, since the Great Tribulation will begin in the middle of the 70th week, it will last throughout the entire second half of the 70th week.

In Daniel 12:7, when the being gave his two answers to the angel's question, he raised both hands toward heaven and swore an oath by God. Usually only one hand is raised when swearing an oath. The fact that this being raised both hands emphasized the solemnity and importance of the oath.[9] Since he put his answer in the form of an oath, and since he based that oath on the eternal God who is sovereign and truthful, he asserted the truthfulness and reliability of his answer in the strongest way possible. He affirmed the absolute certainty of the Great Tribulation's lasting for three and one-half years, until Israel's rebellion against God ends at the end of the 70th week.

The Fourth Indicator. As noted earlier, in Matthew 24:15 and 21 Jesus taught that the Great Tribulation will begin when the overspreading of abominations of Daniel 9:27 takes place in the middle of the 70th week. Jesus' statements indicate that there will be a definite connection between the Great Tribulation and the overspreading of abominations and the activities it initiates.

In addition, we noted earlier that the overspreading of abominations will involve the setting up of some detestable thing (probably an image of the Antichrist) in the future Temple. Again, this activity in the middle of the 70th week will be the starting point of the Antichrist's program of magnifying himself to the level of deity, taking his seat in the new Temple, announcing that he is God, demanding worship of himself, and waging war against the saints.

All of this indicates that two of the things characterizing the Great Tribulation will be the worship of the Antichrist and his warring against the saints. Consequently, any biblical revelation concerning the length of time the Antichrist will be worshiped and will war against the saints will indicate how long the Great Tribulation will last. Several biblical passages reveal this.

First, Daniel 7:21-22 states that the Antichrist will wage war against the saints and prevail against them until the time when the saints are given the rule of the earth for the Millennial Kingdom (cp. 7:25-27). The Scriptures indicate that the Millennial Kingdom will be established in conjunction with the coming of Christ to the earth after the end of the 70th week (Zech. 14:1-9; Rev. 19:11–20:6). Thus, the Antichrist will wage war against the saints through the end of the 70th week. In conjunction with this, it should be noted that Revelation 19:11-20 reveals that the Antichrist (the "beast" in v. 20) will exercise great authority over the other rulers and armies of the world until Christ comes.

Second, Daniel 7:25 states that the Antichrist will "wear out the saints of the most High . . . and they shall be given into his hand until a time and times and the dividing of time." Earlier we showed that this time designation means three and one-half years. Thus, Daniel 7:25 teaches that the

Antichrist will wage war against the saints for three and one-half years. Since, as we noted earlier, he will begin to wage war in the middle of the 70th week, this must be the three and one-half years of the second half of the 70th week, meaning that the Antichrist will war against the saints through the end of the 70th week.

Third, Revelation 13:4-8 indicates that once the Antichrist begins to blaspheme God by claiming deity for himself, to be worshiped, and to war against the saints, he will be given power to continue these activities for 42 months (v. 5), which equals three and one-half years. Since the Antichrist will begin these activities in the middle of the 70th week, we can conclude that he will be worshiped and will war against the saints through the end of the 70th week.

In light of the evidence in the three passages that have been examined, the following comments by Irenaeus, Bishop of Lyons during the last quarter of the second century, are significant:

> But when this Antichrist shall have devastated all things in this world, he will reign for three years and six months, and sit in the temple at Jerusalem; and then the Lord will come from heaven in the clouds, in the glory of the Father, sending this man and those who follow him into the lake of fire; but bringing in for the righteous the times of the kingdom.[10]

Irenaeus was discipled by Polycarp, Bishop of Smyrna, who had been taught by the Apostle John.

Fourth, Daniel 11:36 (having stated that the Antichrist will exalt himself, magnify himself above every god, and blaspheme God) declares that he will "prosper till the indignation be accomplished." The description of these activities is essentially the same as those assigned to the Antichrist in Revelation 13:4-8, which states that he will be worshiped as God, blaspheme God, war against the saints, and be given power to continue for three and one-half years.

In light of this similarity, we can conclude that Daniel 11:36 is teaching that the Antichrist will be worshiped as God and war against the saints until "the indignation be accomplished."

The word translated "be accomplished" means to be brought to a "full end."[11] "The basic idea of this root is 'to bring a process to completion.' "[12]

A study of the term "indignation" throughout Scripture reveals that "the indignation" refers to the period of history during which God is indignant or angry with Israel because of its rebellion against Him. It is the time when God judges Israel, usually at the hands of the Gentiles. For example, the indignation included Israel's conquest and cruel treatment by Assyria (Isa. 10:5, 25) and its conquest and captivity by Babylon (Lam. 2:5-6; Zech. 1:12). Daniel 11:36 indicates that the indignation will also include the time when the Antichrist will exercise great authority in the world, be worshiped as God, and war against the saints.

Putting the meanings of the terms "be accomplished" and "the indignation" together, we can conclude that Daniel 11:36 is teaching that the Antichrist will exercise great authority in the world, be worshiped as God, and war against the saints until the period of history during which God is indignant or angry with Israel because of its rebellion against Him is brought to its full end. When will that occur? In light of the foregoing, it is obvious that it will occur when Israel ends its rebellion against God, which, as indicated earlier, will be at the end of the 70th week (Dan. 9:24; 12:7). Thus, the indignation will be brought to a full end at the end of the 70th week of Daniel.

Since Daniel 11:36 teaches that the Antichrist will be worshiped as God and war against the saints until the indignation is brought to a full end, and since the indignation will be brought to a full end when the 70th week ends, we can conclude that the Antichrist will be worshiped as God and war against the saints through the end of the 70th week.

We have learned that all four of these passages produce the same conclusion: The Antichrist will be worshiped as God and war against the saints through the end of the 70th week of Daniel.

Since, as we noted earlier, the worship of the Antichrist as God and his warring against the saints will characterize the Great Tribulation, and since these things related to the Antichrist will last through the end of the 70th week, we can conclude that the Great Tribulation will last through the end of the 70th week. Beginning in the middle of the 70th week, the Great Tribulation will cover the entire second half of that seven-year period.

THE SHORTENING OF THE GREAT TRIBULATION

But will the Great Tribulation last that long? After having talked about the Great Tribulation (Mt. 24:21), Jesus said, "And except those days should be shortened, there should no flesh be saved; but for the elect's sake those days shall be shortened" (v. 22). Did He mean that God will shorten the Great Tribulation to fewer than 1,260 days and that, therefore, the Great Tribulation will not last to the end of the 70th week?

Earlier we noted that the heavenly being who answered the angel's question concerning the length of the Great Tribulation raised both hands toward heaven and solemnly swore by the eternal God that the Great Tribulation will last for three and one-half years, until Israel's rebellion against God ends at the end of the 70th week. This was his way of asserting the absolute truthfulness and reliability of his answers in the strongest way possible and, therefore, of affirming the absolute certainty that the Great

Tribulation will last for three and one-half years until Israel's rebellion against God ends at the end of the 70th week.

In light of this strong affirmation, we must conclude that Jesus did *not* mean that the Great Tribulation will not last through the end of the 70th week. If He did not mean that, what did He mean?

Mark's record of Jesus' same statement sheds light on its meaning: "And except the Lord had shortened those days, no flesh should be saved; but for the elect's sake, whom he hath chosen, he hath shortened the days" (Mk. 13:20). Two things should be noted about Jesus' statement. First, in the ancient world the verb that is consistently translated "shortened" in the Matthew and Mark passages primarily meant "to cut off."[13] It frequently was used to refer to the cutting off of hands and feet.

Second, the two verbs translated "had shortened" and "hath shortened" in the Mark passage and the verb translated "should be shortened" in the Matthew passage are all in the aorist tense and indicative mood with the augment. Aorist tense verbs have no time significance except when they are in the indicative mood with the augment. That form is used to express past time.[14]

A number of scholars have concluded that since the two verbs in Mark 13:20 are in that form, they are expressing action in the past and therefore have significant bearing on the meaning of Jesus' statement. For example, Ezra P. Gould stated, "The [aorist] tenses put this action in the past—*if the Lord had not shortened the time, no flesh would have been saved*. The language is proleptic, stating the event as it already existed in the Divine decree."[15]

G. B. Winer declared, "The two aorists do not stand for imperfects; the meaning is, *if the Lord had not* (in His decree) *shortened the days, all flesh would have perished*."[16]

Gerhard Delling wrote,

God has already (Mk. 13:20 . . .) 'cut short' the time of the tribulation in Judaea. That is, He has made it shorter than it would normally have been in terms of the purpose and power of the oppressors. If He had not done so, even those who prove themselves to be the elect by their faithfulness, and who have been wonderfully kept thus far, would be brought to physical destruction.[17]

Through these assertions, these scholars indicated that Jesus was teaching that God in the past had already shortened the Great Tribulation. He did so in the sense that in the past He determined to cut it off at a specific time rather than let it continue indefinitely. In His omniscience, God knew that if the Great Tribulation were to continue indefinitely, all flesh would perish from the earth. To prevent that from happening, in the past God sovereignly set a specific time for the Great Tribulation to end.

The Time of the Shortening. When in the past did God shorten the Great Tribulation? Jesus' statement about the shortening in Mark 13:20 clearly indicates that God shortened it sometime *before* Jesus made His statement. Two of the scholars quoted above have expressed their belief that it occurred when He decreed or determined in eternity past what would happen during the course of world history, and the Bible supports this belief, for it teaches that God decreed or determined what will happen during the course of world history (Isa. 14:24-27; 46:9-11; Dan. 9:24, 26-27; 11:36; Lk. 22:22; Acts 2:23; 4:27-28; Eph. 1:11; 3:11). What He has determined cannot be annulled. In Isaiah 14:24-27 God said,

> The LORD of hosts hath sworn, saying, Surely as I have thought, so shall it come to pass; and as I have purposed, so shall it stand: That I will break the Assyrian in my land, and upon my mountains tread him under foot; then shall his yoke depart from off them, and his burden depart from off their shoulders. This is the purpose that is purposed upon the whole earth, and this is the hand that is stretched out upon all the nations. For the LORD of hosts hath purposed, and who shall annul it? And his hand is stretched out, and who shall turn it back?

The Bible also indicates that it was in eternity past that God decreed or determined what would happen during history. It mentions His "eternal purpose" (Eph. 3:11) and His "own purpose . . . before the world began" (2 Tim. 1:9). In Isaiah 46:9-11 God said,

> Remember the former things of old; for I am God, and there is none else; I am God, and there is none like me, Declaring the end from the beginning, and from ancient times the things that are not yet done, saying, My counsel shall stand, and I will do all my pleasure; Calling a ravenous bird from the east, the man that executeth my counsel from a far country; yea, I have spoken it, I will also bring it to pass; I have purposed it, I will also do it.

In this passage God presented evidence to the effect that He alone is the true God. Before the beginning of time He purposed or determined what would happen during the course of history. Everything that He determined He causes to happen (cp. Eph. 1:11, "according to the purpose of him who worketh all things after the counsel of his own will"). Therefore, as God, from the very beginning of time He could declare in advance what would happen throughout history to its very end (cp. Eph. 1:9, "Having made known unto us the mystery of his will, according to his good pleasure which he hath purposed in himself").

In line with what the Bible says about this subject, Henry C. Thiessen wrote, "The decrees are God's eternal purpose. He does not make His plans or alter them as human history develops. He made them in eternity, and, because He is immutable, they remain unaltered (Ps. 33:11; James 1:17)."[18]

Paul Enns stated, "The decrees of God have been established in eternity past and have reference to God's sovereign control over every realm and over all events."[19]

The Apostle Paul taught that one of the things God determined was "the times." In Acts 17:26 he declared that God, who made the world and all things in it, "hath determined the times before appointed." The word translated "determined" sometimes refers to what God decreed.[20] The words translated "the times before appointed" refer to "fixed times."[21] James Hope Moulton wrote that the tenses of the verbal forms in Acts 17:26 indicate that this determination took place "in the Divine plan" before the creation of man.[22] Thus, in this context Paul taught that in eternity past, as part of His eternal plan for history, God decreed or determined fixed times by which to govern man.

It is interesting to note that, just as the verb that is consistently translated "shortened" in Jesus' statement concerning the shortening of the Great Tribulation primarily means "to cut off," so the Old Testament Hebrew verbs that refer to God's decree or determination have the basic meaning of "to cut." For example, that is the basic meaning of the verb translated "determined" in the statement "Seventy weeks are determined upon thy people and upon thy holy city" (Dan. 9:24).[23] God cut a fixed time of 70 weeks (sevens) of years to chasten Israel and end its rebellion against Him.

Another example is found in Daniel 11:36, where the verb translated "determined" in the declaration that the Antichrist "shall prosper till the indignation be accomplished; for that which is determined shall be done" also has the basic meaning of "to cut."[24] "The word connotes the concept of 'determined' and refers to something which cannot be changed. Perhaps the basic idea of 'cut' is evident here in that that which is incised cannot be altered."[25] God cut a fixed time for the Antichrist to prosper and for the indignation to be brought to a full end. This fixed time cannot be changed.

In light of what has been seen, we can conclude that in eternity past God shortened the Great Tribulation in the sense that He decreed or determined to cut it off at a specific time rather than let it continue indefinitely. He sovereignly fixed a specific time for the Great Tribulation to end—when it had run its course for three and one-half years or 42 months or 1,260 days. That fixed time cannot be changed. As we noted earlier in conjunction with Isaiah 46:9-11, everything that God determined in eternity past He causes to happen.

Another truth was noted earlier from Isaiah 46:9-11. From the beginning of time God could declare in advance what would happen during history, because in eternity past He determined what would happen and everything He determined He causes to happen. In many instances God has declared in advance things that He determined in eternity past. Those declarations are the prophecies of future happenings contained in the Bible. Thus, the prophecies already noted in Daniel 12:7—that the Great Tribulation will last for three and one-half years and until Israel's rebellion against God ends at the end of the 70th week—are Old Testament declarations of what God determined in eternity past.

We can conclude that when Jesus spoke of the Great Tribulation's being shortened, He did not mean that it will be cut shorter than the three and one-half years already prophesied before His statement. The tense of the verbs translated "shortened" in the Mark 13:20 record of Jesus' statement indicates that He meant God cut the Great Tribulation short in eternity past when He determined that it will last for the fixed time of three and one-half years.

Since, as noted earlier, the tense of the first verb translated "shortened" in the Matthew 24:22 record of Jesus' statement is the same as the tense of the Mark 13:20 verbs, we can conclude that the Matthew and Mark passages have the same meaning. The second verb translated "shortened" in Matthew 24:22 is a different tense (future) from the others, but that does not nullify this conclusion. That verb simply indicates that in the future God will actually cause to happen what He determined in eternity past and prophesied in the Old Testament.

A number of scholars have recognized this meaning of Jesus' statement. For example, concerning Mark 13:20, John D. Grassmick wrote,

> If the Lord (Yahweh God; cf. 12:29), had not already decided in His sovereign plan to cut short (terminate, not reduce the number of) those days (lit., "the days"; cf. 13:19), no one would survive (esothe, "would be saved"; cf. 15:30-31), that is, be delivered from physical death; this is in contrast with 13:13. But God set limits on the duration of the end-time Tribulation, because of the elect, those redeemed during "those days."[26]

J. Dwight Pentecost stated,

> Christ's words cannot mean that the days will be decreased in number. The phrase "cut short" means "to terminate." If those days with their awful judgments were allowed to continue indefinitely, the human race would be totally destroyed. Christ meant that God will allow that period to run its course but will terminate it according to His timetable so that a remnant will be spared.[27]

Thus, Jesus' statement concerning the shortening of the Great Tribulation does not nullify what was examined earlier. The Great Tribulation will last throughout the entire three and one-half years of the second half of the 70th week and will end when the 70th week ends.

CONCLUSION

This chapter began with the following question: How long will the beginning judgment phase of the Day of the Lord last? In response to this question, this chapter has examined three major areas and produced three major conclusions.

First, we examined the relationship of the Day of the Lord to the Time of Jacob's Trouble and the Great Tribulation and concluded that the Day of the Lord will not be totally separate or distinct from the Time of Jacob's Trouble or the Great Tribulation. The Day of the Lord will at least cover or include the same time period as the Time of Jacob's Trouble and the Great Tribulation.

Then we examined the duration of the Great Tribulation and concluded that it will begin in the middle of the 70th week and last throughout its entire second half. That is, the Great Tribulation will consist of the second three and one-half years or 42 months or 1,260 days of the 70th week and will end when the 70th week ends.

The third area we examined was whether Jesus' statement concerning the shortening of the Great Tribulation meant that the Great Tribulation will not last throughout the entire second half of the 70th week, and we concluded that it did not.

Taken together, these three conclusions produce a fourth one for this chapter. Since the Day of the Lord will at least cover or include the same time period as the Great Tribulation, and since the Great Tribulation will last throughout the entire second half of the 70th week, we can conclude that the beginning judgment phase of the Day of the Lord will at least cover or include the entire second half of the 70th week.

But is that all that the judgment phase of the Day of the Lord will cover or include? To determine the answer to that question, the next chapter will examine two other areas: the end and beginning of the beginning judgment phase of the Day of the Lord.

ENDNOTES

1. Paul Couderc, "Calendar-Year," *The Encyclopedia Americana*, 1969, V, p. 184.

2. C. F. Keil, *Biblical Commentary on Daniel*, in *Biblical Commentary on the Old Testament*, trans. by M. G. Easton (Grand Rapids: Wm. B. Eerdmans Publishing Company, 1959), p. 489.

3. Keil, *Daniel*, pp. 490-91.

4. Ralph H. Alexander, "yad," *Theological Wordbook of the Old Testament*, Vol. I, ed. by R. Laird Harris, Gleason L. Archer, Jr., and Bruce K. Waltke (Chicago: Moody Press, 1980), p. 362.

5. *Ibid.*, p. 363.

6. Otto Proksch, "hagios," *Theological Dictionary of the New Testament*, Vol. I, ed. by Gerhard Kittel, trans. and ed. by Geoffrey W. Bromiley (Grand Rapids: Wm. B. Eerdmans Publishing Company, 1964), p. 89.

7. H. C. Leupold, *Exposition of Daniel* (Grand Rapids: Baker Book House, 1949), p. 412.

8. For a fuller study of the 70-weeks prophecy see: Renald E. Showers, *The Most High God* (Bellmawr, NJ: The Friends of Israel Gospel Ministry, 1982). pp. 115-36.

9. Leon Wood, *A Commentary on Daniel* (Grand Rapids: Zondervan Publishing House, 1973), p. 323.

10. Irenaeus, *Against Heresies*, Book V., chpt. 30, section 3 in *The Ante-Nicene Fathers*, ed. by Rev. Alexander Roberts and James Donaldson (Buffalo: The Christian Literature Publishing Company, 1885), I, p. 560.

11. John N. Oswalt, "kala," *Theological Wordbook of the Old Testament*, Vol. I, ed. by R. Laird Harris, Gleason L. Archer, Jr., and Bruce K. Waltke (Chicago: Moody Press, 1980), p. 439.

12. *Ibid.*

13. Joseph Henry Thayer, *A Greek-English Lexicon of the New Testament*, fourth ed. (Edinburgh: T. & T. Clark, 1955), p. 353.

14. H. E. Dana and Julius R. Mantey, *A Manual Grammar of the Greek New Testament* (New York: The Macmillan Company, 1927), p. 193.

15. Ezra P. Gould, *A Critical and Exegetical Commentary on the Gospel According to St. Mark* of *The International Critical Commentary* (Edinburgh: T. & T. Clark, 1955), p. 247.

16. G. B. Winer, *A Treatise on the Grammar of New Testament Greek*, trans. from German by W. F. Moulton (Edinburgh: T. & T. Clark, 1870), p. 382.

17. Gerhard Delling, "koloboo," *Theological Dictionary of the New Testament*, Vol. III, ed. by Gerhard Kittel, trans. and ed. by Geoffrey W. Bromiley (Grand Rapids: Wm. B. Eerdmans Publishing Company, 1965), pp. 823-24.

18. Henry C. Thiessen, *Lectures in Systematic Theology*, rev. by Vernon D. Doerksen (Grand Rapids: Wm. B. Eerdmans Publishing Company, 1979), p. 100.

19. Paul Enns, *The Moody Handbook of Theology* (Chicago: Moody Press, 1989), p. 203.

20. Thayer, *Lexicon*, p. 453.

21. William F. Arndt and F. Wilbur Gingrich, *A Greek-English Lexicon of the New Testament*, 4th rev. ed. (Chicago: The University of Chicago Press, 1957), p. 725.

22. James Hope Moulton, *A Grammar of New Testament Greek*, Vol. I (Edinburgh: T. & T. Clark, 1906), p. 133.

23. Robert L. Alden, "hatak," *Theological Wordbook of the Old Testament*, Vol. I, ed. by R. Laird Harris, Gleason L. Archer, Jr., and Bruce K. Waltke (Chicago: Moody Press, 1980), p. 334.

24. Leonard J. Coppes, "haras," *Theological Wordbook of the Old Testament*, Vol. I, p. 326.

25. *Ibid.*

26. John D. Grassmick, "Mark," *The Bible Knowledge Commentary—New Testament Edition*, ed. by John F. Walvoord and Roy B. Zuck (Wheaton, IL: Victor Books, 1983), p. 170.

27. J. Dwight Pentecost, *The Words and Works of Jesus Christ* (Grand Rapids: Zondervan Publishing House, 1981), p. 403.

CHAPTER FOUR

THE END AND BEGINNING OF THE BEGINNING JUDGMENT PHASE OF THE DAY OF THE LORD

THE END OF THE JUDGMENT PHASE

The previous chapter demonstrated that the beginning judgment phase of the broad Day of the Lord will at least cover the entire second half of the 70th week of Daniel 9. In addition, the judgment phase must include the Second Coming of Christ immediately after the end of the 70th week, for Joel 3:1-16 and Zechariah 14:1-15 reveal that the Day of the Lord will include the destruction of the armies of the nations by Christ at that time (cp. Rev. 19:11-21). It will also end Satan's day in the world and include his imprisonment in the abyss (Rev. 20:1-3).

Daniel 12:11-12 implies that the judgment phase of the Day of the Lord may extend even beyond the day of Christ's Second Coming. That passage refers to two different periods of time—1,290 days and 1,335 days. Both periods will begin at the same time—the middle of the 70th week, when the Antichrist ends the regular sacrifices at the Temple in Jerusalem and sets up his image there. Since, as we noted earlier, the second half of the 70th week will consist of 1,260 days, both of these periods of time will extend beyond the end of the 70th week and subsequent Second Coming of Christ. The 1,290 days will extend 30 days beyond the end of the 70th week; the 1,335 days will extend 75 days beyond it.

Daniel 12 does not explain the significance of these two sets of days, but the fact that the Bible refers to them seems to indicate that they will end on the dates of important events. At this time, we can make only an educated guess concerning what those events will be. First, the 1,290 days may end on the day that will conclude the judgment to take place after the Second Coming of Christ. The Scriptures teach that Christ will judge Israel and the Gentiles (the people who survive the horrors of the 70th week) after His return and before the establishment of the Millennial Kingdom (Ezek. 20:34-38; Mt. 25:31-46). This judgment will separate the believers from the unbelievers, so that the believers can enter the Millennial Kingdom and the unbelievers can be removed from the earth in judgment. It may take 30 days after the end of the 70th week to finish this judgment, which will have no adverse effect on believers or nature.[1]

Second, perhaps the 1,335 days will end on the day that will begin the Millennial Kingdom. Once the judgment determining who can enter the kingdom has been concluded, it may take another 45 days to form the governmental structure necessary to operate the kingdom.[2] The Bible teaches that the saints will reign with Christ in the Millennial Kingdom (2 Tim. 2:12; Rev. 20:4-6). After the saints and unbelievers have been separated and the unbelievers are removed in judgment, it will take time to appoint saints to different government positions and inform them of their various responsibilities.

Daniel 12:12 says, "Blessed is he that waiteth, and cometh to the thousand three hundred and five and thirty days." This statement makes it apparent that whatever will happen or begin on the 1,335th day is both "good and desirable."[3] The word translated "he that waiteth" means "one who waits earnestly."[4] Certainly the 70th-week saints will wait earnestly for the Millennial Kingdom of God to come as they face the horrors of the war the Antichrist will wage against them during that 70th week.

It may be, then, that the 30 days after the end of the 70th week will involve the judgment described above, which will follow the Second Coming of Christ. If that is so, perhaps that judgment will be part of the broad Day of the Lord judgments. If the Day of the Lord judgments include that 30-day judgment, then the beginning judgment phase of the Day of the Lord will end 30 days after the end of the 70th week. If the broad Day judgments do not include that 30-day judgment, then the judgment phase will end with the judgments at the Second Coming of Christ.

THE BEGINNING OF THE BEGINNING JUDGMENT PHASE

In an earlier chapter we noted that the first phase of the broad Day of the Lord will be a judgment phase.

In light of this, we can conclude that the beginning of the broad Day will also be the beginning of the judgment phase. Since this is true, the discovery of the starting point of the broad Day will also disclose the beginning of the judgment phase.

When will the broad Day of the Lord begin? A significant passage, 1 Thessalonians 5, provides an answer to this question. The Apostle Paul began with a reference to "the times" (the spans or periods of time[5]) and "the seasons" (the decisive or turning points of time[6]) that God determined to accomplish His purpose for world history.[7] In this way, Paul introduced his major subject of verses 1-11—the broad Day of the Lord, a significant future span of time that will include a major turning point of history (the destruction of the rule of Satan and rebellious mankind over the world system and the restoration of God's theocratic kingdom rule over the world system) and that God determined to accomplish His purpose for history.

THE INTRODUCTION OF A NEW SUBJECT

Paul's discussion of the broad Day of the Lord in the opening part of 1 Thessalonians 5 involved the introduction of a new and, therefore, different subject from the Rapture of the church at the end of chapter four. Three things indicate this change of subjects.

First, Paul began verse 1 with a significant combination of two Greek words back to back (*peri de*). In every other instance, when Paul placed this combination at the beginning of a statement, it was to introduce a new subject.

Second, the second word in this combination, *de*, even by itself has the essential significance of introducing a new subject.[8]

Third, the Thessalonians already had a "perfect" (accurate[9]) knowledge concerning the broad Day of the Lord before Paul wrote 1 Thessalonians to them (v. 2), but by contrast they were ignorant concerning the Rapture of the church (4:13-18). It is apparent that when he was with them prior to writing this letter, he had given them exact instructions concerning the Day of the Lord but had not taught them about the Rapture. The implication is that the Rapture event was not part of the subject of the Day of the Lord.

All three factors indicate the same thing—the broad Day of the Lord is a different subject from the Rapture of the church. This difference is significant for four reasons.

First, it indicates that the broad Day of the Lord will not include the Rapture of the church.

Second, we noted earlier that the broad Day will include the Second Coming of Christ; but, since it will not include the Rapture, the Rapture must be a separate event from the Second Coming. Thus, the Rapture must take place at a time different from the Second Coming of Christ immediately after the Great Tribulation.

Third, since the Rapture will not be part of the Day of the Lord, there must be a period of time between the Rapture and the beginning of the broad Day.

Fourth, since the Rapture will not be part of the Day of the Lord, it will not be the starting point of the broad Day.

1 THESSALONIANS 5 AND THE BEGINNING OF THE BROAD DAY OF THE LORD

In 1 Thessalonians 5:2-3, Paul wrote about the coming of the broad Day of the Lord, thus indicating that he was dealing with the beginning of that future period. He described the beginning of the Day of the Lord in three graphic ways.

The First Way. Paul declared that the broad Day of the Lord will come like a thief in the night—suddenly, unexpectedly, when the victims are unprepared (v. 2). A thief depends upon the element of surprise for success. He does not give his intended victims a forewarning of his coming. Paul's point—the unsaved will be given no forewarning of the coming of the broad Day of the Lord—rules out any of the seals of Revelation as being fore-warnings of the beginning of the broad Day. For example, it rules out the sixth seal (Rev. 6:12-14), which will cause great cosmic disturbances and a major earthquake causing the people of the world to flee to the mountains in terror (Rev. 6:15-17). In light of this reaction, if the disturbances of the sixth seal were a precursor to the Day of the Lord, the unsaved thereby would be given a graphic forewarning of its coming and will not be caught by surprise when it comes. Thus, the Day of the Lord would not come unexpectedly like a thief in the night.

The Second Way. Paul stated that the broad Day of the Lord will begin at the same time[10] that the unsaved will claim that they have established a state of "peace and safety" in the world (v. 3).[11] George Milligan asserted that the tense and mood of the verb translated "shall say," together with the word translated "when" in the statement "when they shall say, Peace and safety," indicate "*coincidence of time* in the events spoken of: It is 'at the very moment when they are saying.' "[12]

Milligan also pointed out that the word translated "safety" was rare in the New Testament. He stated that "in the papyri it is found as a law-term: 'bond,' 'security.' "[13] In light of the fact that a covenant is a bond or "formal agreement of legal validity,"[14] it could be that it will be the Antichrist's forcing of a covenant upon Israel at the very beginning of the 70th week (Dan. 9:27), which will cause the unsaved to conclude that they have peace and security.

Thus, Paul was saying that at the same time the unsaved are convinced they have finally reached the elusive goal mankind has always dreamed of achieving through their own efforts, they will experience the opposite of what they are expecting. The Day of the Lord will break upon them with sudden destruction. Paul placed the word "sudden" near the beginning of his Greek clause to emphasize how abruptly the Day of the Lord destruction will come upon the unsaved.[15] Paul also used an emphatic double negative to stress that the unsaved will be totally incapable of escaping the Day of the Lord judgment, implying that they will be incapable of escaping because God has determined that it will be so. God has appointed these unsaved to His Day of the Lord wrath.

We should note that peace will be removed from the earth when the second seal is broken (Rev. 6:3-4). A study of Revelation 6-19 clearly indicates that there will be no peace and safety for the unsaved from the time of the second seal through the Second Coming of Christ immediately after the Great Tribulation. For example, by the end of the fourth seal death will have come to one-fourth of the earth's population through the sword, famine, pestilence, and wild beasts (Rev. 6:8). This will be the opposite of peace and safety. In conjunction with this, it is interesting to note that Jeremiah 14:12-14 and 16:4-5 indicate that the sword, famine, pestilence, and wild beasts are the results of God's withdrawing peace. By contrast, Leviticus 26:4-6; Ezekiel 34:23-30; and Hosea 2:18 teach that peace and safety are characterized by the absence of the sword, famine, and wild beasts.

In addition, when the sixth seal is broken, the unsaved will be so terrified by the resulting cosmic disturbances that they will flee to the caves and rocks of the mountains and plead with them to fall on them and hide them from divine wrath (Rev. 6:12-17). Their terror and resulting action will show that they now realize they have not obtained peace and safety.

In light of these things and Paul's teaching that the broad Day of the Lord will start when the unsaved claim they have peace and safety, we can conclude that the broad Day of the Lord must start at least by the time of the second seal.

The Old Testament indicates that true peace and safety will come when the unique combination of the following four conditions exist in the world:

1. God's regathering of Israel to the homeland (Jer. 32:37; Ezek. 28:25-26; 39:25-29).

2. A great world ruler, the Messiah (Isa. 9:6-7; Jer. 23:5-6; 33:14-16; Ezek. 34:23-30; Mic. 5:2-5; Zech. 9:9-10; 14:9-11).

3. A new Temple in Jerusalem for the worship of God (Ezek. 37:24-28; Hag. 2:9).

4. A covenant of peace made with Israel (Isa. 54:10; Ezek. 34:23-30; 37:24-28).

At the very beginning of the 70th week, the world will appear to have this unique combination of conditions. First, there will be a nation of Israel living securely in the homeland as the result of a regathering (Ezek. 38:8, 11-12, 14). Second, there will be a great world ruler, the Antichrist, who must have significant power and the authority to make a strong covenant with Israel at the start of the 70th week (Dan. 9:27). Third, there will be a new Temple in Jerusalem for the worship of God (Mt. 24:15; 2 Th. 2:4; Dan. 9:27 implies that sacrifices and grain offerings will be offered at the Temple during the first half of the 70th week). Fourth, the Antichrist will make a covenant of peace with Israel at the very start of the 70th week (Dan. 9:27).

Since this combination of conditions at the start of the 70th week will appear to be the prophesied unique combination of conditions in existence when true peace and safety are to come to the world, the unsaved will conclude that they have peace and safety at the start of the 70th week. This fact, along with the fact that the Day of the Lord will come when the unsaved are convinced that they have peace and safety (1 Th. 5:3), brings us to the conclusion that the Day of the Lord will start at the beginning of the 70th week.

We should note a significant thing at this point. Ezekiel 34:23-30 says that when God establishes His covenant of peace with Israel, the covenant will result in safety, peace with nations, and the elimination of harmful beasts and famine. By contrast, when the Antichrist establishes his covenant of peace with Israel, God will inflict the world with conditions opposite of those His covenant of peace will bring. He will unleash war (the sword) [the second seal, Rev. 6:3-4], famine (the third seal, Rev. 6:5-6), and harmful beasts (the fourth seal, Rev. 6:7-8) upon the earth to demonstrate that the Antichrist's covenant of peace is not the covenant of peace that will bring true peace and safety, as foretold in the Old Testament.

The Third Way. Paul asserted that the destruction at the start of the broad Day of the Lord will come just as suddenly as travail (lit., "the birth pang") comes upon a woman who is about to give birth (1 Th. 5:3). Paul used the singular form of "birth pang" and placed the definite article "the" before it. This, together with his emphasis on how the Day of the Lord will start and the suddenness with which its destruction will come, indicates that Paul was referring to the very first birth pang. It is a woman's very first birth pang, not the later hard labor birth pangs, that comes suddenly at the start of the painful process of giving birth. Thus, as we concluded earlier, Paul was teaching that the beginning of the broad Day of the Lord will be characterized by the very first birth pang.

As we also noted earlier, Jesus referred to "the beginning of sorrows" (lit., the beginning of birth pangs) in Matthew 24:5-8. Jesus and Paul used the same word for birth pang. Surely the beginning of birth pangs must include the very first birth pang. Indeed, the very first birth pang must be the start of the beginning of birth pangs.

Since the beginning of the broad Day of the Lord will be characterized by the very first birth pang, which will be the start of the beginning of birth pangs, we can conclude that the broad Day of the Lord will start at the very outset of the beginning of birth pangs.

In the earlier chapter entitled "THE BIRTH PANGS OF THE MESSIAH," we noted that in addition to 1 Thessalonians 5:2-3, other biblical passages (Isa. 13:6-13; Zeph. 1:14-18) indicate that birth pangs will be characteristic of the Day of the Lord. In addition, that same chapter produced the following conclusions: Both the Bible and ancient Judaism teach that the last seven years before the Messiah comes to rule the earth will be characterized by severe birth pangs; Judaism called these the birth pangs of the Messiah. The Bible indicates that these seven years characterized by birth pangs are the 70th week; that they will be divided into two divisions of birth pangs; that the first division will both cover the first half of the seven years and contain the less severe beginning of birth pangs that Jesus called "the beginning of sorrows"; and that the second division will cover the second half of the seven years and contain the later, more severe hard labor birth pangs.

The Bible demonstrates that the beginning of birth pangs and the first four seals are the same thing and, therefore, the first four seals will also be present during the first half of the seven years. Both the Bible and ancient Judaism teach that the world must go through the seven years of birth pangs for the Messianic Age to be born into the world. The Bible indicates that these birth pangs are absolutely necessary to remove Satan, rebellious mankind, and their rule of the world system from the earth so that the Messianic Age can come, and associates birth pangs with the divine wrath, fierce anger, and destruction of the Day of the Lord.

In light of these facts, we can draw several conclusions.

Since the first division of birth pangs will cover the first half of the 70th week and will contain the beginning of birth pangs, and since the broad Day of the Lord will start at the very outset of the beginning of birth pangs, we can conclude that the broad Day of the Lord will start at the beginning of the 70th week and include the beginning of birth pangs.

Since the beginning of birth pangs of Matthew 24 and the first four seals of Revelation 6 are the same thing, and since the broad Day of the Lord will include the beginning of birth pangs, we can conclude that the broad Day of the Lord will also include the first four seals of Revelation 6.

Since the Bible associates birth pangs with the divine wrath, fierce anger, and destruction of the Day of the Lord, and since the broad Day of the Lord will include the beginning of birth pangs of the first half of the 70th week, we can conclude that the divine wrath, fierce anger, and destruction of the Day of the Lord will be associated with the beginning of birth pangs of the first half of the 70th week.

Since the beginning of birth pangs of the first half of the 70th week and the first four seals of Revelation 6 are the same thing, the divine wrath, anger, and destruction of the Day of the Lord will also be associated with the first four seals. The beginning of birth pangs of the first four seals will involve some human instruments and activity, such as warfare (Mt. 24:5-8; Rev. 6:1-8), but in two earlier chapters we demonstrated that the divine wrath, anger, and destruction that will characterize the birth pangs and Day of the Lord will sometimes involve human instruments and activity.

Paul's teaching in 1 Thessalonians 5:2-3 consistently points to the same conclusion: The broad Day of the Lord will start at the beginning of the 70th week.

2 THESSALONIANS 2 AND THE BEGINNING OF THE BROAD DAY OF THE LORD

The Thessalonians' Disturbance. Second Thessalonians 2:2 relates that the Thessalonian Christians were greatly shaken and disturbed by reports that the Day of the Lord had already begun. We should note that Paul used the perfect tense of the verb translated "is at hand." The perfect tense "views action as a finished product" and "signifies action as complete from the point of view of present time."[16] In light of this, James Everett Frame has asserted that the verb does not mean "is coming," "is at hand," or "is near." Instead, it means "has come," "is on hand," or "is present."[17] Thus, the Thessalonian believers had been told that the Day of the Lord had already come and that they were in it.

The fact that the Thessalonians were shaken and disturbed by these reports implies that they were beginning to believe them. How could these believers have been deceived into thinking that the Day of the Lord had already come, when it was obvious that the unprecedented pouring out of God's wrath upon the world had not yet begun? One cause for their deception could have been the persecution they were experiencing from the unbelievers of Thessalonica as a result of their profession of faith in Christ (Acts 17:5-9; 1 Th. 1:6; 2:14; 3:3-4; 2 Th. 1:4-7).

But why would their persecution by unbelievers because they professed faith in Christ prompt them to believe reports that the Day of the Lord had already begun? The only possible answer is that they understood that the time period covered by the Day of the Lord would be characterized, not only by a great outpouring of God's wrath upon the world, but also by the persecution of professors of faith in Christ by unbelievers. The fact that Paul did not correct this understanding indicates that the time period covered by the Day of the Lord will indeed be characterized by the persecution of professors of faith in Christ by unbelievers.

From what source could the Thessalonian Christians have received this understanding? It seems apparent that Paul had been their source of information, for he reminded them that when he was with them in the past, he had taught them about the Day of the Lord (2 Th. 2:2-5; cp. 1 Th. 5:2). It would appear that Paul had taught them that the time period covered by the Day of the Lord would be characterized, not only by a great outpouring of God's wrath, but also by the persecution of professors of faith in Christ by unbelievers.

In Matthew 24:9, Jesus referred to that persecution in conjunction with His discussion of the beginning of birth pangs and before He introduced the subject of the abomination of desolation (v. 15). We presented evidence earlier to the effect that the beginning of birth pangs will occur in the first half of the 70th week and that the abomination of desolation, which will signal the start of the Great Tribulation (vv. 15-21), will take place in the middle of the 70th week. This evidence, together with the chronological order of Jesus' Matthew 24 teaching, implies that the persecution to which Jesus referred in verse 9 will occur during the first half of the 70th week.

In light of this, we can conclude that the persecution of professors of faith in Christ (which will characterize the Day of the Lord) could include the persecution during the first half of the 70th week, and the Day of the Lord therefore could include the first half of the 70th week.

The Revelation of the Man of Sin. In order to prove to the Thessalonians that the Day of the Lord had not begun, Paul presented two things that had not yet happened but that must happen before the Day of the Lord can begin: "first the apostasy" (literal translation) and the revelation of the "man of sin" (v. 3).

Since the revelation of the man of sin is the latter of the two things, it, rather than the apostasy, will take place closer to the beginning of the Day of the Lord. Therefore, when trying to determine when the Day of the Lord will begin, it is more crucial to discern when the man of sin will be revealed than when the apostasy will take place.

Some propose that the revelation of the man of sin will occur in the middle of the 70th week, when he declares himself to be God (Dan. 9:27; 11:36-37; 2 Th. 2:4). On the basis of this proposal and Paul's teaching that the Day of the Lord will not come until the man of sin is revealed, some conclude that the Day of the Lord will not start until sometime after the middle of the 70th week.

There is a significant problem with this proposal, however. In the Scriptures, God has revealed other activities of the man of sin that will precede his declaration to be God and reveal who he is at least three and one-half years before that declaration. First, the man of sin will rise to power as the 11th ruler within the already formed ten-division confederation that will constitute the revived Roman Empire (Dan. 7:7-8, 20, 23-24). Second, as the man of sin rises to power, he will overthrow three of the original ten rulers of the revived Roman Empire (Dan. 7:8, 20, 24). Third, after overthrowing those three rulers, the man of sin will become the dominant ruler of the revived Roman Empire (Dan. 7:20, 24, 26; Rev. 17:12-13, 16-17). Fourth, as the dominant ruler of the revived Roman Empire, the man of sin will establish a seven-year covenant of peace with the nation of Israel, and the establishment of the covenant will be the historic starting point of the 70th week (Dan. 9:27).

If the man of sin is not to be revealed until the middle of the 70th week, why did God reveal these specific activities that will occur at least three and one-half years before the middle of the 70th week and will make the man of sin clearly identifiable?

Since these divinely foretold activities will reveal who the man of sin is, and since they will be performed by the beginning of the 70th week, we can conclude that the man of sin will be revealed by the beginning of the 70th week.

Since the man of sin will be revealed at that time, and since his revelation is the latter of the two things that must occur before the Day of the Lord can begin, we can conclude two things: The Day of the Lord does not have to wait until sometime after the middle of the 70th week to begin; and the Day of the Lord can begin at the start of the 70th week.

The Day of the Lord and the Rapture. Again, Paul's statement in 2 Thessalonians 2:2 implies that the Thessalonians were badly shaken and disturbed by reports that the Day of the Lord had already begun. Their reactions indicate that they understood that the first phase (the beginning judgment phase) of the Day of the Lord will be horrible for those who enter it and was therefore something to be dreaded.

By contrast, the Scriptures teach that the Rapture is to be awaited with eager, comforting anticipation by those who will participate in it (evidence for this will be presented in later chapters).

This great contrast of attitudes toward the beginning judgment phase of the Day of the Lord and the Rapture is another indicator that the Rapture is not the beginning or any part of the Day of the Lord. Rather, it will be a separate event. Therefore, Paul's reference to the Day of the Lord in 2 Thessalonians 2:2 is not a reference to the Rapture.

COSMIC DISTURBANCES AND THE BEGINNING OF THE BROAD DAY OF THE LORD

Future Cosmic Disturbances. Joel 3:2, 9-15 says that the sun, moon, and stars will be darkened when the armies of the nations gather in Israel for war and the Day of the Lord is "near." This implies that there will be great cosmic disturbances immediately before the Day of the Lord.

In Matthew 24:29-30 Jesus taught that the sun and moon will be darkened and the stars will fall from heaven immediately after the Great Tribulation (cp. v. 21) and before His glorious Second Coming in the clouds of heaven.

Revelation 6:12-13 indicates that the sun will become black, the moon will become like blood, and the stars of heaven will fall to the earth when the sixth seal is opened.

Possible Conclusions. All three of these passages present future cosmic disturbances involving the sun, moon, and stars. Do all three refer to the same cosmic disturbances? If so, we might conclude that the sixth seal will immediately follow the Great Tribulation and immediately precede the Second Coming of Christ and the beginning of the Day of the Lord.

If the sixth seal were to follow the Great Tribulation and precede the beginning of the Day of the Lord, the Great Tribulation and the Day of the

Lord would be totally separate from each other. In addition, if the Day of the Lord were to begin after the end of the Great Tribulation (since, as noted in an earlier chapter, the Great Tribulation will not start until the middle of the 70th week), the Day of the Lord would not start until some point in the second half of the 70th week.

There are significant problems with this approach. In an earlier chapter we demonstrated that the Great Tribulation and the broad Day of the Lord will not be separate from each other. The broad Day will include the Great Tribulation.

There are reasons for concluding that the cosmic disturbances related to the beginning of the Joel 3 Day of the Lord and the Second Coming of Christ immediately after the Great Tribulation are not the same as those of the sixth seal. First, the cosmic disturbances of Joel 3 will occur when the armies of the nations have gathered for war in Israel. Those armies will not begin to gather for war until the sixth bowl has been poured out (Rev. 16:12-16), long after the sixth seal—one seal, seven trumpets, and five bowls after the cosmic disturbances of the sixth seal. Thus, the cosmic disturbances of the sixth seal will occur long before the armies of the nations start to gather for war in Israel.

Since the cosmic disturbances of Joel 3 will occur when the armies have gathered, we can conclude that those cosmic disturbances will transpire long after those of the sixth seal and will not be the same as those of the sixth seal.

In light of this, we can further conclude that since the cosmic disturbances of Joel 3 are the ones that will come immediately before the Day of the Lord, those of the sixth seal will not immediately precede the Day of the Lord.

Second, there will be more than one instance of cosmic disturbances in the future. The Scriptures teach that other cosmic disturbances will occur after those of the sixth seal. A third of the sun, moon, and stars will be darkened at the fourth trumpet (Rev. 8:12); the sun will be darkened by smoke from the abyss at the fifth trumpet (Rev. 9:1-2); the sun will scorch people on the earth with fire and fierce heat when the fourth bowl is poured out (Rev. 16:8-9).

The fact that there will be further cosmic disturbances after the sixth seal indicates that the darkening of the heavenly luminous bodies of the sixth seal will be temporary. In order for the later darkenings at the fourth and fifth trumpets to take place, the heavenly luminous bodies must become light again after the sixth seal. Thus, the cosmic disturbances associated with the sixth seal will end sometime before the fourth trumpet; therefore, the cosmic disturbances of the fourth and fifth trumpets and the fourth bowl will not be the same as those of the sixth seal.

Earlier we saw that the cosmic disturbances immediately before the Joel 3 Day of the Lord will occur when the armies of the nations are gathered for war in Israel and that those armies will not start to gather until the sixth bowl. The chronology of Revelation indicates that the sixth bowl will occur after the fourth and fifth trumpets and the fourth bowl, meaning that the cosmic disturbances immediately before the Joel 3 Day of the Lord will not occur until after the fourth and fifth trumpets and the fourth bowl.

Cosmic Disturbances of the 70th Week

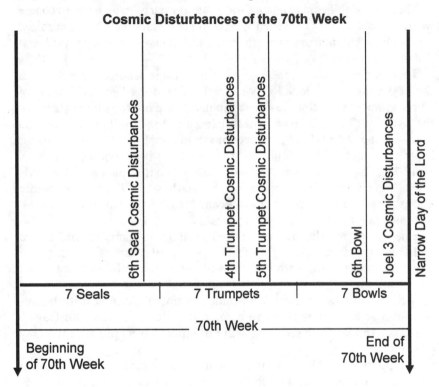

We demonstrated before that the cosmic disturbances associated with the sixth seal will end sometime before the fourth trumpet; therefore, the cosmic disturbances of the fourth and fifth trumpets and the fourth bowl will not be the same as those of the sixth seal. Because this is so, we can conclude that the cosmic disturbances associated with the sixth seal will end before those related to the beginning of the Joel 3 Day of the Lord occur. Therefore, the cosmic disturbances immediately before the Joel 3 Day of the Lord will not be the same as those of the sixth seal.

Third, when the cosmic disturbances of the sixth seal take place, kings, military men, and all other classes of people will run to the caves and rocks of the mountains to hide. They will plead with the mountains and rocks to fall on them and hide them from the presence of God and the wrath of the Lamb (Rev. 6:15-16).

By contrast, when the cosmic disturbances immediately before the Joel 3 Day of the Lord occur after the sixth bowl, the kings and military men will not run and hide. Rather, they will remain assembled together in battle array to boldly attempt war against God, His Messiah, and the holy angels (Ps. 2:1-3; Joel 3:9-16; Zech. 12:2-9; 14:1-6, 12-14). Revelation 19:11-21 indicates that they will be gathered together to make war when Christ comes out of heaven (after the cosmic disturbances that will precede that coming, Mt. 24:29-31) to fight against them. On this occasion, the kings and military men will have Satan, the Antichrist, and the False Prophet with them (Rev. 16:12-16; 19:19-20; 20:1-2). Apparently the presence of these three persons with supernatural powers will cause the kings and military men to react boldly in response to the cosmic disturbances after the sixth bowl and in contrast to their cowardly response to the cosmic disturbances of the sixth seal.

These radically different responses to the cosmic disturbances of the sixth seal and those related to the beginning of the Joel 3 Day of the Lord indicate that the cosmic disturbances of the Day of the Lord are not the same as those of the sixth seal.

Fourth, in Joel 3:1-8 God declared that the gathering of the armies of the nations, which will begin with the sixth bowl and be related to the cosmic disturbances of the Joel 3 Day of the Lord, will occur when it is time for the fortunes of Judah and Jerusalem to be restored. When they gather in Israel, God will destroy the forces of the Gentile world dominion so that He can restore Israel to the place of blessing.

When will the fortunes of Judah and Jerusalem be restored? Certainly not until the persecution of the Jews has ended. A comparison of Daniel 9:27 with Matthew 24:15-21 indicates that the Jews will be forced to flee from Judah when the Antichrist sets himself up as God in the Temple in the middle of the 70th week. Revelation 12:6, 13-17 says that when the Jews flee, Satan will persecute them so severely that God will have to intervene to preserve them for the remaining three and one-half years of the 70th week. Thus, the Jews will be pursued and severely persecuted throughout the entire second half of the 70th week. The previous chapter demonstrated that the persecution of the Jews will not stop until the 70th week ends; therefore, the fortunes of Judah and Jerusalem will not be restored until the end of the 70th week.

Since the Joel 3 gathering of the armies of the nations (which will start with the sixth bowl and will be related to the cosmic disturbances of the Joel 3 Day of the Lord) will occur when it is time for the fortunes of Judah and Jerusalem to be restored (which will not be until the end of the 70th week), the Joel 3 gathering of the armies will not take place until the end of the 70th week. Thus, the cosmic disturbances of the Joel 3 Day of the Lord, which will be related to this gathering of the armies, will not take place until the end of the 70th week. The sixth bowl, which will begin the gathering of the armies, will occur near the end of the 70th week.

Since the sixth bowl will take place near the end of the 70th week—one seal, seven trumpets, and five bowls after the sixth seal—we can conclude that the sixth seal will take place considerably earlier in the 70th week, when a significant time of persecution yet remains for the Jews. Thus, the sixth seal will take place substantially earlier than the restoration of the fortunes of Judah and Jerusalem.

Since the sixth seal will occur substantially earlier than the restoration of the fortunes of Judah and Jerusalem, and since the regathering of the armies will take place when it is time for the fortunes of Judah and Jerusalem to be restored, the sixth seal and the gathering of the armies will occur at considerably different times. This is another evidence that the cosmic disturbances of the sixth seal and those related to the gathering of the armies and the beginning of the Joel 3 Day of the Lord are not the same.

Conclusions. From this examination of cosmic disturbances and the beginning of the broad Day of the Lord, we can conclude that there will be more than one instance of cosmic disturbances in the future. The cosmic disturbances immediately before the beginning of the Joel 3 Day of the Lord and the Second Coming of Christ immediately after the Great Tribulation are not the same as those of the sixth seal. The cosmic disturbances immediately before the beginning of the Joel 3 Day of the Lord and the Second Coming of Christ will occur at the end of the 70th week, but those of the sixth seal will occur and end considerably before then. Thus, the cosmic disturbances of the sixth seal will not immediately precede the beginning of the Day of the Lord.

Earlier we noted that Joel 3 says there will be great cosmic disturbances immediately before the Day of the Lord. In light of this and the fact that these cosmic disturbances will not occur until the end of the 70th week, there appears to be a problem: How can the conclusion produced earlier in this chapter, that the Day of the Lord will start at the beginning of the 70th week, be correct? If the cosmic disturbances to occur immediately before the Day of the Lord do not occur until the end of the 70th week, won't the Day of the Lord start immediately after the end of the 70th week instead of at its beginning? Doesn't Joel 3 contradict the conclusion that the Day of the Lord will start at the beginning of the 70th week?

To find a solution, we must recall an earlier chapter, which demonstrated that in the Scriptures the expression *the Day of the Lord* has a double sense in relationship to the future. First, there is a broad sense referring to an extended period of time involving at least the 70th week plus the Millennium. Second, there is a narrow sense referring to one specific day—the day on which Christ will return to the earth from heaven immediately after the Great Tribulation.

The chapter that presents this double sense of the Day of the Lord also demonstrates that Joel 3 refers to the Day of the Lord in the narrow sense.

It presents the Day of the Lord as one specific day—the day on which Christ will return to the earth. Thus, the cosmic disturbances of Joel 3 are those that will occur at the end of the 70th week immediately before the narrow Day of the Lord. Joel 3 does not indicate that there will be cosmic disturbances before the broad Day of the Lord.

By contrast, the conclusion drawn earlier in this present chapter (that the Day of the Lord will start at the beginning of the 70th week) refers to the broad Day of the Lord, the extended period of time involving at least the 70th week plus the Millennium.

In light of what we have seen, we can conclude that Joel 3 and the conclusion drawn in this chapter refer to two different senses of the Day of the Lord; therefore, Joel 3 does not contradict the conclusion that the broad Day of the Lord will start at the beginning of the 70th week.

CONCLUSIONS

This study has produced several significant conclusions.

1. The beginning judgment phase of the broad Day of the Lord will end either with the judgments at the coming of Christ or on the 30th day after the end of the 70th week.

2. The beginning of the broad Day of the Lord will also be the beginning of its beginning judgment phase.

3. The Rapture of the church will be a separate event from the Day of the Lord.

4. The Rapture must be a different event from the coming of Christ immediately after the Great Tribulation.

5. There must be a period of time between the Rapture and the beginning of the broad Day of the Lord.

6. The Rapture will not be the starting point of the broad Day of the Lord.

7. There will be no forewarning of the beginning of the broad Day of the Lord.

8. The broad Day of the Lord will start at the beginning of the 70th week and will include the beginning of birth pangs and the first four seals of Revelation 6.

9. The divine wrath, fierce anger, and destruction of the broad Day of the Lord will be associated with the beginning of birth pangs and the first four seals.

10. The time period covered by the broad Day of the Lord will be characterized not only by a great outpouring of God's wrath on the world, but also by the persecution of professors of faith in Christ by unbelievers.

11. The man of sin will be revealed by the beginning of the 70th week; therefore, the broad Day of the Lord can start at the beginning of the 70th week.

12. Paul's reference to the Day of the Lord in 2 Thessalonians 2:2 is not a reference to the Rapture of the church.

13. There will be more than one instance of cosmic disturbances in the future.

14. The cosmic disturbances immediately before the beginning of the Joel 3 Day of the Lord and the Second Coming of Christ are not the same as those of the sixth seal of Revelation 6.

15. There will be a considerable amount of time between the cosmic disturbances of the sixth seal and those immediately before the beginning of the Joel 3 Day of the Lord and the Second Coming of Christ.

16. The cosmic disturbances of the sixth seal will not immediately precede the beginning of the Day of the Lord.

17. Joel 3 refers to the narrow Day of the Lord, not the broad Day.

18. Joel 3 does not contradict the conclusion that the broad Day of the Lord will start at the beginning of the 70th week.

Since the beginning of the broad Day of the Lord will also be the start of its beginning judgment phase, and since the broad Day of the Lord will start at the beginning of the 70th week, the beginning judgment phase will start at the beginning of the 70th week. Further, since that phase will end either with the judgments at the Second Coming of Christ or on the 30th day after the end of the 70th week, we can conclude that the beginning judgment phase of the broad Day of the Lord will at least cover and include the entire 70th week.

ENDNOTES

1. Leon Wood, *A Commentary on Daniel* (Grand Rapids: Zondervan Publishing House, 1973), p. 328.

2. *Ibid.*

3. *Ibid.*

4. *Ibid.*

5. Gerhard Delling, "chronos," *Theological Dictionary of the New Testament*, Vol. IX, ed. by Gerhard Friedrich, trans. and ed. by Geoffrey W. Bromiley (Grand Rapids: Wm. B. Eerdmans Publishing Company, 1974), pp. 590-91.

6. Gerhard Delling, "kairos," *Theological Dictionary of the New Testament*, Vol. III, ed. by Gerhard Kittel, trans. and ed. by Geoffrey W. Bromiley (Grand Rapids: Wm. B. Eerdmans Publishing Company, 1965), pp. 460-61.

7. *Ibid.*, IX, p. 590; III, pp. 460-61.

8. A. T. Robertson, *A Grammar of the Greek New Testament in the Light of Historical Research* (Nashville, TN: Broadman Press, 1934), pp. 1184-85.

9. William F. Arndt and F. Wilbur Gingrich, *A Greek-English Lexicon of the New Testament*, 4th rev. ed. (Chicago: The University of Chicago Press, 1957), p. 32.

10. *Ibid.*, p. 592.

11. *Ibid.*, p. 118.

12. George Milligan, *St. Paul's Epistles to the Thessalonians* (London: Macmillan and Co., Limited, 1908), p. 65.

13. *Ibid.*

14. *The American College Dictionary* (New York: Harper & Brothers Publishers, 1947), p. 279.

15. C. F. Hogg and W. E. Vine, *The Epistles to the Thessalonians* (London: Pickering & Inglis, Ltd., 1959), pp. 155-56.

16. H. E. Dana and Julius R. Mantey, *A Manual Grammar of the Greek New Testament* (New York: The Macmillan Company, 1927), p. 200.

17. James Everett Frame, *A Critical and Exegetical Commentary on the Epistles of St. Paul to the Thessalonians* (Edinburgh: T. & T. Clark, 1912), p. 248.

CHAPTER FIVE

THE SEALED SCROLL OF REVELATION 5

THE MAJOR DIVISIONS OF REVELATION

R evelation 1:19 presents the major divisions of the Book of the Revelation. John was told, "Write the things which thou hast seen, and the things which are, and the things which shall be hereafter." This indicates three major divisions.

First, chapter 1 contains John's record of the things he had seen (the glorified Christ and the things related to Him). Second, chapters 2 and 3 present the things that are (things of the present church age in which John was living).

Third, according to Revelation 4:1, after John had seen the things that are, he saw a door opened in heaven and heard a voice saying, "Come up here, and I will show thee things which must be hereafter." This statement indicates that the third major division of Revelation begins with chapter 4 and that chapters 4 through 22 record future events after the things of the church age in chapters 2 and 3. Note that the statement of 4:1 adds the idea that the things that shall be hereafter "must" take place, meaning that the future events foretold in chapters 4 through 22 have been destined by God to happen and therefore are unavoidable.[1]

THE SIGNIFICANCE OF REVELATION 4 AND 5

Chapters 4 and 5 serve as the introduction of the third major division of Revelation. They portray the divine throne room of the universe and set the stage for what is foretold in chapters 6 through 22. They are the key to the purpose of the future events of those chapters.[2]

Seven things related to the purpose of these future events emerge from chapters 4 and 5. First, Revelation 4:8 emphasizes the holiness of God. Day and night four creatures say, "Holy, holy, holy." God's holiness is His quality of being distinct from His creation.[3] When Satan began His revolt against God, he challenged God's holiness by asserting, "I will be like the Most High" (Isa. 14:14). This was Satan's way of saying, "God, You are not unique or different in contrast with Your creation. As one of Your creatures, I shall become just like You." In contrast with this bold challenge, four of God's heavenly creatures continuously assert His holiness.

Second, Revelation 4:8-10 and 5:14 emphasize God's eternality. God is the one "who was, and is, and is to come" (4:8) and "that liveth forever and ever" (4:10). God's eternality indicates that He existed before creation. In contrast with creation, which had a beginning, the eternal God had no beginning. Thus, His eternality makes Him holy (different or unique) in contrast with creation.

Third, Revelation 4:11 emphasizes that God created "all things" that have been created (the heavens, the earth, and everything in them) and that He created these things for His own benefit or purpose (lit., "on account of your will they were and were created").

R. H. Charles declares that in chapter 4 "God the Creator is the centre of worship."[4] As the unique, eternal being who had no beginning, God is the one who had the wisdom and power to create everything for His own sovereign purpose.

Fourth, God's power or authority to rule all of creation is emphasized in two ways in chapters 4 and 5. One, God's throne is mentioned a total of 17 times. The word for throne, when used figuratively, indicates dominion or sovereignty.[5] R. C. H. Lenski wrote concerning chapter 4, "Count how often 'Throne' ('thrones') is repeated in this chapter—this is the great *Throne Vision*, God's rule, power, dominion symbolized to mortal vision."[6]

Two, the doxologies in 4:11 and 5:13 use two words to ascribe great power to God. One of these words sometimes "is designed to stress the power of God which none can withstand and which is sovereign over all."[7] "It denotes the superior power of God to which the final victory will belong."[8]

The other word was used in statements that express "the hope and longing that God will demonstrate His power in a last great conflict, destroying His opponents and saving those who belong to Him. Thus, the righteous wait for God to reveal Himself in His power and definitively to establish His dominion."[9]

These words portray a divine power that is active in history. It shapes and sets a goal for history in accordance with God's own sovereign will and purpose.[10] These words refer to the power God uses to exercise His sovereign rule over His creation.

In light of the usage of these power words, Walter Grundmann explains the significance of the doxologies in Revelation 4 and 5 as follows: "These doxologies in Rev. imply acknowledgment and acceptance of the power of God which has an eschatological character, which destroys hostile powers and which brings the world to perfection."[11]

Revelation 4:11 declares that God is worthy to possess the power or authority to rule all of creation because He created "all things" that have been created, and He created them for His own benefit and sovereign purpose. Since God is the one who created the universe and everything in it, and since He created it for His own benefit and sovereign purpose, it all belongs to Him. As Creator, He alone is its legitimate owner; therefore, the right to rule the entire universe is exclusively His, including the right to use His power to crush any enemy who challenges His rule.

Fifth, the Redeemer and His work of redemption are emphasized through His portrayal as a slain Lamb in Revelation 5:6, 8-9, 12-13 and through the declaration that He has redeemed us by His blood (5:9).

Sixth, Revelation 5:1-9 emphasizes the Redeemer's worthiness to take the scroll from God's hand, break its seven seals, open and read it. He is worthy to do this because of His work of redemption through His death and shed blood.

Seventh, Revelation 5:12-13 points out the Redeemer's worthiness to exercise God's ruling power. There the same power words for God's rule noted earlier are ascribed to Him. In fact, in 5:13 one of those words is used jointly for God and the Redeemer.

Verse 12 indicates that it is as the Lamb that was slain that the Redeemer is worthy, implying that the Redeemer is worthy to exercise God's ruling power because of His redemptive work through His death and shed blood.

We should note that both the Redeemer's worthiness to take the scroll from God's hand, break its seals, open and read it and His worthiness to exercise God's ruling power are the result of His work of redemption.

THE IMPORTANCE OF THE SEALED SCROLL

The major issue in Revelation 5 is finding someone worthy to take the scroll sealed with seven seals from God's hand, break its seals, open and read it (vv. 1-2). (The word translated "book" in these verses refers to a rolled scroll, the type mentioned in Ezekiel 2:9–3:2, not a modern type book[12].)

The facts that this is the major issue, that John wept much when no one was found worthy to do these things with the scroll (5:3-4), and that God's creatures broke into great doxologies when the Redeemer who was worthy took the sealed scroll from God's hand (5:5-14) together indicate that the sealed scroll is a very important document. It ties together the seven things emphasized in Revelation 4 and 5, which are related to the purpose of the future events foretold in chapters 6 through 22. The sealed scroll makes chapters 4 and 5 the key to the purpose of those future events.

In light of what we have seen here, the identification of the sealed scroll is critical. Apart from that identification, it is impossible to understand the significance or purpose of the future events of chapters 6 through 22. With regard to this, Gottlob Schrenk declared that the content of the scroll

must be brought into relation to the whole chain of judicial acts which unfold from c. 6 on and from which there develop organically the visions of the trumpets and bowls. Hence we are not concerned merely with the 6 or 7 seals themselves, but with all the last events up to the consummation.[13]

Whatever the sealed scroll is, its identification must relate to the facts that the unique, eternal God created the universe for His own benefit and sovereign purpose; that therefore He alone has the right to rule the entire universe; and that His right to rule includes the right to use His power to crush any enemy who challenges His rule. In addition, its identification must relate to the importance of the Redeemer and His redemptive work and the fact that the Redeemer is worthy to take the scroll from God's hand, break its seals, open and read it, and exercise God's ruling power because of His work of redemption.

In light of the importance that Revelation 5 attaches to the relationship of the sealed scroll to the Redeemer and His work of redemption, it seems apparent that the scroll is tied significantly to God's program of redemption for the world. In order to understand that program and the identification of the sealed scroll, it will be necessary to examine as background a key program of God.

GOD'S PROGRAM OF LAND REDEMPTION FOR ISRAEL

Several significant principles were involved in God's land redemption program for Israel under the Mosaic law.

The Principle that the Land of Israel Belonged to God

This was the first and foremost principle. In Leviticus 25:23 God declared, "The land is mine." He was its ultimate owner; therefore, "ultimate power over the land" rested with Him as Israel's King (Ps. 149:2; Isa. 43:15).[14] He alone had the right to rule and dispense it for His own benefit and in accordance with His own sovereign purpose.

The Principle of Tenant Possession

God gave His land to the people of Israel to possess as an inheritance forever (Gen. 13:15; 15:7; Dt. 19:14; Josh. 1:2). In spite of that fact, they were not free to regard themselves as its sole owners and authorities. Since God was the ultimate owner of the land, they were responsible to serve as His representatives, administering His rule over the land for His benefit, in accordance with His sovereign purpose, and in obedience to His commands. The Mosaic Law spelled out the details of this arrangement.

Scholars have described this principle in various ways. Max L. Margolis said, "The land, the law declares, properly belongs to YHWH, who is sole landlord, while all the Israelites are but his tenants."[15]

Stephen Herbert Bess wrote,

The proper concept of this divine ownership appears to be that every Israelite proprietor was to regard his holding as deriving from God himself, as though it had been apportioned to him from God . . . each head of a family holding his own land as from God.[16]

Yahweh was king in Israel, and the people conceived of their holdings as fiefs.[17]

Each family, or perhaps each individual, recognized the suzerainty of Yahweh and acknowledged themselves his vassals. The whole relationship harmonized well with the concept of God as the owner of the land and the people as his feudal tenants.[18]

God expressed this relationship in the following statement: "For unto me the children of Israel are servants; they are my servants whom I brought forth out of the land of Egypt: I am the LORD your God" (Lev. 25:55). It is significant that God made this statement in one of the most important chapters expressing His ownership of the land of Israel and regulating the nation's administration of that land.

In essence, God established a theocratic system with Israel under the Mosaic Law. A theocracy is a form of government in which God's rule is administered by one or more representatives over a possession of God in accordance with His sovereign purpose and in obedience to His commands. The ancient rabbis understood that the laws God gave to Israel concerning the land of Israel "were made to promote the idea of theocracy."[19]

The Principle of Not Losing Tenant Possession Forever

Since God was the ultimate owner of the land of Israel, since He had given tenant possession of the land to the people of Israel forever (Gen. 13:15; 2 Chr. 20:7), and since the Israelites were only the tenant administrators of God's land, they were forbidden to sell the land forever. In Leviticus 25:23 God declared, "The land shall not be sold forever: for the land is mine; for ye are strangers and sojourners with me."

Bess explained this principle as follows:

Inasmuch as the land was Yahweh's land, the portion held by an Israelite was inalienable . . . an individual Israelite received his portion by inheritance. There was no other legal method devised whereby he might come into permanent possession of landed property, and there was therefore no proper way in which to dispose of property except to apportion it to his legal heirs.[20]

This prohibition of a permanent sale was on the basis that the property was not actually the possessor's to sell. He could not sell what he did not own.[21]

If, because of mismanagement or other circumstances, an Israelite became so poverty-stricken that he was forced to sell the portion of land that was his tenant possession, he did not sell the ownership of the land. Instead, he sold the tenant possession or administration of the portion of land for a temporary period of time (Lev. 25:15-16, 25-27). Concerning this, Bess wrote, "In actuality, the land was sold only in the sense that the use of the land for a number of years was surrendered so that it might be regarded as a kind of lease."[22]

To prevent the sale of tenant possession or land administration from being permanent, God established the year of Jubilee (Lev. 25:28), which was the 50th year (the year following the seventh sabbatical year) in Israel's God-ordained calendar system (Lev. 25:8-10). Margolis explained the significance of the year of Jubilee as follows:

> The Jubilee year was mainly instituted in order to prevent violent changes in the tenure of lands (Lev. xxv. 23 et seq.). The land, the law declares, properly belongs to YHWH, who is sole landlord, while all the Israelites are but his tenants. Therefore the land must not be sold in perpetuity. It may be leased, or its crops may be sold; but in the Jubilee year the land returns to its original owner.[23]

Thus, God required that a sold tenant possession be returned to the original tenant or his heir in the year of Jubilee (Lev. 25:10, 13, 28; 27:24).[24]

The Principle of Not Losing Tenant Possession to a Person Outside the Original Tenant's Tribe

God commanded, "Neither shall the inheritance be transferred from one tribe to another tribe, but every one of the tribes of the children of Israel shall keep himself to his own inheritance" (Num. 36:9).

God established regulations designed to keep each portion of land permanently in the tribe of the original tenant. Bess referred to one of these regulations as follows: "Concern that no land once allotted to a member of a tribe should ever pass into hands outside the tribe is expressed in Num. 27:8-11."[25] In this passage God commanded that if a man died, his tenant possession could be given only to a member of that family.

But that regulation did not totally solve the problem of tenant possession passing from one tribe to another. If a man's tenant possession was given to his daughter, and that daughter married outside her tribe, her sons would inherit her tenant possession. Her sons would be reckoned as belonging to the tribe of their father, rather than to the tribe of their mother. Thus, their inherited tenant possession, which originally belonged to their mother's tribe, would become the property of their father's tribe (Num. 36:1-4).[26]

To prevent this from happening, God established another regulation in Numbers 36:5-9. Bess gave the following explanation of that regulation:

> In order to prevent the transfer of land in this way from one tribe to another, the daughters of Zelophahad (and other brotherless heirs) were instructed that they might marry only within their own tribe. Every effort was to be made to see that every parcel of ground remain forever in the tribe (and perhaps clan) to which it was originally apportioned.[27]

The Principle of Redemption

The Right of Redemption. After having declared, "The land shall not be sold forever: for the land is mine" (Lev. 25:23), God commanded, "And in all the land of your possession ye shall grant a redemption for the land" (v. 24).

Bess wrote, "An integral part of that system which viewed the proprietorship of land within the framework of tribal ownership was the right of redemption."[28] If, because of poverty, an Israelite sold his tenant possession or a portion of it, he had the right to redeem it back at any time before the year of Jubilee if his circumstances enabled him to do so. In the meantime, his nearest kinsman also had the right and duty to redeem it before the year of Jubilee (Lev. 25:25-26).[29] This right of redemption, including the duty of a kinsman, was another means of keeping tenancy of land within the clan and tribe to which it originally belonged.

The Redemption Price. Whenever the right of redemption was exercised, the original tenant or his kinsman was required to pay a redemption price consisting of "the sum of money equivalent to the rent for the years the lease was yet supposed to run, namely, until the jubilee"[30] (Lev. 25:27).

The Kinsman-Redeemer's Keeping of the Land. We should note that although a kinsman paid the redemption price to redeem his relative's lost land, he did not return the land to the relative before the year of Jubilee. Instead, the kinsman-redeemer kept the land to administer it for his own purposes. Concerning this practice Bess stated,

> Redemption of the land was not a sentimental regulation that the kinsman should assist the needy by preserving the property for his less fortunate relative. The redeemer took the land into his own possession and used it for his own ends. The purpose that was served by the redemption was the retention of the land within the tribe and family. The land did not return to the hands of him who sold it until the jubilee, even when it was redeemed by a kinsman.[31]

An example of this practice is found in Jeremiah 32:6-9, where Jeremiah exercised the right of redemption for his cousin's land. In this instance the cousin did not sell his tenant possession to a person outside the family. Instead, he came to his kinsman, Jeremiah, and asked him to redeem the land directly from him. The cousin said to Jeremiah, "The redemption is thine; buy it for thyself" (v. 8; cp. Ruth 4:8). That statement indicates that once Jeremiah, as the kinsman-redeemer, paid the redemption price, the land was his to administer. It was not returned immediately to the cousin.

The Deeds of Purchase. In conjunction with Jeremiah's payment of the land redemption price, two copies of the deed of purchase were made as legal evidence of the transaction and of Jeremiah's right of tenant possession of the land (Jer. 32:10-16). Concerning the meaning of the word translated "evidence" and "book" in this passage, Richard D. Patterson wrote,

The noun *seper* "writing," "book" came to be used also of important legal documents (Deut 24:1, 3; Isa 50:1; Jer 3:8) or official letters (I Kgs 21:8ff.; II Kgs 19:14; Est 1:22; Jer 29:1ff.). No doubt these were chiefly in the form of scrolls (e.g. Num 5:23; Ps 40:7 [H 8]; cf. Heb 10:7; Isa 34:4; Ezk 2:9), written in columns (Jer 36:23) and occasionally on both sides (Ezk 2:9-10; cf. Rev 5:1).[32]

Jeremiah signed and sealed shut one copy of the scroll deed of purchase and had witnesses sign it, apparently on the outside (Jer. 32:10, 12). Concerning this practice, Weemse wrote,

> For the manner of writing the contract, he who was to buy the ground wrote two instruments; the one to be sealed with his own signet, the other he showed unclosed to the witnesses, that they might subscribe and bear witness of that which was written. *This, the witnesses did subscribe UPON THE BACK of the inclosed instrument.*[33]

No doubt this deed was sealed to prevent anyone from changing its contents. "Besides authenticating a document, the seal often was used as a means of security. Thus, sealed documents could be opened only by authorized persons."[34]

Jeremiah left the second copy unsealed (Jer. 32:11, 13-14) so that it could be read by anyone who wanted to know who had the right of tenant possession to this land.

The Need for the Sealed Scroll Deed. Obviously an unsealed deed of purchase would be vulnerable to tampering or change by unscrupulous people who wanted to deny tenant possession to the rightful person. In light of this risk, there was always the possibility that someone would challenge the reliability of the unsealed deed and the right of tenant possession for the person named in it. It was therefore necessary to have the sealed deed of purchase as irrefutable evidence of who had the right of tenant possession. Sealing "guaranteed that the terms would not be changed."[35]

Gaston Maspero gave an example of an enclosed document being used as evidence.

> Contracts stamped upon clay tablets have been found in Babylonia, enclosed in an envelope of clay, on the outside of which an exact duplicate of the contract was impressed: if in the course of time any disagreement arose, and it was suspected that the outside text had been tampered with, the envelope was broken in the presence of witnesses to see if the inside text agreed with it or not.[36]

The possibility of someone challenging the right of tenant possession would be especially strong in a situation where the kinsman-redeemer did not take actual possession of the land for a long period of time after he had paid the redemption price for it because circumstances removed him for many years to a location far from the land, and usurpers occupied and used that land during his absence. That kind of situation would require the kinsman-redeemer to open and read the sealed scroll deed as irrefutable evidence of his right of tenant possession before he took actual possession of the land.

Such was the situation of Jeremiah. Although he had paid the price of redemption for his cousin's land and thereby had gained the right of tenant possession, he could not take immediate, actual possession of the land for at least two reasons. First, Jeremiah was confined in prison when he paid the price of redemption (Jer. 32:2-3, 8-9). Second, his cousin's land was "already under Babylonian control" when Jeremiah paid for it.[37] Because Israel had rebelled against God so persistently, its land inheritance had been turned over to foreigners (Lam. 5:2; Jer. 32:21-24, 28-36). The Jews (including Jeremiah) would be exiled to other countries, and their land would continue under enemy control for several decades; but then the Jews would be regathered to their homeland, and their land would be restored to their control (Jer. 32:15, 37, 41-44). Because he knew that actual possession of the land could not take place for many years, Jeremiah commanded that both deeds of purchase be placed in a secure place for a long time (Jer. 32:13-15).

The Two Responsibilities of the Kinsman-Redeemer. It is important to note that land redemption in Israel involved two significant responsibilities for the kinsman-redeemer. First, he had to pay the redemption price for the land and thereby obtain the right of tenant possession. Second, after obtaining that right he had to take actual possession of the land and exercise administrative control over it. In situations where the kinsman-redeemer did not take immediate possession of the land for a long period of time, he had to evict any usurpers before he could take actual possession of the land. Sometimes this eviction required the use of force by the kinsman-redeemer when the usurpers resisted removal from the land.

E. W. Bullinger referred to these two responsibilities of the kinsman-redeemer as follows:

> But the payment of the price is only one part of the work of redemption. If the *price* be paid and there be no power to take possession and eject the holder the payment is in vain. And if *power* be put forth and exercised in casting out the usurper, without the previous payment of the redemption price, it would not be a righteous act. So that for the redemption of the forfeited inheritance two things are absolutely necessary, *price* and *power*.[38]

THE IDENTIFICATION OF THE SEALED SCROLL OF REVELATION 5

The relationship of God's program of land redemption for Israel to the sealed scroll of Revelation 5 can be seen through an examination of several parallels between God's program of land redemption for Israel and His program of redemption for the world.

The First Parallel

Just as the land of Israel belonged to God, so the whole earth and everything in it is His. Because God created the earth and everything in it, He is its owner and sovereign King (Ex. 19:5; 1 Chr. 29:11; Ps. 24:1-2; 47:2-3; 7-9). Henry M. Morris wrote, "The earth is permanently God's possession by right of creation."[39]

The Second Parallel

Just as God gave His land of Israel to the people of Israel to possess as an inheritance forever, so He gave His earth to mankind to possess as an inheritance forever (Ps. 115:16; Gen. 1:26-28; Isa. 24:5 ["the everlasting covenant"]). In conjunction with this, it is interesting to note that the biblical term "son" involves the concept of "heir" ("and if a son, then an heir of God," Gal. 4:7). Further, Luke 3:38 indicates that Adam was God's son. As God's son, Adam inherited God's earth.

James Kelly expressed this truth as follows: "What is the history of our earth? God made it 'good,' and it was consigned to Adam as his inheritance."[40]

Along similar lines, Alfred Jenour stated,

> The earth and all things in it were originally given to Adam and his posterity for a possession. This primeval grant is contained in the first chapter of Genesis (ver. 28) . . . Here, then, we have man's original title-deed to the possession of the earth. It was given him by God himself, and is recorded in the very commencement of his Word.[41]

In spite of the fact that God gave the earth to mankind, mankind was not free to regard themselves as sole owner and authority. Since God was the ultimate owner of the earth, mankind was responsible to serve as His representative, administering His rule over the earth for His benefit in accordance with His sovereign purpose and in obedience to His commands (Gen. 2:15-17). God was the landlord; mankind was the tenant possessor. In essence, God established a theocratic system with mankind at the time of creation.

The Third Parallel

The Restriction. Just as the Israelites were forbidden to lose forever their tenant possession or administration of the land portions that were their inheritance, so it was wrong for mankind to forfeit forever their tenant possession or administration of the earth that was their inheritance. It was wrong because God was the ultimate owner of the earth; He had given tenant possession of the earth to mankind forever, and mankind was only the tenant administrator of God's earth. Mankind was not the ultimate owner of the earth; therefore, they did not have the right or authority to forfeit forever tenant possession or administration of God's earth to anyone else.

The Loss of Tenant Possession. In the same manner that an Israelite lost tenant possession or administration of his land inheritance to another person because of mismanagement or, as in the case of the whole nation, to foreign usurpers, because of rebellion against God (Lam. 5:2), there is a genuine sense in which mankind forfeited tenant possession or administration of their earth inheritance to Satan because they followed Satan's lead to rebel against God (Gen. 3).

As a result of getting the first man, Adam, to join his revolt against God, Satan usurped tenant possession of the earth away from its original tenant and has been exercising administrative control of the world system against God ever since. In other words, the theocracy was lost and replaced by a satanocracy. Several things indicate that this is so. For example, Satan had the authority to offer Jesus all the power and glory of the kingdoms of the world (Lk. 4:5-6); Satan declared that it had been delivered (perfect passive verb) to him by someone else (Adam, Lk. 4:6); Jesus called Satan "the prince of this world" (Jn. 12:31; 14:30; 16:11); and Paul called him "the god of this age" (2 Cor. 4:4).

Because mankind forfeited their God-given tenant possession of the earth to Satan, God placed nature under a curse (Gen. 3:17-19). In addition, according to Isaiah 24:5-6, the earth has become defiled and cursed because mankind transgressed God's laws (the regulations that they were to obey in order to administer God's rule over the earth), changed the ordinance (God's ordinance that mankind was to be His representative tenant of the earth, administering His rule His way), and broke the everlasting covenant (the covenant that gave mankind tenant possession or administration of the earth forever). As a result of these actions, creation was made subject to vanity, corruption, groaning, and travails in pain. It can hardly wait until the day when, in conjunction with redemption, it will be released from this curse and defilement (Rom. 8:19-23).

Concerning the fact that mankind forfeited their tenant possession inheritance, Jenour wrote:

> Thus, then, the earth from the moment of Adam's transgression must have become, in respect to man, a forfeited inheritance. And this is in fact everywhere implied . . . It is implied in the promise to Christ, to whom God says, "Ask of me, and I will give thee the heathen for thine inheritance, and the uttermost parts of the earth for thy possession." It is obvious from hence that the inheritance had been forfeited, otherwise the mention of a new heirship would be inappropriate. God having given the world to Adam in the first instance would certainly not have spoken of *another* heir, had not he to

whom it was originally made over lost his title to it. We have, therefore, scriptural authority for asserting that the earth is to be regarded in the light of a *forfeited* or *alienated inheritance*.[42]

Kelly expressed it this way: "But Adam sinned, and so the crown fell from his head; and, by a judicial permission this once fair domain of creation has lapsed into the hands of the usurper, Satan."[43]

The Temporary Nature of the Loss. Just as the loss of their tenant possession inheritance by an Israelite and by the entire nation was temporary, so mankind's loss of their tenant possession inheritance of the earth to Satan is temporary. Evidence for this will be presented later.

The Fourth Parallel

Just as God intended each Israelite tenant inheritance to remain forever the possession of the tribe to which it was given originally, so He intended the tenant inheritance of the earth to remain forever the possession of mankind to whom it was given originally. Thus, parallel to the fact that an Israelite was forbidden to lose his tenant possession inheritance to a person outside his tribe is the fact that it was wrong for mankind to forfeit their tenant possession inheritance to a being outside mankind. But they did forfeit their tenant possession inheritance to Satan, a being outside mankind (Satan is an angel [2 Cor. 11:14], not a human.)

The Fifth Parallel

Just as God established means, including the program of land redemption, to prevent the Israelites' loss of tenant possession from being permanent, so He has established a program of redemption to prevent mankind's loss of tenant possession of the earth to Satan from being permanent.

The Provision of the Kinsman-Redeemer. Parallel to the fact that God established a program for Israel through which a kinsman could redeem a tenant possession of property that had been lost by a relative is the fact that He also has established a program through which a kinsman of mankind redeems both mankind and the tenant possession of the earth, which mankind lost to Satan.

Just as the Israelite redeemer had to be a kinsman (a relative from the same clan and tribe) of the person who lost the tenant possession, so the Redeemer of mankind and their forfeited tenant possession of the earth had to be a kinsman (a relative of the same kind) of mankind. He had to be a human. No angel or any other kind of being would qualify.

Several things indicate that God has provided a qualified kinsman-redeemer for mankind. First, immediately after mankind forfeited their tenant possession inheritance to Satan by following his lead and rebelling against God (Gen. 3:1-7), God promised that the woman's "seed" (a human born of woman during the course of history) would "bruise" Satan (crush the usurper of mankind's inheritance, Gen. 3:15). Second, Paul declared that this promised one was sent forth by God and was "made of a woman" (a human born of woman) to do the work of redemption (Gal. 4:4-5). Third, Hebrews indicates that the one who does the work of redemption is Christ (Heb. 9:12-15) and that He partook of mankind's flesh and blood (not the nature of angels) so that He might "destroy" Satan (Heb. 2:14-16). Fourth, John asserted that Jesus Christ, the Son of God (1 Jn. 2:22), came into the world in human flesh (1 Jn. 4:2) with a literal, physical, human body that could be seen and touched (1 Jn. 1:1), so "that he might destroy the works of the devil" (1 Jn. 3:8).

Fifth, Christ talked about "the regeneration" of the future (Mt. 19:28). The word translated "regeneration" consists of two words. The first word, meaning "back, again, once more, anew," is used "in expressions that denote a falling back into a previous state or a return to a previous activity." It is used for situations in which "a state of being recurs in the same (or nearly the same) way as at first."[44] The second word is "genesis," which means "birth, existence, origin."[45] Thus, the word translated "regeneration" could be translated "back to Genesis" or "Genesis again" and refers to a return to the original state that existed when the earth was born and is recorded in Genesis.

In Matthew 19:28 Jesus declared that "the regeneration" would take place "when the Son of man shall sit on the throne of his glory." His terminology is significant. It indicates that when Christ, as the Son of man (as a human, a kinsman of mankind) rules the earth, there will be a return to the original state that existed when the earth was born, which is recorded in Genesis and involved mankind's tenant possession or administration of the earth as God's representative. Christ taught that He will begin to exercise that rule when He returns in glory with His holy angels (Mt. 25:31). Thus, when Christ returns to the earth immediately after the Great Tribulation and takes over the rule of the earth as the Kinsman-Redeemer, He will restore mankind's forfeited inheritance. The first Adam lost that inheritance; Christ, as "the last Adam" (1 Cor. 15:45), will restore it.

Sixth, in Acts 3:19-21 Peter declared that "the times of refreshing" and "the times of restitution of all things" will come when God sends Christ back to be personally present on the earth. Earlier in his declaration (vv. 13-15), Peter made it clear that Christ was crucified and resurrected, thereby indicating that He was human (a kinsman of mankind) with a physical body.

Arndt and Gingrich stated that the word for "times" in the expression "the times of refreshing" is "one of the chief eschatological terms"[46] and that the entire expression is a reference to "the Messianic Age."[47]

Concerning this same expression, Eduard Schweizer wrote, "The context makes sense only if the 'times of refreshing' are the definitive age of salvation." He asserted that it refers to "eschatological redemption."[48]

Regarding the word translated "restitution" in the expression "the times of restitution of all things," Albrecht Oepke claimed that in ancient secular usage "the basic meaning is 'restitution to an earlier state' or 'restoration.' "[49] Concerning its meaning in Peter's Acts 3:19-21 declaration, he wrote that it

> cannot denote the conversion of persons but only the reconstitution or establishment of things. For the concept of restoration, which is so strong in the term, does not strictly refer to the content of the prophetic promise, but to the relations of which it speaks. These are restored, i.e., brought back to the integrity of creation, while the promise itself is established or fulfilled.[50]

Thus, Peter was referring to the future restoration of the original order of things that God established on the earth at creation.

Concerning the relationship of the expressions "the times of refreshing" and "the times of restitution of all things," Oepke stated that they "stand in correspondence and mutually explain one another."[51] They both refer to the same restoration of the original order of things. However, in light of the fact that these expressions involve two different Greek words translated "times," they refer to two different aspects of that future restoration. The word for "times" in the expression "the times of refreshing" "marks the beginning of the transformation," and the word for "times" in the expression "the times of restitution of all things" "conveys the thought of the lasting nature of the renewed world."[52]

F. F. Bruce wrote that "the restitution" to which Peter referred in Acts 3:21 "appears to be identical with" "the regeneration" to which Jesus referred in Matthew 19:28, and that the restoration involved will include "a renovation of all nature."[53]

In light of what has been seen, we can conclude that in Acts 3:19-21 Peter was referring to the future Messianic Age (the Millennium) that Christ will establish when, in conjunction with His coming and as the kinsman of mankind, He will redeem the earth by restoring the original order of things that God established on the earth at the time of creation. This restoration, to be that of the original creation order, will include restoration of mankind's tenant possession or administration of the earth as God's representative plus removal of the curse and defilement of nature.

The Redemption Price. Just as the Israelite kinsman-redeemer was required to pay a redemption price to redeem the lost inheritance of his relative, so Christ, as the Kinsman-Redeemer of mankind and their tenant possession of the earth, was required to pay a redemption price to redeem mankind's forfeited inheritance. The redemption price He paid was the shedding of His blood (Eph. 1:7; Col. 1:14; 1 Pet. 1:18-19; Rev. 5:9).

The Kinsman-Redeemer's Keeping of the Land. Although an Israelite kinsman-redeemer paid the redemption price to redeem his relative's lost tenant possession inheritance of land, he did not return the administration of the land to the relative who had lost it. Instead, he kept the land and administered it for his own purposes. In like manner, although Christ paid the redemption price to redeem mankind's forfeited tenant possession inheritance of the earth, He will not return the administration of the whole earth to Adam, the man who forfeited it. As the Kinsman-Redeemer and last Adam, Christ will keep the earth to administer it for God's purposes (Rev. 11:15). Christ "shall be king over all the earth; in that day shall there be one LORD, and his name one" (Zech. 14:9).

The Deed of Purchase. In light of the many parallels between God's program of land redemption for Israel and His program of redemption for the world, it seems apparent that the sealed scroll Christ took from the right hand of God in heaven (Rev. 5) is the deed of purchase for mankind's tenant possession or administration of the earth. This implies that just as scroll deeds of purchase were made when Jeremiah paid the redemption price for his cousin's tenant possession of land, so a scroll deed of purchase was made when Christ paid the redemption price for mankind's tenant possession of the earth by shedding His blood on the cross.

The fact that the sealed scroll of Revelation 5 had writing on both the inside and outside (v. 1), in the same manner as Jeremiah's and other deeds of purchase in Israel's land redemption system, indicates that it is a deed of purchase. Joseph A. Seiss wrote concerning this twofold writing on the Revelation 5 scroll:

> This again tends to identify it with these books of forfeited inheritances. Within were the specifications of the forfeiture; without were the names and attestations of the witnesses; for this is the manner in which these documents were attested.[54]

When writing about the revelation 5 scroll, Jenour stated, "We regard it as a COVENANT DEED, the book in which were registered the terms of man's redemption, and his restoration to the dominion of the earth and all those privileges which he had forfeited by transgression."[55]

Both Kelly[56] and Morris[57] asserted that the scroll of Revelation 5 is the title deed to the earth.

In the same manner that Jeremiah's scrolls were legal evidence of his payment of the redemption price and therefore of his right of tenant possession of the land, so Christ's scroll deed is legal evidence of His payment of the redemption price and therefore of His right of tenant possession of the earth. In conjunction with this, Kelly wrote,

> Provision has accordingly been made, not merely for the salvation of man, but for the recovery of his lost inheritance. The redemption price has been

duly paid; and "the evidence of the purchase," represented by the expressive symbol of the sealed book, is exhibited in this vision as in the Divine possession; its formal production at length taking place, because *now*, "He whose right it is," is coming forth to assert it.[58]

The Need for the Sealed Scroll Deed. One of Jeremiah's scroll deeds was sealed to prevent anyone from changing its contents, giving that scroll the nature of irrefutable evidence. Parallel to this is the fact that Christ's scroll deed is sealed with seven seals (Rev. 5:1, 5). Since in the Bible the number seven signifies "what is total or complete"[59], the seven seals on Christ's scroll make it totally secure from tampering or change. Thus, they are the guarantee that Christ's scroll deed is absolutely irrefutable evidence that He is the Kinsman-Redeemer who has the right to take tenant possession of the earth. Gottfried Fitzer wrote that "The seal served as a legal protection and guarantee in many ways, esp. in relation to property."[60]

Jeremiah's scroll deeds were placed in a secure place where they could be preserved for a long period of time, since he did not take actual possession of the land immediately after paying the redemption price for it because circumstances removed him for many years to a location far from the land. In like manner, Christ's scroll deed was placed in a secure place (God's right hand in heaven, Rev. 5:1, 7) for a long period of time because He did not take actual possession of the earth immediately after paying the redemption price for it at the cross, being removed for many years to a location far from the earth (heaven, Acts 1:9-11).

Just as foreign squatters controlled the land of Israel (including the land Jeremiah had purchased) for many years while the Jews and Jeremiah were removed from it, so foreign squatters (Satan and the human members of his kingdom) are controlling the world system during the years Christ is removed from the earth.

The Two Responsibilities of the Kinsman-Redeemer. Just as land redemption in Israel involved two significant responsibilities for the kinsman-redeemer, so the redemption of the earth involves the same two responsibilities for Christ, mankind's Kinsman-Redeemer. First, He had to pay the redemption price for the earth and thereby obtain the right of tenant possession. Second, now that Christ has obtained that right, He must take actual possession of the earth and exercise administrative control over it as the last Adam, God's representative.

Several things presented in Revelation 5 relate directly to Christ's two responsibilities as mankind's Kinsman-Redeemer. First, the three titles assigned to Him (vv. 5-6) portray Him as both the one who has paid the redemption price and the one who will take possession of the earth to rule it.

The first title is "the Lion of the tribe of Judah." The lion in ancient times was "a symbol of power and courage."[61] Historically, the lion has been regarded as the king of the animal domain. Thus, Christ as "the Lion" has power to rule.

This idea is emphasized further by the designation of Christ as the Lion "of the tribe of Judah," which is based on Jacob's prophecy concerning his son, Judah, and his tribal descendants (Gen. 49:8-10). This prophecy declared that Judah would be the ruling tribe of Israel, have the power to defeat its enemies (cp. 2 Sam. 22:41; Ps. 18:40), be characterized by the action of a lion, always have the right to rule, and have all this power and right to rule culminate in its ultimate descendant, the Messiah, to whom the people will gather for leadership and instruction. Wilhelm Michaelis claimed that this prophecy was interpreted in later Judaism "in terms of the Messiah."[62]

We can conclude, then, that in the context of Revelation 5 the title "the Lion of the tribe of Judah" is applied to Christ to indicate that He is the one who has the power and right to defeat Satan and his followers, by evicting them and their rule from the earth, and to take possession of the earth to rule it as the last Adam.

The second title applied to Christ is "the Root of David." This title is based on Isaiah 11:10, which, in its context, talks about "a root of Jesse" (root out of David's father) "in a Messianic sense."[63] Since Jesse was the father of David, the first king from the tribe of Judah, and thereby the father of the royal family of the tribe of Judah, it appears that both of these titles were designed to indicate that the Messiah would be a descendant of the royal family of Judah and therefore would have the right and authority to rule.

The Hebrew word translated "root" in the expression "root of Jesse" "denotes both the relic of past glory and also the hopeful starting-point for a better future."[64] The idea involved is "From the root a fallen tree can renew itself and put forth fresh shoots, Job 14:7-9. The root, then, is the hope of a new beginning after catastrophe."[65]

This idea applies to the expression "root of Jesse" in Isaiah 11:10. When the royal family of the tribe of Judah provided the nation with godly kings, both that family and the nation experienced great glory. However, as a result of ungodly kings and rebellious people, the royal family was cut down, like a tree, from exercising rule, and the nation fell on very hard times through foreign captivity and scattering. Since that captivity, the royal family of Judah has not exercised rule but has remained dormant, just as a stump gives no evidence of having life. The stump of this royal family will spring to life again suddenly when its King (the Messiah or Christ) springs forth from it to rule. "From the pitiable remnant of the house of Jesse there will come forth, as from the remaining stump of a tree, a new shoot which will establish the coming kingdom of peace and righteousness."[66]

Isaiah 11 says that during the Messiah's rule the curse will be removed from creation. Once again animals will be tame and snakes harmless. God will be known throughout the world. The Messiah will be the center of world attention, and even the Gentiles will seek Him as their ruler. The expression "his rest shall be glorious" (v. 10) indicates that the Messiah will impress the world by defeating His enemies and giving the earth rest.[67]

In light of what has been seen, it appears that the title "the root of David" in Revelation 5 is designed to communicate the idea that as a descendant of the royal family of Judah, Christ will defeat His enemies (Satan and his followers), give the earth rest from their rebellious rule and the curse on creation, and rule the entire world with peace and righteousness.

The third title applied to Christ is "the Lamb that was slain." The song recorded in Revelation 5:9-10, which emphasizes Christ's crucifixion and the shedding of His blood, indicates that this title refers to the redemptive work of Christ. When Christ shed His blood on the cross, He functioned as "the Lamb of God, who taketh away the sin of the world" (Jn. 1:29). As the Lamb that was slain, Christ fulfilled the first responsibility of a kinsman-redeemer—He paid the redemption price and thereby obtained the right of tenant possession. In line with this, the song of Revelation 5:9-10 declares that Christ is worthy to take the scroll and open its seals because He was slain and accomplished His redemptive work.

We should note, however, that the Lamb that was slain had seven horns (5:6). Werner Foerster said that in the Old Testament the horn "is a direct term for power."[68] Passages such as Deuteronomy 33:17; 1 Kings 22:11; and Zechariah 1:18-21 indicate that this is so. In later Judaism "the growing of horns on lambs denotes their growing power."[69] In light of the significance of horns, Foerster explained the implication of the seven horns on the Lamb in Revelation 5 as follows: "In accordance with the symbolical meaning of the number seven and of the figure of the horn, the seven horns of the Lamb express the divine plentitude of power."[70] As the slain Lamb of God who paid the price of redemption, Christ has the fullness of divine power necessary to crush His enemies and take over the rule of the earth.

In line with this understanding of the Lamb that was slain and had seven horns, William Barclay wrote,

> Here is the great paradox: the Lamb bears the sacrificial wounds upon it; but at the same time it is clothed with the very might of God which can now shatter and break its enemies. The Lamb has *seven* horns; we have already seen that the number *seven* stands for completeness and perfection; the power of the lamb is perfect, full, complete, beyond withstanding.[71]

Joachim Jeremias asserted that "the statements of Revelation concerning Christ as" Lamb "depict Him as Redeemer and Ruler."[72]

A second thing in Revelation 5 directly related to Christ's two responsibilities as mankind's Kinsman-Redeemer is the statement that Christ "hath prevailed to open the scroll, and to loose its seven seals" (v. 5:5). Otto Bauernfeind stated, concerning the meaning of the word translated "hath prevailed" and the word group to which it belongs, "The word group denotes 'victory' or 'superiority,' . . . the basic sense of genuine superiority and overwhelming success generally remains."[73] He further declared that it is generally assumed that such victory "is demonstrated by an action, by the overthrow of an opposing force."[74] Thus, it appears that Revelation 5:5 is indicating that Christ has authority to open the scroll and loose its seven seals because of a previous victory He gained over Satan and his forces.

Since Revelation 5:9 asserts that Christ is worthy to take the scroll and open its seals because He was slain and has redeemed mankind by His blood, we can conclude that the previous victory Christ gained over Satan and his forces, which gives Him the authority to open the scroll and loose its seven seals, was His redemptive work on the cross. Christ defeated Satan and his forces when He paid the redemption price of His shed blood. Through the payment of that price, Christ defeated Satan and his forces in the sense that He gained the right to take tenant possession of the earth away from them and rule the earth as the last Adam. This truth sheds light on the meaning of Christ's statement just before He went to the cross, "the prince of this world is judged" (Jn. 16:11). Christ's death sealed Satan's doom. At the proper time, determined sovereignly by God, Christ will exercise the right He gained at the cross to throw out the usurper.

Concerning this, Gottlob Schrenk wrote, "Triumphant in His sacrificial death, Christ can execute the divine will up to the the final consummation. Thus the cross is the basis of His ruling power, which can bring the divine lordship to its goal."[75]

A third thing in Revelation 5 relating to Christ's two Kinsman-Redeemer responsibilities is the declaration that those people who have been re-deemed by Christ's blood "shall reign on the earth" (5:9-10). It is important to note that the verb translated "shall reign" is in the future tense in the Greek text and that this declaration will be made when Christ takes the scroll from God's hand. Thus, the redeemed will reign on the earth after Christ takes the sealed scroll.

The significance of this declaration and the future tense of its verb is stated by Jenour,

> Now, why does the ransomed Church in celebrating the praises of its Re-deemer, and declaring his worthiness to open the book, add, at the close of its doxology, "and we shall reign upon the earth," but because the redemption wrought out has reference to the earth, and its restoration to its original possessor? And what makes this the more striking is, the use of the future tense in regard to this anticipated dominion over the earth. It is not said, *we reign*, but we *shall reign; i.e.*, when thou hast opened the sealed covenant deed, and fully established thy right to the purchased possession, and hast put all opposing enemies under thy feet, *then* shall we reign with thee upon the earth.[76]

Thus, once again, Revelation 5 associates Christ's redemptive work with the future rule of the earth. It is interesting to note that the Apostle Paul also declared that church saints "shall reign" (future tense) with Christ (2 Tim. 2:12).

A fourth thing in Revelation 5 relating to Christ's two responsibilities as the Kinsman-Redeemer is the doxologies found in verses 8-13, which were expressed when Christ took the scroll from God's hand (vv. 7-8). The first doxology (vv. 8-10) emphasizes Christ's past payment of the redemption price through the shedding of His blood; but, as noted previously, it includes the rule of the earth by the redeemed. The last part of the doxologies (vv. 11-13) declares that as the redemptive Lamb that was slain, Christ is worthy to receive many significant things, including power. In the Greek text, that power is expressed with different words. Earlier in this chapter we noted that these words refer to God's power to crush His enemies and establish and exercise His sovereign rule over His creation. Thus, the last part of the doxologies of Revelation 5 declares that because Christ has already paid the redemption price, He is worthy to have and exercise God's power to crush Satan and his forces and rule the earth as God's representative.

Taken together, these four things in Revelation 5 indicate three things concerning Christ's two Kinsman-Redeemer responsibilities. First, Christ fulfilled the first responsibility when He paid the redemption price by shedding His blood on the cross and thereby obtained the right to take tenant possession of the earth. Second, because He fulfilled the first responsibility, Christ is worthy to take the scroll, break its seals, open it, have and exercise God's power to crush Satan and his forces, and rule the earth. Third, Christ will do these things, thus fulfilling His second Kinsman-Redeemer responsibility.

Conclusion Concerning the Scroll

The five parallels between God's program of land redemption for Israel and His program of redemption for the earth prompt the following conclusion: The sealed scroll of Revelation 5 is the deed of purchase for mankind's tenant possession or administration of the earth. This deed was made when Christ paid the redemption price by shedding His blood on the cross for mankind's tenant possession of the earth.

THE SIGNIFICANCE OF CHRIST'S ACTION WITH THE SCROLL

John wept much when it appeared that no one was able to take the scroll from God's hand, break its seals, open it, and look at its contents (Rev. 5:2-4). When Christ took the scroll from God's hand, there were tremendous expressions of praise from God's creatures (vv. 7-14). These responses indicate that Christ's action of taking the scroll, breaking its seals, opening it, and looking at its contents will have great significance.

The Need for Evidence. Earlier we noted that in Israel's land redemption system, one deed of purchase was sealed so that it could serve as irrefutable evidence of who had the right of tenant possession, in case that right were challenged in the future. The possibility of such a challenge would be especially strong in a situation where the kinsman-redeemer did not take actual possession of the land for a long period of time after paying the redemption price because circumstances removed him for many years to a location far from the land, and where usurpers occupied and used that land during his absence. Surely in some instances the usurpers would challenge anyone who appeared after many years and claimed to be the kinsman-redeemer with the right to take tenant possession of the land.

Such is the situation of Christ. As we noted earlier, Christ paid the redemption price and thereby obtained the right of tenant possession of the earth many centuries ago, but He did not take actual possession of the earth at that time. Instead, He ascended to heaven, far from the earth, and has remained there ever since. During His absence, Satan and his forces, who usurped tenant possession of the earth when mankind fell, have continued to exercise that tenant possession.

The Scriptures indicate that Satan and his forces will challenge Christ's right to take tenant possession of the earth as the time of His return draws near. Since Christ will take actual possession of the earth in conjunction with His Second Coming immediately after the end of the 70th week and the Great Tribulation, Satan and his forces will issue their challenge during the 70th week (the last seven years before Christ takes possession). That challenge will involve strong, deceptive, violent action. For example, Satan and his forces will wage war against those who testify for Christ and the Word of God during the 70th week (Dan. 7:21-22, 25-27; Rev. 6:9-11; 11:3-10; 13:7). They will put many of these witnesses to death, trying to deny Christ of a following on the earth when He comes.

Since Christ will not crush Satan and his forces and take possession of the earth until the nation of Israel repents (Zech. 12-14; Acts 3:12, 19-21), during the 70th week Satan and his forces will exert great effort to annihilate Israel before it can repent (Dan. 9:27; Mt. 24:15-16; Rev. 12:7-17). They will thereby try to rob Christ of a major key to His defeating His enemies and taking possession of the earth.

By the end of the 70th week, Satan and his forces will have drawn all the rulers and armies of the world into the land of Israel for the battle of Armageddon (Rev. 16:12-16), which will take place at Christ's Second Coming and will pit Satan and his ungodly allies against Christ and His forces (Rev. 19:11–20:3). This will be Satan's ultimate challenge to Christ's right to take tenant possession of the earth and rule it. The combined military might of rebellious mankind will be gathered to the precise location to which Christ will return to take possession of the earth, because Satan will want all the help he can get to try to prevent Christ from exercising His right (Ps. 2:1-3).

Just as a challenge to an Israelite kinsman-redeemer's right of tenant possession of land in such a situation required the kinsman-redeemer to provide irrefutable evidence of his right of tenant possession before he took actual possession of the land, so Satan's challenge to Christ's Kinsman-Redeemer right of tenant possession of the earth will require Christ to provide irrefutable evidence of His right of tenant possession before He takes actual possession of the earth at His Second Coming.

The Israelite kinsman-redeemer's irrefutable evidence consisted of his taking the sealed deed of purchase from its secure place, breaking its seal or seals, opening it, and reading its contents publicly. In like manner, Christ's irrefutable evidence will consist of His taking the sealed deed of purchase of the earth from its secure place (God's right hand), breaking its seven seals, opening it, and looking at its contents (for the purpose of reading publicly).

The significance of Christ's action with the sealed scroll of Revelation 5 is the evidence it provides—that He is the true Kinsman-Redeemer, the one who paid the redemption price in the past and therefore has the right to take tenant possession of the earth.

The Breaking of the Seals. It should be noted that Christ—not Satan, the Antichrist, or rebellious mankind—will break the seals of the scroll deed of purchase. Revelation 5 makes it clear that He alone is worthy to break them, because only the kinsman-redeemer could legitimately break the seal or seals of a deed of purchase, and Christ is the only Kinsman-Redeemer of mankind's forfeited inheritance. Only Christ has paid the redemption price.

Therefore, Christ—not Satan, the Antichrist, or rebellious mankind— will instigate the things that will transpire when the seven seals are broken. In conjunction with this, Martin Kiddle wrote,

> The strong angel's challenge to find some one worthy to open the scroll and to break its seals was much more than to ask for some one capable of *revealing* the world's fate. The demand was for one able not only to disclose God's plan, but to set it in motion, accomplish it, bring it to pass . . . This is clearly implied in the song of praise, when at last the Lamb accepts the challenge and takes the scroll . . . That is why John is careful to note in chaps. vi.-viii. that the enactment of the last things is performed through the Lamb. One by one, He opens the seals, and as each is broken, so God's plan is wrought.[77]

It also should be noted that Christ's breaking of the seven seals is one aspect of His process of providing irrefutable evidence through His action with the scroll. Thus, the things that transpire when Christ breaks the seals will be part of the irrefutable evidence that He is the true Kinsman-

Redeemer with the right, authority, and power to evict Satan and his forces and take tenant possession of the earth.

Some of the things that will transpire when Christ breaks the seals will devastate significant areas of Satan's domain. They will be expressions of God's Day of the Lord wrath or judgment on that domain. Schrenk wrote, "The book with seven seals declares the ways of God in judgment as ordained by His ruling power."[78] Just as an armed force will attack an alien occupying army with a tremendous bombardment before it launches the invasion that will evict that alien army, so Christ, through the breaking of the seals, will attack the domain of Satan and his forces (the alien forces occupying the earth since the fall of mankind) with a tremendous bombardment of divine wrath or judgment before He launches the invasion (His great and terrible Day of the Lord invasion of the earth when He comes with His angels), which will evict Satan and his forces from the earth.

The fact that Satan and his forces will be incapable of stopping this bombardment of their domain will prove that they are not the ultimate authority over the earth. In addition, this bombardment, instigated by Christ through the breaking of the seals, will demonstrate not only that He has power and authority to fulfill the second responsibility of the Kinsman-Redeemer (the taking of tenant possession by eviction of the usurper) but also is preparing to do so. Thus, the breaking of the seals will produce part of the evidence that Christ is the true Kinsman-Redeemer.

In line with this, James Kelly indicated that when Christ takes the scroll and breaks its seals, He will thereby assert His right to recover mankind's forfeited inheritance.[79] He declared that Christ will do this "amidst demonstrations of judgment, affecting every department of nature, as though to shake it from the enemy's grasp."[80] He further stated,

> Here, in the Revelation, the inheritance of the earth, is conveyed to Christ from the Father, by the formal instrument of the sealed book, the opening of the seals of which, is as it were so many judicial stages towards the establishment of His righteous empire.[81]

Similarly, Jenour wrote, "For the opening of the seals is the preliminary act whereby the GOEL, or Redeemer, begins to take possession."[82]

The Reading of the Scroll Deed. A study of Revelation 8 through 18 indicates that the seventh seal will contain the seven trumpet and seven bowl judgments. Thus, when Christ breaks all seven seals of the Revelation 5 scroll, He will thereby instigate the total bombardment of divine wrath or judgment against the domain of Satan and his forces, which will cover the 70th week of Daniel 9 up to Christ's coming immediately after the 70th week and the Great Tribulation.

Thus, by the time Christ comes from heaven to confront Satan and his forces gathered together against Him to deliver their ultimate challenge to His right to take tenant possession of the earth (Ps. 2:1-3; Rev. 19:11-19), all seven seals of the scroll deed of purchase will have been broken, and the scroll deed will be totally open for Christ to read. Christ will read it publicly as the final, conclusive part of the irrefutable evidence that He is the true Kinsman-Redeemer of mankind's forfeited inheritance and has the right to evict Satan and his forces and take tenant possession of the earth. After presenting this evidence and thereby declaring His right, Christ will proceed to rid the earth of Satan and his forces and take the rule of the earth (Rev. 19:19–20:6).

Psalm 2 presents the same scenario. Verses 1-3 describe the rebellious world forces gathered together to try to prevent God's Messiah from taking tenant possession or administration of the earth. Verse 7 records that when the Messiah confronts this challenge, He will declare what God has already decreed concerning Him: "Thou art my Son."

Earlier in this chapter we noted that the biblical term "son" involves the concept of "heir" (Gal. 4:7). Thus, as God's Son, the Messiah is the heir of an inheritance given to Him by God. Psalm 2:8 presents God's description of that inheritance: "I shall give thee the nations for thine inheritance, and the uttermost parts of the earth for thy possession." Verse 9 states that when the rebel forces gather against Him, "Thou shalt break them with a rod of iron; thou shalt dash in pieces like a potter's vessel."

In light of what has been seen, we can conclude that Psalm 2 is saying that on the day when the Messiah comes to confront the rebel forces gathered to challenge His right to take tenant possession of the earth, He will declare what God has already decreed concerning Him (i.e., that, as His Son, the Messiah has the right to inherit the people and uttermost parts of the earth as His possession). Once the Messiah has delivered that declaration and thereby given irrefutable evidence of His right, He will proceed to crush the rebel forces.

CONCLUSIONS

The unique, eternal God created the universe for His own benefit and sovereign purpose; therefore, only He has the right to rule the entire universe, and that right includes the right to crush any enemy who challenges His rule.

God gave mankind tenant possession of the earth as an inheritance with the intention that mankind function as God's representative, administering God's rule over the earth in accordance with His will. This was a theocratic arrangement.

Mankind forfeited their tenant possession of the earth by following Satan's lead and rebelling against God. As a result, the theocracy was lost. Satan usurped the tenant possession of the earth and has continued to rule the world system ever since mankind's fall.

God purposed to restore the theocracy, which would require the redemption of mankind's forfeited inheritance. To do so, God sent His Son, Jesus Christ, into the world to become a man so that, as a kinsman, He could redeem mankind's tenant possession of the earth. Christ paid the redemption price for mankind and their inheritance by shedding His blood on the cross, thereby fulfilling the first responsibility of the Kinsman-Redeemer.

When Christ paid the redemption price, a scroll deed of purchase for mankind's tenant possession of the earth was prepared, sealed with seven seals (to guarantee its security against change, so that it could serve as irrefutable evidence in the future), and placed in a safe location—God's right hand.

Christ did not take tenant possession of the earth immediately after paying the redemption price but ascended to heaven, far from the earth, and has remained there for many centuries. During His absence, Satan and his forces have continued to exercise tenant possession of the earth as usurpers.

Seven years before His coming to the earth, Christ will take the sealed scroll deed of purchase from God's hand in preparation for the fulfillment of the second responsibility of the Kinsman-Redeemer—the eviction of Satan and his forces and the taking of the earth's tenant possession.

Satan and his forces will strongly challenge Christ's right to take tenant possession. In order to give irrefutable evidence of His right as the Kinsman-Redeemer, Christ will take the scroll, break its seals, open it, and read it. As He breaks the seven seals, Christ will instigate a tremendous seven-year bombardment of divine wrath or judgment against the domain of Satan and his forces in preparation for His coming invasion to evict these enemies. This seven-year bombardment is described in Revelation 6–18. Through this bombardment Christ will prove that He has the power and authority to fulfill the second responsibility of the Kinsman-Redeemer.

On the day of His Second Coming to the earth, when Christ confronts Satan and his forces gathered in Israel to try to prevent His return to take possession of the earth (Rev. 19:11-19), He will read publicly the open scroll deed of purchase—the final, conclusive evidence that He is the true Kinsman-Redeemer and has the right to evict His enemies and take tenant possession of the earth.

After Christ has read the scroll deed, He will evict Satan and his forces from the earth (Rev. 19:20–20:3). Then He will take tenant possession of the earth and, together with redeemed mankind, will rule the earth in accordance with God's will as the last Adam, God's representative, for a thousand years (Rev. 20:4-6). Thus, God will have fulfilled His purpose of restoring the theocracy to the earth through the Kinsman-Redeemer, Jesus Christ. After this purpose has run its full course on the earth, God will judge Satan and his forces for eternity, destroy the present heaven and earth, and create new ones for the future eternal state (Rev. 20:7–22:21).

This chapter has produced several conclusions.

1. The sealed scroll of Revelation 5 is the deed of purchase for mankind's forfeited inheritance of tenant possession of the earth.

2. The scroll is strongly related to God's purpose and program of redemption for the earth, the importance of the Kinsman-Redeemer, Jesus Christ, His redemptive work, and His worthiness to take the scroll, break its seals, open it, read it, and exercise God's ruling power because of His work of redemption.

3. The scroll ties together the seven things that were noted near the beginning of this chapter, which are emphasized in Revelation 4 and 5.

4. The scroll is the key to understanding the significance or purpose of the future events of Revelation 6 through 22, which constitute the fulfillment of the Kinsman-Redeemer's second responsibility—the eviction of God's enemies from the earth and the taking of its tenant possession.

5. Breaking the seven seals of the scroll is Christ's work. Only He is worthy to do it, since He alone is the Kinsman-Redeemer.

6. Through breaking the seven seals, Christ will instigate a tremendous bombardment of divine wrath or judgment against the domain of Satan and his forces for the last seven years before His Second Coming.

7. Christ's action of taking the scroll from God's hand, breaking its seven seals, opening it, and reading it proves that He is the true Kinsman-Redeemer who has the right to evict Satan and his forces and take tenant possession of the earth.

ENDNOTES

1. William F. Arndt and F. Wilbur Gingrich, *A Greek-English Lexicon of the New Testament*, 4th rev. ed. (Chicago: The University of Chicago Press, 1957), p. 171.

2. W. Robert Cook, *The Theology of John* (Chicago: Moody Press, 1979), p. 160.

3. See the articles on the holiness of God by Renald E. Showers in the December/January 1986-1987 and February/March 1987 issues of *Israel My Glory* magazine, published by The Friends of Israel Gospel Ministry, Bellmawr, NJ.

4. R. H. Charles, *A Critical and Exegetical Commentary on the Revelation of St. John*, Vol. I, in *The International Critical Commentary* (Edinburgh: T. & T. Clark, 1920), p. 134.

5. Arndt and Gingrich, *A Greek-English Lexicon of the New Testament*, p. 365.

6. R. C. H. Lenski, *The Interpretation of St. John's Revelation* (Columbus, OH: Lutheran Book Concern, 1935).

7. Wilhelm Michaelis, "kratos," *Theological Dictionary of the New Testament*, Vol. III, ed. by Gerhard Kittel, trans. and ed. by Geoffrey W. Bromiley (Grand Rapids: Wm. B. Eerdmans Publishing Company, 1965), p. 907.

8. *Ibid.*, p. 908.

9. Walter Grundmann, "dunamis," *Theological Dictionary of the New Testament*, Vol. II, ed. by Gerhard Kittel, trans. and ed. by Geoffrey W. Bromiley (Grand Rapids: Wm. B. Eerdmans Publishing Company, 1964), p. 295.

10. *Ibid.*, pp. 292, 306.

11. *Ibid.*, p. 307.

12. Gottlob Schrenk, "biblion," *Theological Dictionary of the New Testament*, Vol. I, ed. by Gerhard Kittel, trans. and ed. by Geoffrey W. Bromiley (Grand Rapids: Wm. B. Eerdmans Publishing Company, 1964), p. 618.

13. *Ibid.*, pp. 618-19.

14. Stephen Herbert Bess, *Systems of Land Tenure in Ancient Israel*, unpublished Ph. D. dissertation, University of Michigan, 1963, p. 52.

15. Max L. Margolis, "Agrarian Laws," *The Jewish Encyclopedia*, Vol. I, managing ed., Isidore Singer (New York: Funk and Wagnalls Company, 1901), p. 241.

16. Stephen Herbert Bess, *Systems of Land Tenure in Ancient Israel*, p. 86.

17. *Ibid.*, p. 112.

18. *Ibid.*, p. 113.

19. Judah David Eisenstein, "Sabbatical Year and Jubilee," *The Jewish Encyclopedia*, Vol. X, managing ed., Isidore Singer (New York: Funk and Wagnalls Company, 1905, 1909), p. 605.

20. Stephen Herbert Bess, *Systems of Land Tenure in Ancient Israel*, p. 98.

21. *Ibid.*, p. 121.

22. *Ibid.*, p. 80.

23. Max L. Margolis, *The Jewish Encyclopedia*, p. 241.

24. Stephen Herbert Bess, *Systems of Land Tenure in Ancient Israel*, p. 120.

25. *Ibid.*, p. 66.

26. *Ibid.*

27. *Ibid.*, p. 67.

28. *Ibid.*, p. 74.

29. Max L. Margolis, *The Jewish Encyclopedia*, p. 241.

30. Stephen Herbert Bess, *Systems of Land Tenure in Ancient Israel*, p. 80.

31. *Ibid.*

32. Richard D. Patterson, "seper," *Theological Wordbook of the Old Testament*, Vol. II, ed. by R. Laird Harris, Gleason L. Archer, Jr., and Bruce K. Waltke (Chicago: Moody Press, 1980), p. 633.

33. Weemse on the Judicial Law of Moses, chapter 30, as quoted in Joseph A. Seiss, *The Apocalypse* (New York: Charles C. Cook, 1913), Vol. I, p. 273.

34. T. H. Weber, *New Catholic Encyclopedia*, Vol. XIII, 1967, p. 14.

35. Norman C. Habel, *Jeremiah, Lamentations* in *Concordia Commentary* (St. Louis: Concordia Publishing House, 1968), p. 254.

36. Gaston Maspero, *The Dawn of Civilization*, p. 732, as quoted in A. W. Streane, *The Book of the Prophet Jeremiah together with The Lamentations* (Cambridge: The University Press, 1926), p. 201.

37. Charles H. Dyer, "Jeremiah," *The Bible Knowledge Commentary—Old Testament Edition*, ed. by John F. Walvoord and Roy B. Zuck (Wheaton, IL: Victor Books, 1985), p. 1173.

38. E. W. Bullinger, *The Apocalypse or "The Day of the Lord"* (London: Eyre and Spottiswoode, 1935), p. 243.

39. Henry M. Morris, *The Revelation Record* (San Diego: Creation-Life Publishers, 1983), p. 96.

40. James Kelly, *The Apocalypse Interpreted in the Light of "The Day of the Lord"* (London: James Nisbet and Co., 1849), Vol. I, p. 288.

41. Alfred Jenour, *Rationale Apocalypticum* (London: Thomas Hatchard, 1852), Vol. I, pp. 203-04.

42. *Ibid.*, pp. 204-05.

43. James Kelly, *The Apocalypse Interpreted*, Vol. I, p. 288.

44. Arndt and Gingrich, *A Greek-English Lexicon of the New Testament*, p. 611.

45. *Ibid.*, p. 154.

46. *Ibid.*, p. 396.

47. *Ibid.*, p. 63.

48. Eduard Schweizer, "anapsuxis," *Theological Dictionary of the New Testament*, Vol. IX, ed. by Gerhard Friedrich, trans. and ed. by Geoffrey W. Bromiley (Grand Rapids: Wm. B. Eerdmans Publishing Company, 1974), p. 664.

49. Albrecht Oepke, "apokatastasis," *Theological Dictionary of the New Testament*, Vol. I, ed. by Gerhard Kittel, trans. and ed. by Geoffrey W. Bromiley (Grand Rapids: Wm. B. Eerdmans Publishing Company, 1964), p. 389.

50. *Ibid.*, p. 391.

51. *Ibid.*

52. *Ibid.*

53. F. F. Bruce, *Commentary on the Book of the Acts* (Grand Rapids: Wm. B. Eerdmans Publishing Company, 1954), footnote 36, p. 91.

54. Joseph A. Seiss, *The Apocalypse*, Vol. I, p. 273.

55. Alfred Jenour, *Rational Apocalypticum*, Vol. I, p. 202.

56. James Kelly, *The Apocalypse Interpreted*, Vol. I, p. 285.

57. Henry M. Morris, *The Revelation Record*, p. 96.

58. James Kelly, *The Apocalypse Interpreted*, Vol. I, p. 289.

59. Karl Heinrich Rengstorf, "hepta," *Theological Dictionary of the New Testament*, Vol. II, ed. by Gerhard Kittel, trans. and ed. by Geoffrey W. Bromiley (Grand Rapids: Wm. B. Eerdmans Publishing Company, 1964), p. 628.

60. Gottfried Fitzer, "sphragis," *Theological Dictionary of the New Testament*, Vol. VII, ed. by Gerhard Friedrich, trans. and ed. by Geoffrey W. Bromiley (Grand Rapids: Wm. B. Eerdmans Publishing Company, 1971), p. 940.

61. Wilhelm Michaelis, "leon," *Theological Dictionary of the New Testament*, Vol. IV, ed. by Gerhard Kittel, trans. and ed. by Geoffrey W. Bromiley (Grand Rapids: Wm. B. Eerdmans Publishing Company, 1967), p. 251.

62. *Ibid.*, p. 252.

63. Christian Maurer, "rhiza," *Theological Dictionary of the New Testament,* Vol. VI, ed. by Gerhard Kittel, trans. and ed. by Geoffrey W. Bromiley (Grand Rapids: Wm. B. Eerdmans Publishing Company, 1968), p. 986.

64. *Ibid.*

65. *Ibid.*

66. *Ibid.*

67. Leonard J. Coppes, "nuah," *Theological Wordbook of the Old Testament*, Vol. II, ed. by R. Laird Harris, Gleason L. Archer, Jr., and Bruce K. Waltke (Chicago: Moody Press, 1980), p. 562.

68. Werner Foerster, "keras," *Theological Dictionary of the New Testament*, Vol. III, ed. by Gerhard Kittel, trans. and ed. by Geoffrey W. Bromiley (Grand Rapids: Wm. B. Eerdmans Publishing Company, 1965), p. 669.

69. *Ibid.*, p. 670.

70. *Ibid.*

71. William Barclay, *The Revelation of John* (Philadelphia: The Westminster Press, 1960), Vol. 1, p. 217.

72. Joachim Jeremias, "arnion," *Theological Dictionary of the New Testament*, Vol. I, ed. by Gerhard Kittel, trans. and ed. by Geoffrey W. Bromiley (Grand Rapids: Wm. B. Eerdmans Publishing Company, 1964), p. 341.

73. Otto Bauernfiend, "nikao," *Theological Dictionary of the New Testament*, Vol. IV, ed. by Gerhard Kittel, trans. and ed. by Geoffrey W. Bromiley (Grand Rapids: Wm. B. Eerdmans Publishing Company, 1967), p. 942.

74. *Ibid*.

75. Gottlob Schrenk, "biblion," *Theological Dictionary of the New Testament*, Vol. I, p. 619.

76. Alfred Jenour, *Rational Apocalypticum*, Vol. I, pp. 211-12.

77. Martin Kiddle, *The Revelation of St. John* (New York: Harper and Brothers Publishers, n.d.), p. 96.

78. Gottlob Schrenk, "biblion," *Theological Dictionary of the New Testament*, Vol. I, p. 619.

79. James Kelly, *The Apocalypse Interpreted*, Vol. I, p. 289.

80. *Ibid*.

81. *Ibid*., p. 295.

82. Alfred Jenour, *Rationale Apocalypticum*, Vol. I, p. 213.

CHAPTER SIX

OBSERVATIONS RELATED TO THE SEALS

SEALS AND SECURITY

The previous chapter indicated that seals often were used as a means of security. A major function of some seals was to make objects secure from tampering or change by unscrupulous people. For example, a seal was placed on the stone covering the opening of the lions' den to prevent anyone from rescuing Daniel (Dan. 6:17). Sealed objects could be opened legitimately only by authorized people.

Two important things should be noted concerning this function of seals, however. First, they were intended to make the object to which they were applied secure, not some other object. In light of this, we should observe that the seven seals of Revelation 6-8 were applied to the sealed scroll of Revelation, not to people. Thus, as noted in the previous chapter, those seven seals were intended to make the sealed scroll of Revelation 5 secure from tampering or change, rather than people.

Second, seals made an object secure when they were applied and as long as they remained intact. That security was removed, however, when the seals were broken. In light of this, we note that in Revelation 6-8 Christ did not apply the seven seals to the scroll of Revelation 5, nor did He keep those seals intact. Instead, He did the opposite. He broke the seven seals and thereby removed the security they were designed to provide. Thus, His breaking of the seven seals has nothing to do with making people secure.

THE SEALS AND THE SEALED SCROLL OF REVELATION 5

All seven seals of Revelation 6-8 are part of the same sealed scroll (Rev. 5:1-2, 5, 9). The previous chapter demonstrated that the sealed scroll is the deed of purchase for mankind's lost tenant possession inheritance of the earth.

In addition, that chapter demonstrated two things concerning the relationship of the seals to the sealed scroll. First, all seven seals had the same purpose—making the scroll totally secure from tampering or change and thereby providing a sevenfold guarantee of its integrity, so that the scroll could serve as irrefutable evidence that Christ is the true Kinsman-Redeemer who has the right to evict Satan and his forces and take tenant possession of the earth.

Second, when Christ breaks the seven seals, the resultant things that will transpire will be part of the irrefutable evidence that He is the true Kinsman-Redeemer.

These two things, together with the identification of the sealed scroll and the fact that all seven seals are part of the same sealed scroll, indicate that all seven seals are part of the same program—Christ's program of fulfilling the second responsibility of the Kinsman-Redeemer.

As noted in the previous chapter, the things that result from Christ's breaking of all seven seals will demonstrate that He has the power and authority to fulfill the second responsibility of the Kinsman-Redeemer (taking tenant possession of the earth by crushing and evicting the usurpers, Satan and his forces).

All seven seals of Revelation 6-8 are therefore part of Christ's Kinsman-Redeemer program. Although, as shall be seen later, Satan and rebellious mankind will carry on activity within that program, the seven seals are not part of their program.

CHRIST'S BREAKING OF THE SEALS

In Revelation 6-8, Christ alone breaks all seven seals. Not one seal will be broken by Satan, the Antichrist, or rebellious mankind. Indeed, Revelation 5 clearly indicates that only Christ is worthy to take the scroll from God's hand and break its seven seals. In the previous chapter we noted that Christ alone is worthy to break the seals because only the kinsman-redeemer could break the seals of a deed of purchase, and Christ is the only Kinsman-Redeemer of mankind's forfeited tenant possession inheritance of the earth. Only He has paid the redemption price, meaning that only He can instigate the things that will transpire when all seven seals are broken.

But doesn't this conclusion present a serious problem, particularly in conjunction with the breaking of the first and fifth seals? To find the answer to this question, we must examine the first and fifth seals.

THE FIRST SEAL

Identification of the Rider of the First Seal

When Christ breaks the first seal, a rider on a white horse will appear, having a bow and crown and going forth to conquer (Rev. 6:1-2). In spite of the fact that Christ will ride on a white horse at His coming to the earth (Rev. 19:11), several things indicate that the rider of the first seal will not be Christ. First, this rider has a bow; Christ will have a sword (19:15).

Second, this rider wears one crown; Christ will have many crowns (19:12). Third, this rider wears the conqueror's crown (*stephanos*); Christ will have a different kind of crown—the crown of kings (*diadema*).[1] Fourth, the conquering activity of this rider will occur at least as early as the time the first seal is broken; Christ will not come riding out of heaven until six seals, seven trumpets, and seven bowls later.

An earlier chapter demonstrated that the beginning of birth pangs of Matthew 24 and the first four seals of Revelation 6 are the same thing and will occur during the first half of the seven years of the 70th week. In light of the fact that the beginning of birth pangs will involve false messiahs, it would appear that the rider of the first seal will be a false messiah.

The words "conquering and to conquer," describing the activity of this false messiah (Rev. 6:2), indicate that he will be a great man of war. His activity during the first half of the 70th week will be characterized by a driving compulsion to conquer the whole world and bring it under his dominion. Because this same conquering activity will be characteristic of the Antichrist during the first half of the 70th week (Dan. 11:38-44), it seems apparent that the rider of the first seal will be the Antichrist, the ultimate false messiah.

The Problem of a Divided House

If Christ is the one who will instigate the things that occur when all seven seals are broken, since the breaking of the first seal will turn the Antichrist loose on the world as a conqueror, is Christ therefore the one who will turn the Antichrist loose on the world? Yes, He is.

But doesn't that pose a serious problem? Wouldn't God's house be divided and opposing itself if Christ were to turn loose the dominant world ruler of the 70th week, who will be energized and controlled by God's great enemy, Satan (2 Th. 2:9-10) and who will blaspheme God, declare himself to be God, desolate Israel, and wage war against the saints (Dan. 7:21, 25; 9:27; 11:36-37; 2 Th. 2:3-4; Rev. 13:4-8)?

God's house would not be divided and opposing itself if Christ's turning the Antichrist loose would serve God's sovereign purpose. Consider the following: Was God's house divided and opposing itself when God turned over His righteous servant, Job, to be attacked by Satan (Job 1:8-12; 2:3-6)? Did God have a sovereign purpose for doing this?

When God raised up the Pharaoh who severely abused Israel (Ex. 9:16; Rom. 9:17) and hardened that Pharaoh's heart so that He refused to obey God's command to let Israel go (Ex. 9:1, 12; 10:1), didn't God have a sovereign purpose for this, even though it appeared to oppose His will?

In spite of the fact that God despises the practices of homosexuality, lesbianism, murder, and the hatred of Himself, didn't He turn ancient Gentiles over to these practices as an expression of His wrath against them because they had willfully rejected His revelation to them (Rom. 1:18-32)?

Was God thereby opposing Himself by giving up people to practices He despises? Obviously not, because He had a sovereign purpose for doing it. Other biblical examples could be given in which God, because of sovereign purposes, did things that appeared to oppose Himself.

Parallel to these examples, in spite of the fact that God will despise the Antichrist, He will have Christ turn him loose to conquer the world through the breaking of the first seal because He will have several sovereign purposes for that action.

Biblical Evidences

There are at least two biblical evidences to the effect that God will have Christ turn the Antichrist loose to conquer the world.

The First Evidence. In Genesis 6:3 God indicated that it was His Spirit who strove with lawless mankind (vv. 5, 11-13) in the days before the Noahic flood. The word translated "strive" means "to govern"; "it embodies the idea of government, in whatever realm,"[2] meaning that the Holy Spirit has one of the same responsibilities or functions as government—the restraint of lawlessness in the world (Rom. 13:3-6; 1 Pet. 2:13-14). Thus, the Holy Spirit's restraint of lawlessness has been a significant factor in the administration of God's rule over the world. Since this restraining work of the Spirit belongs to the administration of God's rule over the world, and since God is sovereign, only God has the authority to remove that restraint.

Second Thessalonians 2:3 and 8 says that the Antichrist will be characterized by lawlessness. In verse 3 the word translated "sin" in the expression "that man of sin" literally means "lawlessness"[3]; thus, the expression "that man of lawlessness" indicates that the Antichrist will be the ultimate expression of human lawlessness. In verse 8 the word translated "wicked" in the expression "that wicked" literally means "lawless one"[4] and refers to the Antichrist as the epitome of human lawlessness.

In 2 Thessalonians 2:6-8 Paul indicated that the mystery of lawlessness (the word translated "iniquity" in the expression "the mystery of iniquity" in v. 7 literally means "lawlessness"[5]) was already working in his day. Nevertheless, some restraint (the word translated "what withholdeth" in v. 6 literally means "the restraining"[6]) was preventing the Antichrist, the ultimate expression of that lawlessness, from being revealed until the right time. Further, Paul declared that the person causing that restraint would continue it until he, as the restrainer, would be "taken out of the way" (v. 7). Once the restrainer would be removed, the lawless one—the Antichrist—would be revealed (v. 8).

Since, as noted earlier, God's Holy Spirit has the function of restraining humanity's lawlessness, and since the Antichrist will be the ultimate expression of human lawlessness, it would appear that Paul was indicating in 2 Thessalonians 2:6-8 that the restraining work of the Holy Spirit is the restraint that prevents the Antichrist from being revealed until the right time. The Holy Spirit will continue that restraining work until He, as the restrainer, is removed, at which time the Antichrist will be revealed.

Since, as noted earlier, only God has the authority to remove the Holy Spirit's restraint, and since the Antichrist will be revealed once that restraint is removed, we can conclude that it will be through divine activity that the Antichrist will be turned loose to conquer the world.

The Second Evidence. In Zechariah 11:15-17 God declared that He would raise up a "foolish" and "idol" shepherd. God's description of this shepherd helps to identify him. The word translated "foolish" (v. 15) refers to a person who is morally perverted, insolent (rude, disrespectful, insulting), and impatient with discipline. He does not fear God. He feels that his own way is without error, and he is overbearing in his attitude since he feels he has all the answers.[7]

These characteristics will be true of the Antichrist. He will be morally perverted, for he will lie (2 Th. 2:11) and kill godly people (Dan. 7:21, 25; Rev. 13:7). He will be insolent toward God and will not fear Him, for he will speak monstrous, blasphemous things against Him (Dan. 11:36; Rev. 13:5-6). He will be impatient with discipline and feel that his own way is without error, for he "shall do according to his will" (Dan. 11:36). He will be overbearing in his attitude and feel that he has all the answers, for he "shall exalt himself, and magnify himself" (Dan. 11:36) and will "think to change the times and the laws" (Dan. 7:25).

This shepherd will also be an "idol" shepherd (Zech. 11:17). The word translated "idol" means "something worthless (particularly as an object of worship), gods, idols" and "is used primarily in Scripture to describe vain objects of worship, i.e. the gods of this world."[8] These worthless gods or idols "even included people in whom men trusted but who were deceitful and of no value (Job 13:4; Isa. 19:3; Zech. 11:17)."[9] Thus, the shepherd of Zechariah 11:15-17 will be a person who, through deceit, will convince people to put their trust in him as a god, even though he is not a god.

Certainly this will be true of the Antichrist. In spite of the fact that he will be a man, he will claim to be God (Dan. 11:36-37; 2 Th. 2:4). He will use "lying wonders," "all deceivableness of unrighteousness" ("every kind of wicked deception"[10]), and a "lie" to convince people to put their trust in him as God (2 Th. 2:9-11). Many people will believe his false claim, place their trust in him, and worship him as God (2 Th. 2:11; Rev. 13:3-4, 8).

Zechariah 11:16 says that instead of shepherding the people of Israel in a loving, caring way, the foolish, idol shepherd will decimate them cruelly for his own selfish purposes. This too will be true of the Antichrist. During the second half of the 70th week of Daniel 9, he will desolate the people of Israel (Dan. 9:27; 12:11; Mt. 24:15-23).

All of these characteristics indicate that the foolish idol shepherd of Zechariah 11:15-17 will be the Antichrist. F. Duane Lindsey wrote, "This is a prophecy of the end-time Antichrist who will do the very opposite of Christ the True Shepherd (cf. John 5:43)."[11]

It is important to note that God declared He will raise up the foolish, idol shepherd (Zech. 11:16). Concerning the meaning of the verb "raise up" in this specific verse, Brown, Driver, and Briggs stated the following: "Raise up = bring on the scene."[12] Since this evil shepherd will be the Antichrist, God thereby indicated that He will bring the Antichrist on the world scene.

God's Purposes

God will have specific purposes for bringing the Antichrist on the world scene.

One purpose will be the punishment of Israel. In Zechariah 11 God foretold the future judgment of Israel because it would reject its good Shepherd, the Messiah. In His first coming, the Messiah would serve as a good Shepherd to the nation. He would bless it, seek to unify it under His leadership, and oppose its false shepherds (vv. 7-8). But the nation would reject the Messiah as its Shepherd in a contemptuous way. It would pay Him 30 pieces of silver (the sum paid for a worthless slave, one gored by an ox) to show Him the value it placed on His shepherding ministry. That silver would be thrown down in the Temple to be given to a potter (vv. 10-13; cp. Mt. 26:14–27:10).

As a result of His rejection, the Messiah would turn the Jews over to division (v. 14) and death from starvation, pestilence, war, and cannibalism (the horrors suffered during the Roman siege of the nation, 67-70 A.D., v. 9), and God would send Israel a false shepherd (the Antichrist) who, as noted earlier, would try to annihilate the nation (vv. 15-17; cp. Dan. 9:27). That desolation of Israel by the Antichrist will be part of God's judgment of the nation because it rejected its Messiah in His first coming. Thus, when God brings the Antichrist on the world scene, it will be a significant form of His wrath upon Israel.

A second purpose will be the repentance of Israel. For centuries Israel's stiff-necked rebellion against God and His Messiah has been so stubborn and persistent that nothing short of the severest persecution in Israel's history will break that rebellion and bring the nation to genuine repentance.

In an earlier chapter, we noted that the future unprecedented time of Great Tribulation will not end until God has completely shattered the obstinate rebellion of Israel against Himself (Dan. 12:6-7). God will bring the Antichrist on the world scene to play a major role in shattering that rebellion. He will use the Antichrist's desolation of the nation (including his part in drawing the armies of the nations against Israel by the end of the 70th week, Rev. 16:12-16) as a means of backing Israel so tightly into a corner that it will have no means of escaping total annihilation unless it repents. At that darkest time in all its history, the nation will repent (Zech. 12:2, 10–13:1).

A third purpose will be the judgment of the world. Isaiah 3:1-15 indicates that sometimes God judges rebellious people by removing good leaders or rulers and giving them oppressive rulers. Thus, there are times when God gives people the kind of rulers they deserve.

During the 70th week, God will inflict on the rebellious world a ruler who will be the ultimate expression of its own spirit of lawlessness. As we noted earlier, the Antichrist will be the epitome of human lawlessness. That rebellious nature will make him an oppressive, dictatorial tyrant who will subject the world to his self-centered whims, causing the world to suffer the horrible consequences of the same spirit of lawlessness that prompts it to rebel against God. Thus, God will judge the world by giving it the kind of ruler it deserves. When God brings the Antichrist on the world scene, it will be a form of His wrath.

A fourth purpose will be the exposure of the world's unbelief. God will bring the Antichrist on the world scene and permit him to make his claim to be God to demonstrate mankind's unbelief, which will be graphically displayed through the great multitudes of people who will believe the Antichrist's lie and worship him (2 Th. 2:10-12; Rev. 13:3-8). This exposure of unbelief will demonstrate the need for the world to be judged.

A fifth purpose will be the instigation of the final showdown between Christ and Satan's forces and the defeat of those forces. When God brings the Antichrist on the world scene, it will cause the conflict of the ages between God and Satan's forces to rise to the peak of intensity (Rev. 6–18). This will be God's way of setting the stage for the grand climax of that conflict when Christ comes out of heaven as God's victorious conqueror to crush Satan's forces (Rev. 19:11–20:3). Just as God raised up Pharaoh, who despised and stubbornly resisted Him and tried to annihilate His people, to demonstrate His awesome power through him and thereby impress the world with Himself (Ex. 9:16; Rom. 9:17), so He will bring the Antichrist on the world scene for a similar purpose.

Thus, God will have several purposes for turning the Antichrist loose on the world when Christ breaks the first seal.

THE FIFTH SEAL

Revelation 6:9-11 indicates that the fifth seal is related to believers who have been martyred because of their persistent public witness and declaration of God's Word. In light of this, if Christ is the one who will instigate the things that will transpire when all seven seals are broken, does this mean that when Christ breaks the fifth seal, He will instigate the martyrdom of His own saints who have been faithful to Him?

In response to this question, it is important to note what John did and did not see when Christ broke the fifth seal. Revelation 6:9-11 indicates that John did not see believers being martyred when the fifth seal was broken. Instead, he saw the disembodied souls of believers who had been slain already. The verb form translated "were slain" (v. 9) is in the Greek perfect tense. H. E. Dana and Julius R. Mantey explain the significance of the perfect tense as follows:

> The perfect is the tense of complete action . . . It implies a process, but views that process as having reached its consummation and existing in a finished state. The point of completion is always antecedent to the time implied or stated in connection with the use of the perfect.[13]

This means that the slaying of this particular group of believers had already been completed before John saw their souls under the altar. In line with this, A. T. Robertson, who has been acclaimed as America's premier Greek authority of the 20th century, indicates that the verb form translated "were slain" in Revelation 6:9 represents action that was completed before the action of the main verb "saw" in John's statement "I saw."[14]

The fact that John did not see believers being slain, but instead saw the disembodied souls of saints who had been slain before he saw them, forces the conclusion that when Christ breaks the fifth seal, it will not cause the martyrdom of those saints.

THE SEVEN SEALS AND
THE DAY OF THE LORD WRATH

The Absence of the Word "Wrath"

Within the scope of the seven seals, the word "wrath" does not appear until the sixth seal (Rev. 6:16-17). The biblical text does not use the word "wrath" for the first five seals. Does this absence of the word force the conclusion that the first five seals will not involve God's Day of the Lord wrath?

No, it does not. The absence of a word does not guarantee the absence of the concept related to that word. For example, the word "Trinity" is totally absent from the Bible, but the concept of the Trinity is very much present. The real issue is not the absence or presence of a word, but the absence or presence of a concept.

Does the Bible contain the concept that all seven seals will involve God's Day of the Lord wrath? There are several evidences indicating that it does.

General Evidences

There are at least two evidences that all seven seals in general will involve God's Day of the Lord wrath.

The First Evidence. The seven seals have a consistent pattern of having things in common. As noted earlier, all seven are part of the same sealed scroll; all seven have the same purpose or function with regard to that scroll; all seven will be part of the irrefutable evidence that Christ is the true Kinsman-Redeemer; all seven will be broken by Christ; and all seven will be part of the same program of Christ's evicting Satan and his forces and taking tenant possession of the earth.

In light of this consistent pattern of all seven seals having things in common, it would appear that if any one of the seals involves God's Day of the Lord wrath, then all of the seals will involve it. The sixth seal will involve it (evidence for this will be presented later). In addition, there can be no doubt that the seventh seal will involve that wrath, for it will contain the seven trumpets and seven bowls.

The Second Evidence. Christ's purpose for breaking all seven seals coincides with three things: the definition and objects of God's wrath, the key administrator of God's wrath in Revelation, and the biblical concept of the Day of the Lord. In a thorough study article on the wrath of God, Johannes Fichtner gave the following excellent definition: "The wrath of God is the onslaught of the holy God asserting and establishing His absolute claim to dominion."[15]

In the same article, Gustav Stahlin indicated that the objects of the future wrath of God portrayed in Revelation are all nations (including Israel), all classes of people, Satan and his evil angelic powers, all of whom oppose God.[16] Concerning these objects of God's wrath, Stahlin wrote,

> One of the marks of the richness of the depiction in Rev. is that God's wrath is also against devils and powers which oppose God, as is made plain by the revelation of God in Christ, . . . and in this connection we are given the picture of two antithetical forces of wrath. The devil with his great wrath—Rev. 12:17 has the image of the angry dragon—and along with him the angry nations (11:18) fight against God and His kingdom. This is the great eschatological wrath which opposes the wrath of God. It is described in colours taken from the Psalter. The drama of revelation can thus be understood in large measure as a battle between two wraths.[17]

Stahlin made comments concerning the wrath of Christ that relate significantly to the issue of the key administrator of God's wrath in Revelation. He stated that Christ's wrath "is not just human anger. It always has about it something of the nature of God's wrath."[18] Christ's wrath "is the wrath of the Ruler of the world provoked by rebels against God."[19] It "is the wrath of the eschatological Judge who has full power to destroy."[20] Christ "in wrath destroys His foes."[21] Concerning Revelation, Stahlin declared, "The last book takes up again in its own forceful and vivid way this picture of the wrathful King and Judge of the last days."[22]

These comments by Stahlin, which are based upon a thorough study of the wrath of Christ and God, indicate that the exercise of Christ's wrath involves the exercise of God's wrath. Christ directs this wrath against those who oppose God. Revelation portrays Christ as the judge and ruler of the world, exercising this wrath to destroy God's foes in the last days. In other words, Revelation portrays Him as the God-Man who, although incarnated in human flesh, exercises God's wrath as His representative, crushing God's enemies in order to restore and rule over God's theocratic kingdom on the earth. Thus, Christ is the key administrator of God's wrath in Revelation.

In an earlier chapter it was noted that the biblical concept of the Day of the Lord is as follows: The Day of the Lord will involve God's intervention into the course of world events to judge His enemies, end their rule over the world system, evict them from the earth, and accomplish His purpose for history by restoring His theocratic kingdom rule on the earth through the last Adam, Jesus Christ. God thereby will demonstrate who He is—the sovereign God of the universe.

The previous chapter indicated that Christ will break all seven seals to demonstrate that He has the power and authority to evict God's enemies, take tenant possession of the earth, and administer God's rule as His representative. That chapter noted that during the 70th week of Daniel 9, Satan and his forces will use strong, deceptive, violent action to challenge Christ's right to do these things. As a result, Christ will have to use force in the fulfillment of His second responsibility as the Kinsman-Redeemer. As He breaks the seals, He will unleash a tremendous bombardment of divine wrath on the domain of Satan and his forces before He invades the earth at His coming to evict God's enemies and take tenant possession. Thus, Christ's breaking of the seven seals, with their outpouring of divine wrath, will be a significant part of His asserting and establishing the truthfulness of His claim to be the true Kinsman-Redeemer, the one who has the right to take back the rule of the world on behalf of God.

Christ's purpose for breaking all seven seals coincides, then, with the definition of God's wrath ("the onslaught of the holy God asserting and establishing His absolute claim to dominion"), the objects of God's wrath (Satan and his forces, including all nations, people, and angels who oppose God), the key administrator of God's wrath in Revelation (Christ), and the biblical concept of the Day of the Lord (God's intervention into world events to judge and evict His enemies and restore His theocratic kingdom rule on the earth through Jesus Christ).

Specific Evidences

It is obvious that the seventh seal will involve the wrath of God, because it will consist of the seven trumpets and seven bowls. An examination of the first six seals reveals specific evidences to the effect that they too will involve the wrath of God.

The First Seal (Rev. 6:1-2). Earlier in this chapter three things were demonstrated relative to the first seal: The rider of the first seal will be the Antichrist; Christ is the one who will turn the Antichrist loose on the world; and this turning loose of the Antichrist will be a form of God's wrath on rebellious Israel and the Gentiles.

In conjunction with this, the following statement by Stahlin is significant: "The Bible regards many pagan peoples and rulers as executors of God's wrath. They are this even when, like the devil, they consciously fight against God and His people . . . This is the picture of political powers in Rev."[23]

An example of such a pagan ruler was Nebuchadnezzar, king of Babylon. In spite of his proud opposition (Dan. 3-4), God used him to administer His wrath on Judah (2 Chr. 36:16-17; Ezra 5:12; Jer. 32:28-32) and called him "my servant" (Jer. 25:9; 27:6).

The Second Seal (Rev. 6:3-4). The rider of the second seal will be given a great sword and will remove peace from the earth. This description indicates that when the second seal is broken, great warfare will be brought to the earth. As we noted in an earlier chapter, it will be equal to the wars and rumors of wars, nation rising against nation, and kingdom against kingdom in Jesus' beginning of birth pangs statements in Matthew 24:6-8.

Obviously this warfare will involve extensive human activity; however, the Scriptures clearly indicate that the wars of nations are often the weapons of God's wrath. For example, God declared that "an assembly of great nations" would be "the weapons of his indignation" and "wrath" against Babylon (Jer. 50:9, 13, 25; Isa. 13:1-5). God raised up Syria and Philistia as instruments of His anger against Israel (Isa. 9:11-12). He used Assyria as "the rod" of His anger and wrath against Israel (Isa. 10:5-6).

In line with this, Fichtner wrote, "The weapons of God's wrath and agents of His chastisements are the nations when there is ref. to them as" weapons of indignation or rod of anger. "This vivid image expresses the common OT view that God vents His wrath through earthly powers . . . Yahweh delivers up the people of His anger to the Assyrian . . . The nations are also instruments of His wrath against other nations to execute judgment."[24]

The Third Seal (Rev. 6:5-6). The rider of the third seal holds a balance in his hand. Verse 6 indicates that food is the commodity to be weighed in the balance, and money will buy only one-eighth the normal quantity of food.[25] The implication is that prices will be very high because of scarcity of food. Thus, when the third seal is broken, it will bring famine to the world. As we noted in an earlier chapter, this will be equal to the famines in Jesus' beginning of birth pangs statements in Matthew 24:7-8.

We should note that when the third seal is broken, a voice in the midst of the four beasts speaks. The person speaking determines the prices of food and sets limits on the famine—he administers the famine. Revelation

4 indicates that God sits on the throne in the midst of the four beasts, and Revelation 5:6 portrays Christ as a Lamb standing in the midst of the four beasts. In light of this, the voice in the midst of the beasts must belong to either God or Christ; therefore, either God or Christ, not mankind or Satan, will administer the famine associated with the third seal.

The Scriptures teach that God uses famine as an expression of His wrath against rebellious mankind (Jer. 21:5-7, 9; 42:17-18, 22; 44:8, 11-13; Ezek. 5:11-17; 7:3, 8, 14-15). For this reason, Fichtner referred to "Yahweh's wrath, which finds expression in drought and famine."[26] In light of this and the fact that either God or Christ will administer the famine associated with the third seal, it seems apparent that this famine will involve an outpouring of divine wrath.

The Fourth Seal (Rev. 6:7-8). The rider of the fourth seal is Death, and he is followed by a partner, Hell (vv. 7-8). Together they are given power to inflict death upon one-fourth of the world's population through means of the sword, hunger (famine), death (in this context referring to pestilence[27]), and beasts. What relationship, if any, do the sword, famine, pestilence, and beasts of the fourth seal have to God's Day of the Lord wrath? To determine the answer to this question, several things must be observed.

First, the Hebrew Old Testament used six major words for the anger or wrath of God. Gerard Van Groningen summarized the significance of these words as follows:

> Of the six main synonyms referring to anger, the strongest, probably, are *qesep* which often refers to the Lord's anger, and *hema* and *haron* both of which refer to a burning and consuming wrath. The noun *ap* taking its meaning of 'anger' from the dilation of the nostrils is the most widely used word of the class. It is used for anger both of God and men and often with verbs like "kindle" *hara*. The word *ebra* emphasizes the overflowing or excess of anger. It and the weaker words *za'am* "indignation" and *ka'as* "vexation" are not used as often.[28]

Second, the Apostle John used the Old Testament extensively in the Revelation. Henry Barclay Swete claimed that "of the 404 verses of the Apocalypse there are 278 which contain references to the Jewish Scriptures."[29] Further, Swete stated that "more than half of his references to the Old Testament belong to the Psalms, the prophecies of Isaiah and Ezekiel, and the Book of Daniel."[30] Twenty-nine Old Testament references in Revelation are from the prophecy of Ezekiel.[31]

Concerning John's use of the Old Testament in Revelation, Swete declared that there are "references in which it is clear the he has in view certain books and passages, and is practically quoting from them."[32]

Third, scholars recognize that when John wrote Revelation 6:8 concerning the sword, famine, pestilence, and beasts of the fourth seal, he had in view Ezekiel 5:17 and 14:21. For example, Swete indicated this correlation between Revelation 6:8 and Ezekiel 14:21.[33] In addition, Wilhelm Michaelis asserted that Revelation 6:8 is "unmistakably influenced by the fourfold series" in Ezekiel 5:17 "and especially" by the sword, famine, beast, and pestilence "in Ez. 14:21."[34]

Ezekiel 5:17 states, "so will I send upon you famine and evil beasts, and they shall bereave thee; and pestilence and blood shall pass through thee; and I will bring the sword upon thee. I, the LORD, have spoken." Ezekiel 14:21 says, "For thus saith the Lord GOD, How much more when I send my four severe judgments upon Jerusalem, the sword, and the famine, and the evil beast, and the pestilence, to cut off from it man and beast?"

Fourth, the context of Ezekiel 5:17 (vv. 12-16) indicates that the famine, beasts, pestilence, and sword of that passage are expressions of God's wrath. Verses 13 and 15 use two of the six synonyms for God's wrath noted above—*hema* (translated as "fury" and "furious rebukes") and *ap* (translated as "anger").

The context of Ezekiel 14:21 (v. 19) indicates that the sword, famine, beast, and pestilence of that passage are also expressions of God's wrath. Verse 19 uses one of the six words for God's wrath noted above—*hema* (translated as "fury").

Fifth, it is important to note that these two words (*hema* and *ap*) for God's wrath, which are used for the expressions of God's wrath in the two Ezekiel passages upon which the fourth seal of Revelation 6:8 is based, are used as well for expressions of God's Day of the Lord wrath against Israel and the Gentiles.

In Ezekiel 7 both *hema* ("fury," v. 8) and *ap* ("anger," vv. 3, 8) are used together with *ebra* ("wrath," v. 19) and *haron* ("wrath," vv. 12, 14) for "the day of the wrath (*ebra*) of the Lord" (v. 19; cp. vv. 7, 10, 12). Here God's wrath is against Israel (vv. 2, 7, 23, 26-27), and it should be noted that this *hema, ap, ebra, haron* wrath of the Day of the Lord involves the sword, famine, and pestilence (v. 15).

The fact that the Scriptures teach that Israel as well as the Gentiles are subject to God's Day of the Lord wrath has been recognized by many scholars. For example, Johannes Fichtner wrote,

> Prophetic preaching . . . increasingly looks beyond historical interpretation to the message of eschatological wrath and judgment in which Yahweh will make good His claim in face of all opposing powers and bring history to an end. The earlier prophets proclaim this judgment not merely on the Gentiles but also on the people of God which has turned aside from Him. In this sense they can speak of the day of Yahweh, the day of wrath, as an eschatological event, Am. 5:18-20; Is. 2:6-21; Zeph. 1:15, 18. For Israel there is no escaping it, except that individuals may be sheltered by timely conversion, Zeph. 2:1-3.[35]

Zephaniah uses *ebra* ("wrath," 1:15, 18) for "the great day of the LORD" (1:14) and "the day of the LORD's wrath" (1:18) against all mankind in general (1:2-3), including Judah and Jerusalem (1:4, 10, 12). In Zephaniah 2, *ap* ("anger," vv. 2-3) is used together with *haron* ("fierce," lit. "fierceness of," v. 2) for "the day of the LORD's anger" (vv. 2-3) against Israel ("nation not desired," v. 1) and the Gentiles (vv. 4-15). Zephaniah 3 uses *ap* ("anger," v. 8) together with *haron* ("fierce," lit. "fierceness of," v. 8) and *za'am* ("indignation," v. 8) for "the day that I rise up to the prey" against the nations, the kingdoms, all the earth (v. 8). Zephaniah 3:8 must be a reference to God's gathering of the armies of all the nations of the world for His wrathful judgment as described in Joel 3 and Zechariah 12–14. An earlier chapter demonstrated that this will transpire at the end of the 70th week.

In Isaiah 13, *ap* ("anger," vv. 3, 9, 13) is used together with *ebra* ("wrath," vv. 9, 13) and *haron* ("fierce," lit. "fierceness of," vv. 9, 13) for "the day of the LORD" (vv. 6, 9) and "the day of his fierce anger" (v. 13) against Babylon (vv. 1, 19) through the Medes (v. 17). It should be noted that this wrath involves the darkening of the stars, sun, and moon (v. 10) and birth pangs (v. 8).

Ezekiel 38 uses *hema* ("fury," v. 18) and *ap* ("face," v. 18) together with *ebra* ("wrath," v. 19) for "that day" (v. 19) when God will pour out His wrath against the armies of six nations that will attack Israel with a massive military invasion (vv. 1-16). Note that this outpouring of *hema, ap, ebra* divine wrath will involve the sword (v. 21), pestilence (v. 22), and beasts (39:4).

This invasion and judgment are to occur after a restoration of the Jews to their homeland (38:8, 12) and when they feel so safe and secure that they will have no defenses of their own for their protection (38:8, 11, 14). Israel, which began to be restored to its homeland in 1948, will feel safe and secure as the result of establishing a binding covenant with the Antichrist at the beginning of the 70th week (Dan. 9:27). But the Antichrist will turn against Israel in the middle of the 70th week and, as noted in an earlier chapter, will desolate it during the second half of that seven-year period. Thus, Israel will feel safe and secure only during the first half of the 70th week. It would appear that this invasion and judgment of Ezekiel 38 will take place during the first half of the 70th week. Thus, there will be an outpouring of God's *hema, ap,* and *ebra* wrath during the first half of the 70th week, and it will involve the sword, pestilence, and beasts.

Psalm 2 uses *ap* for God's wrath ("wrath," v. 5) and Christ's wrath ("wrath" and "angry," v. 12) together with *haron* (God's "great displeasure," v. 5). In this instance, these words refer to the wrath that God and Christ will pour out on the Gentile rulers and their armies at Armageddon at Christ's Second Coming after the 70th week.

Isaiah 34 uses *hema* ("fury," v. 2) together with *qesep* ("indignation," v. 2) for "the day of the LORD's vengeance" (v. 8) against all nations and their armies (v. 2). It should be noted that this wrath will involve cosmic disturbances (v. 4).

Isaiah 63 uses *hema* ("fury," vv. 3, 5, 6) and *ap* ("anger," vv. 3, 6) for Christ's treading of the Gentiles in the winepress (vv. 2-3, 6) in "the day of vengeance" (v. 4) at His coming. Revelation 14:14-20 relates Christ ("the Son of man," v. 14) to "the great winepress of the wrath of God" (vv. 19-20), and Revelation 19:11-21 indicates that at His coming Christ "treadeth the winepress of the fierceness and wrath of Almighty God" (vv. 13-15).

Ezekiel 30 uses *hema* ("fury," 15) for "the day of the LORD" (vv. 1-3) wrath against Gentiles (vv. 3-5) through Babylon (vv. 10-11, 24-25). It should be noted that this wrath involves the sword (vv. 4-6, 11, 17, 24-25) and birth pangs ("great pain," vv. 4, 9, 16).

Psalm 110:5 uses *ap* ("wrath") for Christ (the Lord at the LORD's right hand, vv. 1, 5) striking through Gentile kings "in the day of his wrath" at His coming (cp. Ps. 2; Rev. 19:11-21).

These passages demonstrate that the words *ap* and *hema* are used for the Day of the Lord wrath in the Old Testament; that the Day of the Lord wrath involves the sword, famine, pestilence, beasts, and human agents (such as the Medes and Babylon); that the Day of the Lord wrath will come upon Israel and the Gentiles; and that some of the Day of the Lord wrath will transpire during the first half of the 70th week.

We can conclude, then, that the Day of the Lord wrath includes *ap* and *hema* wrath, the same kind of wrath referred to in the contexts of Ezekiel 5:7 and 14:21, which involves the sword, famine, pestilence, and beasts. Thus, the sword, famine, pestilence, and beasts of Ezekiel 5:7 and 14:21 are expressions of the Day of the Lord kind of wrath.

In light of this and the fact, as noted above, that John had Ezekiel 5:7 and 14:21 in view when he wrote about the fourth seal in Revelation 6:8, we can conclude that the sword, famine, pestilence, and beasts of the fourth seal also are expressions of the Day of the Lord kind of wrath. This conclusion seems to be confirmed by the fact that in Ezekiel 14:21 God called the sword, famine, pestilence, and beasts "my four severe judgments."

Another significant evidence that the fourth seal will involve an outpouring of God's wrath is that the rider of the fourth seal is Death, and the Scriptures present a significant relation between death and God's wrath. This is especially true of the Old Testament.

Stahlin wrote, "The OT is especially impressive in the way in which it establishes the fundamental relation between the wrath of God and death (e.g., Ps. 90:7-11)."[36] Similarly, Fichtner stated that "when existence is at stake, the man of the old covenant detects the wrath of his God."[37]

It is interesting to note that the Psalm 90 passage to which Stahlin referred uses *ap* ("anger," v. 7), *hema* ("wrath," v. 7), and *ebra* ("wrath," v. 9) for the wrath of God involved with death. Since, as noted earlier, these same words are used for God's Day of the Lord kind of wrath, we can conclude that the wrath of God involved with death is the Day of the Lord kind of wrath.

Since the Day of the Lord kind of wrath is involved with death, and since the rider of the fourth seal is Death and has the power to administer death to one-fourth of the world through the sword, famine, pestilence, and beasts, we can conclude that when the rider of the fourth seal administers that death, he will be exercising God's Day of the Lord kind of wrath.

The First Four Seals. Evidences of the wrath of God have been given for each of the first four seals individually. In addition, there is evidence for the wrath of God in the first four seals collectively. Such evidence was presented in an earlier chapter, which demonstrated that God's Day of the Lord wrath will be associated with the first four seals.

Numerous scholars have concluded that the first four seals collectively will involve an outpouring of God's wrath on Satan's earthly domain. For example, William Barclay asserted the following concerning Revelation 6:

> The horses and their riders are the instruments of the avenging judgment of God . . . The four horses and their riders stand for four great destructive forces which are in the times before the end to be despatched against the evil world by the holy wrath of God . . . This picture tells . . . of the coming of the terrors of the wrath of God on the world.[38]

The Fifth Seal (Rev. 6:9-11). As we noted earlier, when the fifth seal was broken by Christ, John did not see believers being martyred. Instead he saw the disembodied souls of believers who had been slain already, before the fifth seal was broken.

Obviously, the killing of these saints during the first half of the 70th week will involve the evil activity of Satan's forces in the world as they wage war against God by attacking His people. In light of this killing by Satan's forces before the fifth seal is broken, what relationship will the fifth seal itself have to the wrath of God? It will be related in at least two ways.

First, the fifth seal will reveal one reason why Satan's forces will deserve more divine wrath poured out on them through the remaining seals, trumpets, and bowls.

Second, the martyred saints of the fifth seal asked God how long He would delay His judgment of those who had killed them. In essence, they were pleading with Him to avenge their blood. It is interesting to note that they addressed God as *despotes* ("Lord," v. 10). The ancient Greeks used this word politically to refer to people who intruded into a land already occupied by someone else in order to take possession of it, and also to refer to an absolute ruler who had "an unlimited possibility of the exercise of power unchecked by any law."[39] In the Greek Bible it is used to emphasize God's authority and omnipotence (unlimited power), especially as revealed through His acts in history.[40]

In light of these usages, it would appear that when the martyred saints addressed God as *despotes*, it had the following significance in the context of the fifth seal: The first four seals will involve revelations of God's *despotes* authority and omnipotence in history, because they will involve outpourings of God's wrath on Satan's earthly domain, which Satan and his forces will not be able to check. Through these outpourings, God will begin His intrusion into the world already occupied by Satan and his forces in order to take eventual possession of it.

The martyred saints of the fifth seal will be living and dying during the first four seals. Thus, before they are martyred they will witness various aspects of this revelation of God's *despotes* authority and omnipotence against His enemies. Having thereby observed the fact that God has begun to exercise His *despotes* authority and omnipotent power against Satan's domain, once they have been martyred, they will ask God how long He will delay using this authority and power specifically to avenge their blood against those who killed them.

The answer to their question (v. 11) indicates that God will assure these martyred saints that He will use His *despotes* authority and power to avenge their blood through further outpouring of His wrath, once the total number of saints who are to be martyred have been killed.

It should be noted that in the Greek text of verse 11, the expression translated "that they should rest yet for a little season" is a purpose clause, indicating that this expression is not part of God's answer to their question. Instead, it expresses the purpose for God's answer. To enable these troubled saints to rest for a little season, God will respond that He will delay avenging their blood only until the total number of saints who are to be martyred have been killed. Thus, God's answer will assure them that He certainly will avenge their blood.

In light of this, we can conclude that the second way in which the fifth seal will be related to the wrath of God is its guarantee of further outpouring of God's wrath after the first four seals.

The Sixth Seal (Rev. 6:12-17). Several things indicate that the sixth seal will also involve an outpouring of God's wrath. First, the magnitude of the earthquake and cosmic disturbances that will occur when Christ breaks the sixth seal (vv. 12-14) forces the conclusion that this will be an awesome expression of the wrath of God, not the work of unregenerate mankind.

Second, these traumatic phenomena of the sixth seal will cause all classes of unregenerate people (the mighty as well as the lowly) to hide in the dens and rocks of the mountains and plead with the mountains and rocks to fall on them and hide them from the face of God and the wrath of the Lamb (vv. 15-16). In addition, the unregenerate interpretation of the significance of these events will be, "The great day of his wrath is come, and who shall be able to stand?" (v. 17). These responses clearly indicate that unregenerate mankind will be convinced that these cataclysmic phenomena are expressions of God's wrath directed against them. Certainly this would not be their conclusion if they were the ones causing these catastrophic disturbances.

The following comments by J. B. Smith are significant in conjunction with this: "In ancient times all such physical disturbances were viewed with alarm as evidence of divine wrath and judgment. At any rate, man learns his utter helplessness in the face of such demonstrations in the universe."[41]

Third, Isaiah 2:10-22 foretold the future time when people, including the proud and lofty, will flee in terror to hide in the holes of the rocks and caves of the earth "for fear of the LORD, and for the glory of his majesty, when he ariseth to shake terribly the earth" (v. 21). It is obvious that Isaiah was describing what John saw in conjunction with Christ's breaking of the sixth seal and that Isaiah therefore was foretelling the sixth seal of Revelation 6:12-17. We should note that Isaiah indicated he was writing about the Day of the Lord, from which we can conclude that the Day of the Lord (the broad Day, not the narrow Day) will include the sixth seal, and that seal will involve the Day of the Lord wrath.

A Wrong Conclusion. It is important to note that it is the unregenerate, who will be living on the earth when the sixth seal is broken, who will say, "The great day of his wrath is come" (v. 17). The Apostle John did not say this; he simply recorded what they will say. Their statement reveals their conclusion in light of the awesome expression of God's wrath, which they will experience in conjunction with the sixth seal. It is also important to note that this is the statement and conclusion of the unregenerate because they often draw wrong conclusions concerning the works of God.

In an earlier chapter we demonstrated that the narrow or "great and terrible day of the LORD" (in contrast with the broad Day of the Lord) will be the specific day on which Christ comes from heaven to the earth. Since great cosmic disturbances will be involved with that day (Joel 2:30-31; Mt. 24:29-30), and since, in response to the great cosmic disturbances of the sixth seal, the unregenerate will conclude that "the great day of his wrath is come," it appears that they will conclude that the narrow Day of the Lord has come with the breaking of the sixth seal.

There are reasons to believe that this conclusion of the unregenerate will be wrong. First, in the earlier chapter we demonstrated that "the great and terrible day of the LORD" will not take place until after the armies of the nations have gathered in Israel for Armageddon. These armies will not begin to gather for this "battle of that great day of God Almighty" until the sixth bowl has been poured out (Rev. 16:12-16). Thus, "the great and terrible day of the LORD" will not take place until sometime after the sixth bowl has been poured out, which will not occur until one seal, seven trumpets, and five bowls after the sixth seal has been broken. Thus, "the great and terrible day of the LORD" will not take place until many events have occurred after the sixth seal has been broken.

Second, in an earlier chapter we demonstrated that the cosmic disturbances related to "the great and terrible day of the LORD" are not the cosmic disturbances related to the sixth seal. The cosmic disturbances related to that day will take place at the end of the 70th week, but the cosmic disturbances of the sixth seal will take place a considerable length of time before then. Thus, the unregenerate will be mistaken when, in response to the cosmic disturbances of the sixth seal, they conclude that "the great and terrible day of the LORD" has come.

Third, the cosmic disturbances involved with the sixth seal will cause the unregenerate to flee in terror to the mountains to hide from God's wrath (Rev. 6:12-17). By contrast, the cosmic disturbances involved with "the great and terrible day of the LORD" will not cause them to flee and hide. Instead, when Christ comes out of heaven, the rulers and armies of the nations will be gathered together with the Antichrist and the False Prophet, ready for battle in bold, defiant rebellion against God and Christ (Rev. 19:11-19). Apparently the display of supernatural powers associated with the Antichrist and the False Prophet (2 Th. 2:9-10; Rev. 11:7-10; 13:4, 11-15), along with the presence of Satan and his angels on the earth during the second half of the 70th week (Rev. 12:7-17), will cause this radical change in the unregenerate between the time of the sixth seal and the time of Christ's coming. This radical difference indicates that "the great and terrible day of the LORD" will not occur in conjunction with the sixth seal. Therefore, the unregenerate will be wrong in their conclusion that it has come at that time.

CONCLUSION

This chapter has produced several significant conclusions.

1. The seven seals were intended to make the sealed scroll of Revelation 5, not people, secure.

2. Christ's breaking of the seven seals has nothing to do with making people secure.

3. All seven seals of Revelation 6–8 are part of Christ's Kinsman-Redeemer program, not part of the program of Satan or rebellious mankind.

4. Christ—not Satan, the Antichrist, or rebellious mankind—will instigate the things that occur when all seven seals are broken.

5. The rider of the first seal will be the Antichrist, not Christ.

6. God's house will not be divided and opposing itself when Christ turns loose the Antichrist upon the world, because that turning loose will serve God's sovereign purposes.

7. The restraining work of the Holy Spirit is the restraint that prevents the Antichrist from being revealed until the proper time.

8. Only God has the authority to remove the Holy Spirit's restraint; therefore, it will be divine activity that will turn the Antichrist loose to conquer the world.

9. In Zechariah 11:15-17 God indicated that He will bring the Antichrist on the world scene as the foolish, idol shepherd who will decimate Israel.

10. God's purposes for bringing the Antichrist on the world scene are to punish Israel for its rejection of its good Shepherd (Messiah) in His first coming; to shatter Israel's rebellion and bring them to repentance; to judge the lawless world by giving it the kind of lawless ruler it deserves; to expose the world's unbelief and thereby demonstrate the necessity of the world's judgment; to instigate the final showdown between Christ and Satan's forces; and to defeat those forces.

11. Christ's breaking of the fifth seal will not cause the martyrdom of saints.

12. The absence of the word "wrath" from the first five seals does not require the conclusion that the first five seals will not involve God's Day of the Lord wrath.

13. All seven seals consistently have the same significant things in common; therefore, if any of them involves the Day of the Lord wrath, then all seven will involve it. The sixth and seventh seals will involve the Day of the Lord wrath; thus, all seven will involve it.

14. The purpose for Christ's breaking all seven seals coincides with the definition of God's wrath ("the onslaught of the holy God asserting and establishing His absolute claim to dominion"), with the objects of God's wrath (Satan and his forces, including all nations, people, and angels who oppose God), with the key administrator of God's wrath in Revelation (Christ), and with the biblical concept of the Day of the Lord (God's future intervention into world events to judge and evict His enemies and restore His theocratic kingdom rule on the earth through Christ).

15. The sword, famine, pestilence, and beasts of Ezekiel 5:7 and 14:21 are expressions of the Day of the Lord kind of wrath.

16. Since the fourth seal of Revelation 6 is based upon Ezekiel 5:7 and 14:21, the sword, famine, pestilence, and beasts of the fourth seal are also expressions of the Day of the Lord kind of wrath.

17. There are specific evidences to the effect that the first six seals will involve the wrath of God.

ENDNOTES

1. Richard Chenevix Trench, *Synonyms of the New Testament* (Grand Rapids: Wm. B. Eerdmans Publishing Company, 1960), pp. 78-81.

2. Robert D. Culver, "din," *Theological Wordbook of the Old Testament*, Vol. I, ed. by Laird Harris, Gleason L. Archer, Jr., and Bruce K. Waltke (Chicago: Moody Press, 1980), p. 188.

3. William F. Arndt and F. Wilbur Gingrich, *A Greek-English Lexicon of the New Testament*, 4th rev. ed. (Chicago: The University of Chicago Press, 1957), p. 71.

4. *Ibid.*

5. *Ibid.*

6. *Ibid.*, p. 423.

7. Louis Goldberg, "ewil," *Theological Wordbook of the Old Testament*, Vol. I, ed. by R. Laird Harris, Gleason L. Archer, Jr., and Bruce K. Waltke (Chicago: Moody Press, 1980), p. 19.

8. Jack B. Scott, "elil," *Theological Wordbook of the Old Testament*, Vol. I, ed. by R. Laird Harris, Gleason L. Archer, Jr., and Bruce K. Waltke (Chicago: Moody Press, 1980), p. 46.

9. *Ibid.*

10. Arndt and Gingrich, *A Greek-English Lexicon of the New Testament*, p. 81.

11. F. Duane Lindsey, "Zechariah," *The Bible Knowledge Commentary—Old Testament Edition*, ed. by John F. Walvoord and Roy B. Zuck (Wheaton, IL: Victor Books, 1985), p. 1566.

12. Francis Brown, S. R. Driver, and Charles A. Briggs, *A Hebrew and English Lexicon of the Old Testament* (Oxford: Clarendon Press, 1975), pp. 878-79.

13. H. E. Dana and Julius R. Mantey, *A Manual Grammar of the Greek New Testament* (New York: The Macmillan Company, 1927), p. 200.

14. A. T. Robertson, *A Grammar of the Greek New Testament in the Light of Historical Research* (Nashville: Broadman Press, 1934), pp. 909-10, 1118.

15. Johannes Fichtner, "orge," *Theological Dictionary of the New Testament*, Vol. V, ed. by Gerhard Friedrich, trans. and ed. by Geoffrey W. Bromiley (Grand Rapids: Wm. B. Eerdmans Publishing Company, 1967), p. 407.

16. Gustav Stahlin, "orge," *Theological Dictionary of the New Testament*, Vol. V, pp. 438-39.

17. *Ibid.*, p. 439.

18. *Ibid.*, p. 427.

19. *Ibid.*

20. *Ibid.*, p. 429.

21. *Ibid.*

22. *Ibid.*

23. *Ibid.*, p. 441.

24. Fichtner, "orge," p. 400.

25. W. E. Vine, *An Expository Dictionary of New Testament Words* (London: Oliphants Ltd., 1940), Vol. III, pp. 52-53.

26. Fichtner, "orge," p. 400.

27. Arndt and Gingrich, *A Greek-English Lexicon of the New Testament*, pp. 351-52.

28. Gerard Van Groningen, "qesep," *Theological Wordbook of the Old Testament*, Vol. II, ed. by R. Laird Harris, Gleason L. Archer, Jr., and Bruce K. Waltke (Chicago: Moody Press, 1980), p. 808.

29. Henry Barclay Swete, *The Apocalypse of St. John* (Grand Rapids: Wm. B. Eerdmans Publishing Company, n.d.), p. cxl.

30. *Ibid.*, p. cliii.

31. *Ibid.*, footnote.

32. *Ibid.*, pp. cliii-cliv.

33. *Ibid.*, p. cxliv.

34. Wilhelm Michaelis, "romphaia," *Theological Dictionary of The New Testament*, Vol. VI, ed. by Gerhard Friedrich, trans. and ed. by Geoffrey W. Bromiley (Grand Rapids: Wm. B. Eerdmans Publishing Company, 1968), p. 996.

35. Johannes Fichtner, "orge," *Theological Dictionary of the New Testament*, Vol. V, p. 401; see also pp. 398-99, 403, 438.

36. Gustav Stahlin, "orge," *Theological Dictionary of the New Testament*, Vol. V, pp. 443-44.

37. Johannes Fichtner, "orge," *Theological Dictionary of the New Testament*, Vol. V, p. 399.

38. William Barclay, *The Revelation of John* (Philadelphia: The Westminster Press, 1960), Vol. 2, pp. 3-4.

39. Karl Heinrich Rengstorf, "despotes," *Theological Dictionary of the New Testament*, Vol. II, ed. by Gerhard Kittel, trans. and ed. by Geoffrey W. Bromiley (Grand Rapids: Wm. B. Eerdmans Publishing Company, 1964), p. 44.

40. *Ibid.*, pp. 45, 47.

41. J. B. Smith, *A Revelation of Jesus Christ* (Scottdale, PA: Herald Press, 1961), p. 126.

PART II

BIBLICAL INFERENCES FOR THE PRETRIBULATION RAPTURE OF THE CHURCH

CHAPTER SEVEN

THE IMMINENT COMING OF CHRIST

THE MEANING OF "IMMINENT"

The concept of the imminent coming of Christ is a significant inference for the Pretribulation Rapture of the church. To understand this concept, we must examine the meaning of the term "imminent."
The English word "imminent" comes from the Latin verb "immineo, imminere," which means to "overhang" or "project."[1] In light of this, the English word "imminent" means "hanging over one's head, ready to befall or overtake one; close at hand in its incidence."[2] Thus, an imminent event is one that is always hanging overhead, is constantly ready to befall or overtake a person, is always close at hand in the sense that it could happen at any moment. Other things *may* happen before the imminent event, but nothing else *must* take place before it happens. If something else must take place before an event can happen, that event is not imminent. The necessity of something else taking place first destroys the concept of imminency.

When an event is truly imminent, we never know exactly when it will happen. In line with this, A. T. Pierson stated, "Imminence is the combination of two conditions, viz,: certainty and uncertainty. By an imminent event we mean one which is certain to occur at some time, uncertain at what time."[3]

Since we never know exactly when an imminent event will occur, three things are true. First, we cannot count on a certain amount of time transpiring before the imminent event happens; therefore, we should always be prepared for it to happen at any moment.

Second, we cannot legitimately set a date for its happening. As soon as we set a date for an imminent event, we destroy the concept of imminency because we thereby say that a certain amount of time must transpire before that event can happen. A specific date for an event is contrary to the concept that the event could happen at any moment.

Third, we cannot legitimately say that an imminent event will happen soon. The term "soon" implies that an event must take place "within a short time (after a particular point of time specified or implied)."[4] By contrast, an imminent event may take place within a short time, but it does not have to do so in order to be imminent. Thus, "imminent" is not equal to "soon."

This is illustrated by the fact that the next coming of Christ was just as imminent when the New Testament was written as it is today. However, today, some two thousand years later, that coming has not occurred yet. Thus, from today's historical perspective, it is obvious that although the next coming of Christ was imminent in New Testament times, it certainly was not soon then.

The relationship of "imminent" to "expectant" should be noted. The term "imminent" is an adjective used to describe the nature of an event. It depicts the kind of event that is always hanging overhead and could happen at any moment. By contrast, the term "expectant" is an adjective used to describe people's attitude toward an event (i.e., looking forward to, looking out for, or waiting for the happening of an event[5]). People could have this attitude toward either imminent or non-imminent events. *The Oxford English Dictionary* gives the following example of a person who had such an attitude toward an imminent event: "1877 Kinglake *Crimea* (ed. 6) V, i, 235, 'From moment to moment he was an expectant of death.' "[6]

THE CONCEPT OF THE IMMINENT COMING OF CHRIST

In light of the meaning of the term "imminent" and the fact that the next coming of Christ has not happened yet, we can conclude that the concept of the imminent coming of Christ is that His next coming is always hanging overhead, is constantly ready to befall or overtake us, is always close at hand in the sense that it could happen at any moment. Other things may happen before Christ's coming, but nothing else must happen before it takes place. If something else must happen before it can take place, then it is not imminent. The necessity of something else taking place first destroys the concept of the imminent coming of Christ.

Because we do not know exactly when Christ will come, three things are true. First, we cannot count on a certain amount of time transpiring before Christ's coming; therefore, we should always be prepared for that event to happen at any moment. Second, we cannot legitimately set a date for Christ's coming. Third, we cannot legitimately say that Christ's coming will happen soon. Again, it may happen soon, but it does not have to in order to be imminent.

Christians should have an expectant attitude toward Christ's coming. Since it is imminent and therefore could happen at any moment, believers should constantly look forward to, look out for, or wait for that event.

THE NEW TESTAMENT AND THE IMMINENT COMING OF CHRIST

Does the New Testament teach the imminent coming of Christ? J. G. Davies, the Edward Cadbury Professor of Theology at the University of

Birmingham, stated that the expectation of Christ's "imminent coming" is "so vivid in the New Testament."[7]

Many other Bible scholars have concluded that the New Testament does indeed teach the imminency of Christ's coming. J. Barton Payne declared, "In fact, no natural reading of Scripture would produce any other conclusion."[8]

In order to demonstrate that many have drawn this conclusion, this section will quote the statements of a significant number of Bible scholars based upon their study of various New Testament passages related to the coming of Christ.

Before presenting these statements, this author wants to emphasize that his purpose for quoting these people is to demonstrate that numerous Bible scholars from various church and theological backgrounds have come to the same conclusion; namely, that the New Testament teaches the imminent coming of Christ. It is not his intention to give the impression that because these scholars have come to that conclusion, they also believe that the New Testament teaches a Pretribulation Rapture of the church. To this author's knowledge, many of the scholars quoted do not advocate a Pretribulation Rapture.

The quotations will be presented in conjunction with the New Testament passages upon which they are based.

In addition to quotations of various scholars, in some instances exegetical factors will be presented as evidences that some New Testament passages do teach the imminent coming of Christ.

1 Corinthians 1:7

The Text. "So that ye come behind in no gift, waiting for the coming of our Lord Jesus Christ."

Quotation. Concerning the latter part of this statement, Gordon D. Fee stated that Paul had an "ever present" concern about Christ's "imminent return."[9]

1 Corinthians 4:5

The Text. "Therefore, judge nothing before the time, until the Lord come, who both will bring to light the hidden things of darkness, and will make manifest the counsels of the hearts; and then shall every man have praise of God."

Comments. In this context (1 Cor. 3:8–4:5), Paul referred to the future time when all Christians will stand before the Judgment Seat of Christ in conjunction with His coming (cp. Rom. 14:10-12; 2 Cor. 5:10).

Quotation. On the basis of this passage, Johannes Schneider wrote, "Paul lives in expectation of the imminent coming again of Christ."[10]

1 Corinthians 15:51-52

The Text. "Behold, I show you a mystery: We shall not all sleep, but we shall all be changed, In a moment, in the twinkling of an eye, at the last trump; for the trumpet shall sound, and the dead shall be raised incorruptible, and we shall be changed."

Quotations. In conjunction with these statements, Rudolf Bultmann said, "Believers are still subject, of course, to physical death, though in the early days of imminent expectation of the *parousia* it is seen that this fate will not overtake all Christians."[11] (The word *parousia* is one of the words in the Greek New Testament for the future coming of Christ.)

Gaston Deluz declared, "Christ's return is always imminent; we must never cease to watch for it. The first Christians thought it so near that they faced the possibility of Jesus' return in their lifetime. Paul thinks he too may perhaps be alive when it happens."[12]

A. L. Moore, in his book entitled *The Parousia in the New Testament*, asserted,

> Paul does not write as one who will certainly be dead at the Parousia, but as one who awaits the Parousia as an event which might occur at any moment and therefore he reckons with the possibility of his being alive at that time; but this does not mean that he included himself amongst those who would necessarily be alive at its coming.[13]

R. C. H. Lenski stated, "The simple fact is that Paul did not know when Christ would return. He was in the exact position in which we are. All that he knew, and all that we know, is that Christ may come at any time."[14]

1 Corinthians 16:22

The Text. "If any man love not the Lord Jesus Christ, let him be Anathema Maranatha."

Comments. The significant part of this statement in relationship to Christ's coming is the term "Maranatha," which was one of several "eschatological statements concerning Christ's coming . . . within the framework of early Christian tradition."[15] It was distinctive among these statements because it was an Aramaic expression.[16] It had the form of a petition.[17] The *Didache* (10.6), an ancient Christian manual of worship, used this petition in statements that were to be made at the end of the communion service. This usage helps to clarify the meaning of this expression, especially in light of Paul's reference to the future coming of Christ in conjunction with the observance of communion (1 Cor. 11:26).

Leon Morris said the term "Maranatha" consists of three Aramaic words: "Mar" ("Lord"), "ana" ("our"), and "tha" ("come"); thus, the entire term meant "our Lord, come."[18] In light of this meaning, Charles J.

Ellicott declared that "Maranatha" was "practically equivalent to" the expression "The Lord is at hand" in Philippians 4:5.[19]

William Barclay explained the significance of Paul's using this Aramaic term in a letter to the Greek church:

> It is strange to meet with an Aramaic phrase in a Greek letter to a Greek Church. The explanation is that that phrase had become a watchword and a password. It summed up the vital hope of the early Church, and Christians whispered it to each other, identified each other by it, in a language which the heathen could not understand.[20]

In the same vein, K. G. Kuhn declared that "the untranslated Aram. term is meaningful only if it is a fixed formula" that began in the Palestinian Christian community and then was adopted untranslated by the Greek-speaking Christians.[21] In light of this beginning and adoption of the term, Kuhn drew the conclusion that "maranatha is an important and authentic witness to the faith of the primitive Palestinian community.[22]

Leon Morris asserted that the term "Maranatha" "must have expressed a sentiment that the early Church regarded as supremely important, else it would never have been taken over in this way by the Greek-speaking Christians."[23]

It would appear, then, that the fixed usage of the term "Maranatha" by the early Christians was a witness to their strong belief in the imminent return of Christ. If they knew that Christ could not return at any moment because of other events or a time period that had to transpire first, why did they petition Him in a way that implied that He could come at any moment?

Quotation. Archibald Robertson and Alfred Plummer made the following statement concerning the significance of the term "Maranatha" in 1 Corinthians 16:22: "It warns them that at any moment they may have to answer for their shortcomings."[24]

Philippians 3:20

The Text. "For our citizenship is in heaven, from which also we look for the Savior, the Lord Jesus Christ."

Quotations. The word translated "look for" is a strong compound. The observations of several scholars concerning its emphasis and implications are significant. H. A. A. Kennedy wrote, "The compound emphasizes the intense yearning for the Parousia . . . The dominant influence of this expectation in Paul's thinking and working is only beginning to be fully recognized."[25]

Alfred Plummer declared that the first part of the compound word translated "look for" "implies disregard of other things and concentration on one object."[26]

F. F. Bruce said,

But they did eagerly wait for their Savior, the Lord Jesus Christ, to come from heaven. This expectation was a constant element in the primitive apostolic preaching: the Thessalonian converts, for example, were taught to wait for the Son of God "to come from heaven—His Son Jesus, . . . who rescues his people from the coming judgment" (1 Thess. 1:10).[27]

James Montgomery Boice stated that "the expectation of the Lord's personal and imminent return gave joy and power to the early Christians and to the Christian communities"[28]

Comments We should note that Paul included himself among those who had this attitude toward Christ's coming. Thus, Philippians 3:20 indicates that the expectation of Christ's coming was so intense for Paul and the other Christians of New Testament times that it was the primary focus of their concentration. Would it have been so if there were no possibility of an any-moment coming?

Philippians 4:5

The Text. "Let your moderation be known unto all men. The Lord is at hand."

Quotations. James Moffatt asserted that in the context of Philippians 4:5 the expression "the Lord is at hand" "means the imminent arrival of the Lord rather than his spiritual presence within the Church."[29]

William Hendriksen said that Paul's statement indicated that "it behooves every one to be ready, working, watching at all times.[30]

Pat Edwin Harrell pointed out that in Paul's declaration

the imminence of the Lord's return is used as a motivation for Christian conduct. This does not mean that the apostle contemplated that return tomorrow. In another place in this letter he admits the possibility that he might die before this anticipated event transpires (cf. 1:23) and he reveals plans he has made (2:23). While the Lord's return may not be here, it is near and the Christians must conduct themselves accordingly.[31]

F. W. Beare declared, "The Apostle is not speaking of the nearness of the Lord in his abiding presence with us, but of the imminence of his coming."[32]

Martyn Lloyd-Jones wrote, "In all we do we must always remember that the Lord may return at any time. His coming is always at hand, yes, but we do not know when, and so we must always live in the realisation that he is coming."[33]

Alfred Plummer stated that "at any moment they may have to answer for their conduct."[34]

1 Thessalonians 1:10

The Text. "And to wait for his Son from heaven, whom he raised from the dead, even Jesus, who delivered us from the wrath to come."

Comments. This is the only place where the word translated "to wait for" is used in the New Testament. W. E. Vine said that the "word carries with it the suggestion of waiting with patience and confident expectancy."[35]

Quotations. Concerning the fact that the Thessalonian Christians were waiting for Christ's coming from heaven, James Everett Frame said, "The nearness of the thing expected is suggested by the very idea of waiting."[36]

D. Edmond Hiebert wrote,

> In 1 Thessalonians 1:10 the Thessalonian believers are pictured as waiting for the return of Christ. The clear implication is that they had a hope of His imminent return. If they had been taught that the Great Tribulation, in whole or in part, must first run its course, it is difficult to see how they would be described as expectantly awaiting Christ's return. Then they should rather have been described as bracing themselves for the Great Tribulation and the painful events connected with it.[37]

Comment. To express it another way, the Thessalonian Christians were expectantly waiting for the coming of Christ, not for the coming of the Antichrist.

2 Thessalonians 3:10-12

The Text. "For even when we were with you, this we commanded you, that if any would not work, neither should he eat. For we hear that there are some who walk among you disorderly, working not at all but are busybodies. Now them that are such we command and exhort, by our Lord Jesus Christ, that with quietness they work, and eat their own bread."

Comments. There was a problem in the Thessalonian church. Some of the believers had stopped working and were expecting their fellow believers to supply their daily needs. The language Paul used in verse 10 indicates that these idlers had stopped earning their own livelihood, not because they were incapable of working but because they had willfully determined not to work.

In addition to refusing to work, these people were "busybodies" (v. 11). Leon Morris explained this as follows:

> These people were not simply idle, they were meddling in the affairs of others. We may conjecture that they were trying to do one or both of two incompatible things, namely, to get their living from others, and to persuade those others to share their point of view about the second advent, and so persuade them to stop working also.[38]

What prompted such disorderly conduct? Morris is convinced that Paul gave a clue to the answer in his command and exhortation to these people to work "with quietness" (v. 12).

> The root trouble apparently was their excitability. The thought of the nearness of the Parousia had thrown them into a flutter, and this had led to

unwelcome consequences of which their idleness was the outstanding feature.[39]

Frame agrees with this conclusion. He wrote that the expression "with quietness" "is to be understood as the opposite . . . of the feverish excitement of mind stimulated by the belief that the *Parousia* was at hand."[40]

It seems apparent, then, that these idle Christians believed in the imminent coming of Christ; however, they had concluded wrongly that "imminent" equals "soon." Thus, instead of believing that Christ *could* come soon, they were convinced that He definitely *would* come soon, and work was therefore no longer necessary for them.

Why did the Thessalonian Christians believe in the imminent coming of Christ? It must have been because they had been taught the imminent coming of Christ by a person whose authority they trusted. It would appear that Paul is the one who taught them the imminent coming of Christ. His negative reaction to their actions, however, implies that their wrong conduct was the result of a perversion of his teaching (cp. vv. 6, 10). Contrary to them, Paul did not equate "imminent" with "soon" and think, therefore, that work was unnecessary.

In light of this condition at Thessalonica, D. Edmond Hiebert made the following excellent application:

> This situation carries a warning to people today who are prone to be chasing about to hear some new truth, such as the latest view in eschatology, while failing to order their own lives according to the truth that they already know. The best preparation for our Lord's return is the faithful performance of our present duties in the furtherance of His cause.[41]

Titus 2:13

The Text. "Looking for that blessed hope, and the glorious appearing of the great God and our Savior, Jesus Christ."

Comments. The word translated "looking" has the sense of "to await" and is "used of the subject of Christian expectation."[42]

Concerning the concept of hope, Donald Guthrie wrote, "In the New Testament *hope* does not indicate merely what is wished for but what is assured."[43]

Paul described this particular hope as "blessed." In the New Testament this word "refers overwhelmingly to the distinctive religious joy which accrues to man from his share in the salvation of the kingdom of God."[44]

According to the Greek text, the expression "the glorious appearing" should be translated "appearing of the glory."[45] The full expression "the appearing of the glory of the great God and our Savior, Jesus Christ" does not refer to some event separate from the blessed hope. Instead, it describes the event that is that hope.[46] Thus, the Christians' hope is the appearing of the divine glory that belongs to God and Christ. Surely Christians will see that glory in Christ when He comes to rapture the church.

In light of these observations, we can conclude that in the context of Titus 2 Paul was saying the following in verse 13: Grace is teaching Christians to live sober, righteous, godly lives in this present age in conjunction with their expectant waiting for the appearing of the divine glory in Christ when He comes to rapture the church. The assurance of that appearing is a source of great joy to Christians because that appearing will bring incredibly happy changes for them, such as the loss of their sin nature and the reception of an immortal body.

Quotations. On the basis of Titus 2:13, Marvin R. Vincent states, "That which is *accepted* in faith, is *awaited* expectantly."[47]

Newport J. D. White indicated that Paul "describes the glad expectancy which is the ruling and prevailing thought in the lives of men looking for their Lord's return."[48]

William Barclay wrote,

> The dynamic of this new life is the expectation of the coming of Jesus Christ. When a royal visit is expected, everything is cleansed and decorated, and made fit for the royal eye to see. The Christian is the man who is always prepared for the coming of the King of kings.[49]

Comment. Why should Christians always be prepared for Christ's coming, unless that coming could take place at any moment?

James 5:7-9

The Text. "Be patient therefore, brethren, unto the coming of the Lord . . . Be ye also patient, establish your hearts; for the coming of the Lord draweth near. Murmur not one against another, brethren, lest ye be judged; behold, the judge standeth before the door."

Comments. It is important to note two things in conjunction with this passage. First, the Epistle of James was written to Jewish Christians, not to non-Christian Jews. Everett F. Harrison gave several evidences for this conclusion:

> It is clear that the Epistle of James would not have been received into the canon if the early church had understood it to be directed to Jews in general. It is equally clear that the epistle itself contains items that could hardly have been included in a document intended for non-Christians. Faith in the Lord Jesus Christ is presupposed (2:1). This in turn makes "the coming of the Lord" (5:7) a reference to Christ's coming rather than to some future intervention of the Lord God of Israel. The same is true of the description of the readers as born or brought forth by the word of truth (1:18). This is better understood as an allusion to regeneration than to creation. The good name that has been called upon the readers (2:7) is almost certainly that of Christ. Some interpreters see here an allusion to Christian baptism.[50]

In addition, James addressed his readers as "brethren" a total of 15 times (just as he addressed Jewish Christian apostles and elders as "brethren" at the first church council [Acts 15:13]), and "he bases his authority upon the fact that he is a 'servant of God and of the Lord Jesus Christ' (1:1)."[51] Certainly non-Christian Jews in James' day would have rejected his authority as a servant of the Lord Jesus Christ.

Robert G. Gromacki further described those to whom James wrote ("the twelve tribes which are scattered abroad" [1:1]) as follows:

> The most plausible view is that James wrote to Christian Jews who were scattered throughout the Roman empire. They were perhaps once residents of Palestine, but persecution or lack of job opportunities forced them out of that locale. James would have personally known many who were driven out of Jerusalem in the persecution prompted by Stephen's martyrdom (Acts 8:1-4; 11:19). He would have also known those Jewish pilgrims who were saved on the day of Pentecost (Acts 2:9-11) and those diaspora Jews who worshiped in nationality-centered synagogues in Jerusalem (Acts 6:9). At this time Jews still knew their tribal ancestry (Luke 2:36; Phil. 3:5). Since Peter later wrote to the diaspora Jewish Christians "through Pontus, Galatia, Cappadocia, Asia, and Bithynia" (I Peter 1:1), it may be that James wrote to Christian Jews in the East, possibly Babylon or Persia. This would further explain the late acceptance of the book by the Western churches."[52]

The identification of those to whom James wrote his epistle is important because the fact that it was written to Jewish Christians means that the coming of the Lord and the potential judgment to which James referred in 5:7-9 have implications for Christians and should concern them.

The second important thing to note about James 5:7-9 is the fact that the Greek verbs translated "draweth near" (v. 8) and "standeth" (v. 9) are in the perfect tense and indicative mood, meaning that each of these verbs refers to an action that was completed before James wrote his epistle and that continues on in that completed state.[53] The implication is that Christ's coming drew near before James wrote his epistle, and His coming continues to be near. In addition, Christ as judge began to stand before the door before James wrote his epistle, and Christ as judge continues to stand before the door. In other words, Christ's coming was imminent in New Testament times and continues to be imminent. James wanted to impress his readers with the fact that Christ could come through the door at any moment and cause them as Christians to stand before Him at the Judgment Seat of Christ. He could do so today.

In line with this, Herbert Preisker stated that the verb translated "draweth near" in the expression "the coming of the Lord draweth near" is used in James 5:8 "for a situation of tense eschatological expectation."[54] He further declared that in the early days of Christianity that verb and its related adverb expressed "hope of the imminence of the coming world."[55]

Quotations. On the basis of James 5:7-9, various scholars have made the following statements.

Robert G. Bratcher: "*the judge is standing at the doors*: this is another way of speaking of the imminent coming of the Lord."[56]

M. F. Sadler:

> The Lord had laid it upon His disciples that they should be ever looking for a coming which might be expected at any moment after His departure, and yet might be long delayed.

> If the Apostles had believed that the Lord would come late in the ages, . . . there would have been no need for them to watch; but if they believed that the Lord might return in the "evening" that is, very shortly after His departure, it was very needful to watch, and so they did.[57]

James B. Adamson: "The imminence of the Parousia is another strong argument for the Epistle's early date"[58], and "*At the door* is a picture of imminent judgment, and an incentive to patience."[59]

Frank E. Gaebelein: James "does not treat the subject at length. He simply declares it as an inescapable fact, emphasizing, as he does so, its imminence."[60]

Vernon D. Doerksen: "The perfect 'is at hand,' literally meaning 'has drawn nigh,' denotes imminency,"[61] and "The picture of imminent judgment is as much an incentive to patience as is the coming of Christ to bring deliverance."[62]

E. C. Blackman: "Endurance is necessary, but there is encouragement for those who have to face trials in the thought that the coming of the Lord is imminent."[63]

J. A. Motyer:

> His return is *at hand*. It has been so from the day of the apostles. James was not mistaken even though he lived over 1,000 years ago. The return of the Lord was then at hand; the return of the Lord is now at hand. We live in the last days, the days of the imminent return . . . the pressure upon us of that return is not to promote curiosity as to the date and circumstances, but to promote the life of holiness and of fruitfulness, so that we may be ready to meet the Lord.[64]

C. Leslie Mitton: "James clearly believed, as others of his time did, that the coming of Christ was imminent."[65]

Spiros Zodhiates: "When this verb is used of time, it speaks of imminence. James tells us that this blessed event of the second coming of the Lord will come any time, is imminent . . . Our hearts will be propped up if we live in the constant expectation of His coming."[66]

David P. Scaer: "The early church was caught up with the lively hope of the imminent return of Jesus."[67]

Douglas J. Moo:

The accusation that James has erred on this matter rests on the supposition that James believed that the *parousia* must *necessarily* occur within a very brief period of time. But there is no reason to think that this was the case. The early Christians' conviction that the *parousia* was "near", or "imminent", meant that they fully believed that it *could* transpire within a very short period of time—not that it *had to*.[68]

Homer A. Kent, Jr.: "James was referring to the return of Christ, which he thought might occur at any time."[69]

Harold T. Bryson: "He expected the Lord to return any day while he lived . . . The idea in the New Testament is imminence. To lose sight of the nearness of the Lord's return is to depart from the New Testament as well as to doubt its certainty,"[70] and "The expression 'standing at the doors' implies the Lord's imminent entrance into history to make a distinction between what is good and what is bad."[71]

Peter H. Davids: "That the judge . . . , who alone has the right to criticize the Christians (4:11-12) and who will judge the complaining Christian (e.g. 1 Cor. 3:10-17; 2 Cor. 5:10), stands before the door is an image, not of the place of judgment (i.e. the city gate, . . .), but of its imminence."[72]

Simon J. Kistemaker: "The reminder of the Lord's imminent return is necessary so that the readers will not lose heart in difficult circumstances."[73]

1 John 2:28

The Text. "And now, little children, abide in him, that, when he shall appear, we may have confidence and not be ashamed before him at his coming."

Comments. John commanded believers to abide in Christ (the verb translated "abide" is in the imperative or command mood).[74] This verb means "remain, continue, abide" and is used "of someone who does not leave the realm or sphere in which he finds himself."[75] This meaning, together with the fact that John used the present tense, indicates that John was commanding Christians to continuously abide in Christ.

John stated that Christians should continuously abide in Christ so that they can face Him with confidence and not be ashamed when He comes (*parousia*).

The Greek word translated "when" in the expression "when he shall appear" introduces an element of uncertainty relative to Christ's coming. John did not mean by this that the fact of Christ's coming was uncertain. Instead, he meant that the time of His coming was uncertain, and "this is the reason for steadfast abiding in Him."[76] John's point was that Christ's coming "might be while they all still lived."[77]

In light of what has been seen, we can conclude that John's statements imply that Christ could come at any moment; therefore, Christians should continuously be ready for His coming by constantly having their lives in order.

Quotations. On the basis of 1 John 2:28, various scholars have made the following statements.

A. E. Brooke:

The nearness of the day affords a new motive for the effort to which they are urged. The nearer the Parousia of their Lord the greater the need of constancy . . . If that happens which, as circumstances have shown, may befall them now at any moment, they must be in a position not to be ashamed, when the object of their longing expectation is there.[78]

Charles H. Spurgeon:

The date of that coming is concealed. When he shall come, no man can tell. Watch for him, and be always ready, that you may not be ashamed at his advent. Should a Christian man go into worldly assemblies and amusements? Would he not be ashamed should his Lord come and find him among the enemies of the cross? I dare not go where I should be ashamed to be found should my Lord come on a sudden. Should a Christian man ever be in a passion? Suppose his Lord should there and then come; would he not be ashamed at his coming? One here says of an offender, "I will never forgive her; she will never darken my doors again." Would you not be ashamed if the Lord Jesus came, and found you unforgiving? Oh, that we may abide in him, and never be in such a state that his coming would be unwelcome to us! Beloved, so live from day to day in duty and in devotion, that your Lord's coming would be timely. Go about your daily business and abide in him, and then his coming will be a glorious delight to you.[79]

George G. Findlay:

Christ is to be manifested in His promised advent,—*when* we know not, but it may be soon; and we must appear before Him, with shame or confidence. Abiding in Him, we shall be prepared whenever He may come. If the present should prove to be the world's last hour and the Lord should appear from heaven while we are yet on earth, how welcome His appearing to those who love Him and keep His word![80] Christ stands waiting to return. At any moment the heavens may open and He "may be manifested," . . . The Christian man, susceptible to these impressions, will surely ask himself, "What if my Lord should now appear? how should I meet Him, if He came to-day: with joy or grief; with shame or rapture?" This is a test that Christ's servants might often with advantage put to themselves.[81] In this one instance St John writes of the *parousia*, as St Paul has done so frequently, and builds on the anticipation of a definitive return of the Lord Jesus. The fact that he does speak of it in this way, though but once, and that he lays a solemn stress on the expectation, proves his agreement with the prevalent eschatology of the Church.[82]

Robert S. Candlish:

Let me be ever asking myself, at every moment, If he were to appear now, would I have confidence? . . . Let us then be always abiding in him; every day, every hour, every instant; even as we would wish to be found abiding in him, were he to appear this very day, this very hour, this very instant. He is about to appear; to appear suddenly; to come quickly.[83]

Revelation 3:11; 22:7, 12, 20

The Text. "I come quickly."

Quotations. On the basis of these repeated assertions by Christ, various scholars have made the following statements.

J. Barton Payne stated that the word translated "quickly"

means, not "soon," but "swiftly, all at once," that is before one can be aware and make preparations . . . It should therefore be clear at the outset that imminency does not mean that Christ's coming *must* be soon . . . His day *could* be soon, "close at hand in its incidence." Does this mean then that it could be so soon as to happen right away, at any time? This is the thought that is associated with imminency, "ready to befall or overtake one."[84]

Archibald Thomas Robertson: " '*I come*' (*erchomai*). Futuristic present middle indicative, 'I am coming' (imminent) . . . We do not know how soon 'quickly' is meant to be understood. But it is a real threat."[85]

Edward Schick: "Christ in this context repeats the announcement of his imminent advent."[86]

W. Lincoln: "Also it is quite evident that He would have us live in the constant expectation of His advent being imminent."[87]

Leon Morris: "The imminence of the coming is repeated."[88]

J. B. Smith:

This corresponds with the note of imminency in the latter part of Revelation 1:3, "for the time is at hand."[89] This is the second occurrence of the note of imminence in the concluding section (cf. verse 7). It occurs again in verse 20 in climactic and intensified form: "Surely I come quickly."[90]

Merrill C. Tenney: "Nowhere is a date set, nor was there any definite promise that the consummation would occur within the lifetime of the first century Christians. Nevertheless, the possibility of the Lord's advent was always present."[91]

J. A. Seiss:

Nor is it here alone, but throughout the New Testament in general, that such expressions are used. Everywhere is the promised Apocalypse of the Lord Jesus represented as close at hand, liable to occur at any time. The impression thus made upon the early Christians was, that Christ might come at any day or hour, even in their own lifetime. Exactly when he would come, was nowhere told them . . . Ever, as the Church moves on through time, and above all in the days in which we live, the next thing for every Christian to be looking for in this world is the coming of Christ to fulfill what is written in this Book. The Bible tells of nothing between us and that day.[92]

Comments. In more than one of these passages, Christ introduced His assertions "I come quickly" with the expression "behold." The word translated "behold" was used to arouse "the attention of hearers or readers."[93] In His last assertion (22:20) He used the introductory expression "surely" to convey "solemn assurance."[94] Thus, through these assertions Christ intended to do two things: arouse the attention of Christians to the fact that His coming could happen at any moment; and give believers solemn assurance of the fulfillment of His promise of His imminent return.

Revelation 22:17, 20

The Text. "And the Spirit and the bride say, Come. And let him that heareth say, Come" (v. 17).
"Amen. Even so, come, Lord Jesus" (v. 20).

Comments. In response to Christ's arousing attention to His assertions, "I come quickly" (vv. 7, 12), the Holy Spirit (who gave revelation concerning the coming of Christ through the apostles and New Testament prophets [Jn. 16:13]), and the church (Christ's bride, who, like the Jewish bride, waits eagerly for her betrothed bridegroom to come for her after an extended period of separation) both exclaimed, "Come" (v. 17). The verb translated "Come" is in the imperative mood, indicating that the Spirit and church were so eager for Christ to come that they commanded Him to fulfill His promise to come quickly.

In addition, individual Christians, who, through the public reading of Revelation, heard Christ's promise to come quickly, were commanded to demand Him to fulfill that promise (v. 17).[95]

In response to Christ's solemn assurance of the fulfillment of His promise of His imminent return, John exclaimed, "Amen! Come, Lord Jesus!" (v. 20, lit. trans.). "Amen" was John's way of strongly expressing his conviction that Christ would indeed fulfill His promise to come quickly. Because John was so convinced, he too commanded Christ to come.

Quotations. Concerning the church's response to Christ's promise to come quickly, A. T. Robertson stated, "There is intense longing (19:7) of God's people for the consummation of the marriage of the Lamb and the Bride."[96] Johannes Schneider wrote, "The Church of Christ lives in yearning expectation of His coming again (22:17, 20)."[97]

Concerning John's response as the author of Revelation (v. 20), Schneider said, "The author expects the speedy return of Christ."[98] Leon Morris declared,

> *Amen* is the transliteration of a Hebrew or Aramaic participle with a meaning like "confirming." It indicates assent to what the previous speaker has said.

This is reinforced with the prayer, *come, Lord Jesus* . . . Charles points out
that the Greek here is the equivalent of the Aramaic transliterated as
Maranatha in 1 Corinthians xvi.22.[99]

Comment. If the Holy Spirit, the church, and the Apostle John knew that
Christ could not return at any moment because of other events or a time
period that had to transpire first, why did they command Him in a way that
implied that He could come at any moment?

Conclusion

This examination of exegetical evidences and the statements of scholars
based on New Testament passages prompts the conclusion that the New
Testament church, including the apostles, had the fervent expectancy that,
although Christ's coming might not happen for a long time, it could take
place at any moment. Not only does the New Testament indicate that this
was the expectancy of the church, but, in addition, the New Testament
taught that the church should have that expectancy continuously and
therefore should constantly be watching and prepared for Christ's coming
at any moment. Thus, we can conclude that the New Testament does indeed
teach the imminent coming of Christ.

In line with this conclusion, Payne wrote, "If expectancy is present and
the time, though perhaps long, *could* be short, then the doctrine of His
imminent appearing must follow."[100]

In addition, in his book *The Parousia in the New Testament*, A. L. Moore
made the following statement in the chapter entitled "The New Testament
Insistence on the Imminence of the Parousia": "In this chapter we pass from
the conclusion that Jesus and the early church appear to have awaited an
actual Parousia of the Son of Man to the fact that this expectation appears
to be coupled with an insistence on its imminence."[101]

Moore also stated that imminency "accounts, too, for the otherwise
irreconcilable juxtaposition of exhortations to watch expectantly beside
warnings to patient endurance in face of the possibility of a delay."[102] The
concept that Christ's coming is imminent is the only thing that can harmo-
nize and make sense of these two emphases of the New Testament, which
would be contradictory apart from imminency.

A BRIEF HISTORY OF BELIEF
IN THE IMMINENT COMING OF CHRIST

The purpose of this section is to demonstrate the fact that significant
individuals and groups at different periods of church history have believed
in the imminent coming of Christ.

The Primitive Church

We have presented evidence from the New Testament that the primitive church (the church of the time of the apostles) believed in the imminent return of Christ. In addition to that evidence, the statements of a number of scholars are helpful.

Concerning the *parousia* or coming of Christ, *The Oxford Dictionary of the Christian Church* says, "Primitive Christianity believed the event to be imminent and this belief has been revived from time to time in the history of the Church."[103]

Albrecht Oepke wrote,

Primitive Christianity waits for the Jesus who has come already as the One who is still to come. The hope of an imminent coming of the exalted Lord in Messianic glory is, however, so much to the fore that in the NT the terms are never used for the coming of Christ in the flesh.[104]

Thus, terms such as *parousia* are never used in the New Testament for Christ's first coming (when He was incarnated in human flesh).

J. Barton Payne declared that "belief in the imminency of the return of Jesus was the uniform hope of the early church."[105] He further stated that the early Christians "were waiting, eagerly awaiting, His imminent appearing."[106]

The Post-Apostolic Church

A number of church leaders and other Christians between the time of the apostles and the Council of Nicea (325 A.D.) believed in the imminent coming of Christ, as evidenced by some of the writings of that period along with the statements of scholars.

Writings. *First Epistle of Clement*, 23 (written around 96 A.D. by Clement, a bishop of the church in Rome who knew some of the apostles personally): "Of a truth, soon and suddenly shall His will be accomplished, as the Scripture also bears witness, saying, 'Speedily will He come, and will not tarry.' "[107]

Epistle to Polycarp, 3 (written by 107 A.D. by Ignatius, a bishop of the church in Antioch of Syria and a student of the Apostle John): "Weigh carefully the times. Look for *Him* who is above all time."[108]

Epistle of Barnabas, 20 (written perhaps around 130 A.D. by an unknown author): "The Lord is near, and His reward."[109]

Didache, chapter 16, section 1 (written as early as 70 to 90 A.D. or as late as 120 to 180 A.D. by an unknown author): "Watch for your life's sake. Let not your lamps be quenched, nor your loins unloosed; but be ye ready, for ye know not the hour in which *our Lord* cometh."[110]

Shepherd of Hermas, chapter 3, sections 9, 7 (written between 90 and 150 A.D. by Hermas, a brother of Pius, a bishop of the church in Rome): "All things around the tower must be cleansed lest *the Master* come suddenly and find the places about the tower dirty and be displeased."[111] In this statement Hermas used the word "tower" as a reference to the church.

Dialogue with Trypho, 52 (written around 155 A.D. by Justin Martyr, one of the earliest church apologists): "Those out of all the nations who are pious and righteous through the faith of Christ, look for *His future appearance*."[112]

Statements of Scholars. Payne said, "The ante-Nicene fathers, in other words, were committed to the concept of the imminence of their Lord's return."[113]

Robert G. Clouse wrote, "The early church holding this premillennial view looked for the imminent return of Christ as witnessed by the writings of Papias, Irenaeus, Justin Martyr, Tertullian, Hippolytus, Methodus, Commodianus, and Lactantius."[114]

J. L. Neve declared,

> The time of the Apostolic Fathers, like that of primitive Christianity, was thoroughly eschatological in tendency. Men had the consciousness that they were living in the last times. The immediate return of Jesus was anticipated. It was this expectation which held the congregations together.[115]

Concerning the church's "expectation of an immediate Second Advent of Christ" during this period of time, G. Roger Huddleston asserted,

> That this belief was widespread is admitted on all hands, and obviously it would afford a strong motive for renunciation since a man who expects this present order of things to end at any moment, will lose keen interest in many matters commonly held to be important.[116]

The Church from 325 A.D. to the Reformation

Belief in the imminent coming of Christ began to be questioned by some church leaders at the end of the second century.[117] When persecution against the Christians stopped and the union of church and state occurred in the 300s A.D., "the hope of the church underwent a radical transformation."[118] As a result, belief in the imminent coming of Christ "had ceased to be of any great influence by the fourth century."[119] It continued to have little influence in the major part of organized Christendom throughout medieval times and the Renaissance until the Reformation.

The Church from the Reformation to the Present

The Reformation. The Protestant Reformation of the 1500s revived the early church's belief in the imminent coming of Christ.[120] John Calvin, the reformation leader in Geneva, Switzerland, is an example of the reformers who believed and taught imminency. Payne stated that "in the writings of

Calvin are found some of the clearest formulations of the classical Christian hope of the Lord's imminent appearing."[121]

Heinrich Quistorp, in his book entitled *Calvin's Doctrine of the Last Things*, wrote that Calvin's "precise concern is to see that believers are always ready and stand constantly 'in a state of tense expectation like a soldier at his sentry duty.' " (Here Quistorp quotes from one of Calvin's statements in *Corpus Reformatorum*, 80, 168).[122]

That this is an accurate appraisal of Calvin's concern is evident from his following statements: "As Christ has now appeared, no other attitude is possible for believers but to await in keen vigilance His second coming" (*Corpus Reformatorum*, 83, 274).[123] Commenting on Paul's statements in 1 Thessalonians 4:15, Calvin wrote,

> by speaking in the first person he makes himself, as it were, one of the number of those who will live until the last day, he means by this to arouse the Thessalonians to wait for it, nay more, to hold all believers in suspense, that they may not promise themselves some particular time.[124]

With reference to Christ's statements about His coming, Calvin said, "Besides, as he has promised that he will return to us, we ought to hold ourselves prepared, at every moment, to receive him, that he may not *find us sleeping*,"[125] and "He wished them to be uncertain as to his coming, but yet to be prepared to expect him every day, or rather every moment."[126]

William Tyndale, who translated the Pentateuch and New Testament into the English language in the 1500s, said concerning Christ's coming, "We are commanded to look every hour for that day," and "Christ and His Apostles taught no other, but warned to look for His coming again every hour."[127]

The 1600s. During the 1600s, the reformers' belief in the imminent coming of Christ was continued by the Puritans and Covenanters.[128] The Westminster Confession, produced in England during the 1640s by the Westminster Assembly, which had an overwhelming majority of Presbyterian Puritan members[129], declared that men should "shake off all carnal security and be always watchful, because they know not at what hour the Lord will come" (xxxiii, 3).[130]

The 1700s. During the 1700s, a major reaction against belief in the imminent return of Christ arose through the development and spread of the Postmillennial view of the Millennium. According to Postmillennialism, in the future Christianity will rule the world for a millennium (a thousand years) before Christ comes.[131] "Postmillennialism thus automatically postponed any hope of Christ's imminent appearing for a minimum of a thousand-plus years."[132]

In spite of this major reaction, during the 1700s there were significant Christians who continued to hold and teach the belief of the imminent coming of Christ. For example, George Whitefield, the great English preacher who played a major role in the evangelical spiritual awakenings in Great Britain and America during the 1700s, declared,

> "Where is the promise of His coming?" But perhaps today, perhaps this midnight, the cry may be made . . . Let that cry, Behold, the Bridegroom cometh! be continually sounding in your ears, and begin now to live as though you were assurd [sic] that this night you were to go forth to meet Him.[133]

In addition, John Wesley, the founder of Methodism who also played a major role in the evangelical spiritual awakening in Great Britain during the 1700s, stated, "Perhaps He will appear as the dayspring from on high, before the morning light. Oh, do not set us a time—expect Him every hour. Now He is nigh, even at the doors."[134]

Thomas Coke, the first Methodist bishop in America and successor of John Wesley as the leader of English Methodism after the latter's death, said concerning Christ's coming, "We ought to be in constant and hourly expectation of it."[135]

The 1800s. In spite of the dominant influence of Postmillennialism during the 1800s, that period experienced several significant expressions of belief in the imminent coming of Christ. The Plymouth Brethren movement, which started in Ireland during the 1820s and spread to England and other nations initially under the leadership of John Nelson Darby, vigorously held and taught that belief.

Charles Haddon Spurgeon, the outstanding English Baptist preacher and pastor of Metropolitan Tabernacle in London, preached the imminent coming of Christ, as evidenced by the following sermon statements:

> The Scripture has left the whole matter, as far as I can see, with an intentional indistinctness, that we may be always expecting Christ to come, and that we may be watching for his coming at any hour and every hour . . . He may not come for a thousand years; he may come tonight . . . It is clear that, if it were revealed that a thousand years must elapse before he would come, we might very well go to sleep for that time, for we would have no reason to expect that he would come when Scripture told us he would not . . . We know not when we are to expect his coming; we are not to lay down, as absolutely fixed, any definite prediction or circumstance that would allow us to go to sleep until that prediction was fulfilled, or that circumstance was apparent . . . He may come now; he may come to-morrow; he may come in the first watch of the night, or the second watch, or he may wait until the morning watch; but the one word that he gives to you all is, "Watch! Watch! Watch!" that whenever he shall come, you may be ready to open to him, and to say, in the language of the hymn we sang just now,—"Hallelujah! Welcome, welcome, Judge divine!" So far I know that we are Scriptural, and therefore perfectly safe in our statements about the Lord's Second Advent.
>
> Brethren, I would be earnest on this point, for *the notion of the delay of Christ's Coming is always harmful*, however you arrive at it, whether it be by

studying prophecy, or in any other way . . . Do not, therefore, get the idea that the Lord delayeth his Coming, and that he will not or cannot come as yet. Far better would it be for you to stand on the tiptoe of expectation, and to be rather disappointed to think that he does not come . . . He will come in his own time, and we are always to be looking for his appearing.[136]

Oh, beloved, let us try every morning to get up as if that were the morning in which Christ would come; and when we go up to bed at night, may we lie down with this thought, "Perhaps I shall be awakened by the ringing out of the silver trumpets heralding his Coming. Before the sun arises, I may be startled from my dreams by the greatest of all cries, 'The Lord is come! The Lord is come!' " What a check, what an incentive, what a bridle, what a spur, such thoughts as these would be to us! Take this for the guide of your whole life. Act as if Jesus would come during the act in which you are engaged; and if you would not wish to be caught in that act by the Coming of the Lord, let it not be your act.[137]

People of the Tabernacle, you are set to watch to-night just as they did in the brave days of old! Whitefield and Wesley's men were watchers; and those before them, in the days of Luther and Calvin, and backward even to the days of our Lord. They kept the watches of the night, and you must do the same, until—"Upstarting at the midnight cry, 'Behold your heavenly Bridegroom nigh,' " you go forth to welcome your returning Lord.[138]

The rise of the Bible school movement, faith mission boards, and Bible and prophecy conferences in the latter part of the 1800s greatly aided the spread of the doctrine of the imminent coming of Christ. Many of the Bible schools, faith mission boards, and conferences that began at that time held and taught that belief.

The 1900s. During the 1900s, belief in the imminent coming of Christ has continued to be held and taught by many Bible Schools, faith mission boards, and Bible and prophecy conferences. It is also held by new theological seminaries, by publications, and by radio broadcasters.

CONCLUSIONS

The Truthfulness of Imminency. Through exegetical factors and quotations of scholars, this chapter has given evidence for the conclusion that the New Testament does teach the imminent coming of Christ.

In addition, this chapter has demonstrated that significant individuals and groups at different periods of church history from apostolic times to the present have believed in Christ's imminent coming.

In light of what has been seen, it is the conviction of this author that the doctrine of the imminent return of Christ is truly biblical and should be believed by all Christians.

The Practical Effect of Imminency. The imminent coming of Christ should have an incredible practical effect on the lives of individual Christians and the church as a whole. The fact that the glorified, holy Son of God could step through the door of heaven at any moment is intended by God to be the most pressing, incessant motivation for holy living and aggressive ministry (including missions, evangelism, and Bible teaching) and the greatest cure for lethargy and apathy. It should make a difference in every Christian's values, actions, priorities, and goals. Several of the New Testament passages examined and scholars quoted earlier in this chapter indicated that. In addition, in 1 John 3:2-3 the apostle emphasized the impact that the truth of Christ's coming should have on Christians living now: "we know that, when he shall appear, we shall be like him; for we shall see him as he is. And every man that hath this hope in him purifieth himself, even as he is pure."

Many students of the Scriptures have recognized this practical effect, which, according to the New Testament, the truth of the imminent coming of Christ is intended to have on Christians. For example, H. A. A. Kennedy wrote,

> In truth, it may be said that the early Christian belief in the nearness of the Second Advent was one of the most momentous and inspiring influences for holiness in the primitive Church. It was a call to watchfulness and prayer, a call to strenuous effort and solemn preparation. Perhaps it did more than any other impulse to raise the life of the young Christian community to a lofty level, and to keep it there. For they lived in the expectation of Christ, their returning Lord, as those who must buy up the time.[139]

A. L. Moore, who, as noted earlier, emphasized the insistence of the New Testament on the imminence of the *parousia*, stated,

> It is therefore hoped to show how directly relevant the Parousia hope is for the life of the church. The Parousia hope was, we believe, one of the driving forces behind the early church's life and obedience and behind its missionary zeal. Perhaps by probing these questions and problems again, some light may be shed on the motive which should drive the church to the same primary tasks with urgency and responsibility, and yet with freedom and confidence.[140]

James Montgomery Boice, who, as noted earlier, described the effect that belief in the imminent coming of Christ had on the early Christians, said, "The greatest consequence of belief in the return of the Lord Jesus Christ should be a purification of our conduct."[141]

F. W. Beare asserted, "Christians are to live 'like men who are awaiting their Master' (Luke xxi. 36); and their conduct and character are determined by that expectation."[142]

The Implication of Imminency. The concept of the imminent coming of Christ has a strong implication on the time of the Rapture of the church. Early in this chapter we demonstrated that in light of the meaning of the term "imminent," the concept of the imminent coming of Christ involves the following principles: Christ could come at any moment. Other things *may* happen before His coming, but nothing else *must* happen before it takes place. If something else must happen before Christ's coming can take place, then Christ's coming is not imminent. The necessity of something else taking place first destroys the concept of the imminent coming of Christ. We cannot count on a certain amount of time transpiring before Christ's coming.

In light of the concept of the imminent coming of Christ and the fact that the New Testament does teach His imminent coming, we can conclude that the Pretribulation Rapture view is the only view of the Rapture of the church that comfortably fits the New Testament teaching of the imminent coming of Christ. It is the only view that can honestly say that Christ could return at any moment, because it alone teaches that Christ will come to rapture the church before the 70th week of Daniel 9 or the Tribulation period begins and that nothing else must happen before His return.

All the other views teach that at least part of the 70th week must transpire before Christ can come to rapture the church. The Midtribulation Rapture view claims that one-half (the first three and one-half years) of the 70th week must elapse before Christ can come. Its pre-wrath derivative position teaches that approximately three-fourths of the 70th week must run its course before Christ can come. The Posttribulation Rapture view asserts that the entire 70th week (all seven years) must pass before Christ can come. Thus, none of these views can honestly say that Christ could come at any moment. In reality, then, all of these views are saying that we can count on a certain amount of time transpiring before Christ's coming and therefore destroy the New Testament teaching of the imminent coming of Christ.

We can conclude, then, that the concept of the imminent coming of Christ strongly infers a Pretribulation Rapture of the church and therefore is significant evidence in favor of that view.

ENDNOTES

1. D. A. Kidd, *Collins Latin Gem Dictionary* (London: Collins, 1957), p. 158.

2. "imminent," *The Oxford English Dictionary*, 1901, V, 66.

3. Arthur T. Pierson, *Our Lord's Second Coming as a Motive to World-Wide Evangelism* (published by John Wanamaker, n.d.).

4. "soon," *The Oxford English Dictionary*, 1989, XV, 1011.

5. "expectant" and "expectance," *The Oxford English Dictionary*, 1897, III, 423.

6. *Ibid*.

7. J. G. Davies, *The Early Christian Church* (Garden City, NY: Anchor Books, 1967), p. 132.

8. J. Barton Payne, *The Imminent Appearing of Christ* (Grand Rapids: Wm. B. Eerdmans Publishing Company, 1962), p. 102.

9. Gordon D. Fee, *The First Epistle to the Corinthians* (Grand Rapids: William B. Eerdmans Publishing Company, 1987), p. 42.

10. Johannes Schneider, "erchomai," *Theological Dictionary of the New Testament*, Vol. II, ed. by Gerhard Kittel, trans. and ed. by Geoffrey W. Bromiley (Grand Rapids: Wm. B. Eerdmans Publishing Company, 1964), p. 674.

11. Rudolph Bultmann, "thanatos," *Theological Dictionary of the New Testament*, Vol. III, ed. by Gerhard Kittel, trans. and ed. by Geoffrey W. Bromiley (Grand Rapids: Wm. B. Eerdmans Publishing Company, 1965), p. 18.

12. Gaston Deluz, *A Companion to I Corinthians*, ed. and trans. by Grace E. Watt (London: Darton, Longman & Todd, 1963), p. 248.

13. A. L. Moore, *The Parousia in the New Testament* (Leiden: E. J. Brill, 1966), p. 118.

14. R. C. H. Lenski, *The Interpretation of St. Paul's First and Second Epistle to the Corinthians* (Columbus, OH: Wartburg Press, 1946), p. 737.

15. Johannes Schneider, "erchomai," *Theological Dictionary of the New Testament*, Vol. II, p. 674.

16. *Ibid*.

17. *Ibid*.

18. Leon Morris, *The First Epistle of Paul to the Corinthians* (Grand Rapids: Wm. B. Eerdmans Publishing Company, 1970), p. 248.

19. Charles J. Ellicott, *St. Paul's First Epistle to the Corinthians* (London: Longmans, Green, and Co., 1887), p. 344.

20. William Barclay, *The Letters to the Corinthians* (Philadelphia: The Westminster Press, 1956), p. 188.

21. K. G. Kuhn, "maranatha," *Theological Dictionary of the New Testament*, Vol. IV, ed. by Gerhard Kittel, trans. and ed. by Geoffrey W. Bromiley (Grand Rapids: Wm. B. Eerdmans Publishing Company, 1967), p. 470.

22. *Ibid*.

23. Leon Morris, *The First Epistle of Paul to the Corinthians*, p. 247.

24. Archibald Robertson and Alfred Plummer, *A Critical and Exegetical Commentary on the First Epistle of St Paul to the Corinthians* (Edinburgh: T. & T. Clark, 1914), p. 401.

25. H. A. A. Kennedy, "The Epistle to the Philippians," *The Expositor's Greek Testament*, Vol. 3 (London: Hodder and Stoughton Limited, n.d.), p. 463.

26. Alfred Plummer, *A Commentary on St. Paul's Epistle to the Philippians* (London: Robert Scott, 1919), p. 84.

27. F. F. Bruce, *Philippians* (San Francisco: Harper & Row, Publishers, 1983), p. 108.

28. James Montgomery Boice, *Philippians* (Grand Rapids: Zondervan Publishing House, 1971), p. 247.

29. James Moffatt, *The First Epistle of Paul to the Corinthians* (New York: Harper and Brothers Publishers, n.d.), p. 283.

30. William Hendriksen, "Exposition of Philippians" in *New Testament Commentary* (Grand Rapids: Baker Book House, 1962), p. 194.

31. Pat Edwin Harrell, *The Letter of Paul to the Philippians* (Austin, TX: R. B. Sweet Co., Inc., 1969), p. 137.

32. F. W. Beare, *A Commentary on the Epistle to the Philippians* (London: Adam & Charles Black, 1959), p. 146.

33. Martyn Lloyd-Jones, *Life of Peace* (London: Hodder & Stoughton, 1990), p. 162.

34. Alfred Plummer, *A Commentary on St. Paul's Epistle to the Philippians*, p. 93.

35. W. E. Vine, "anameno," *An Expository Dictionary of New Testament Words*, Vol. IV (London: Oliphants Ltd., 1940), p. 194.

36. James Everett Frame, *A Critical and Exegetical Commentary on the Epistles of St. Paul to the Thessalonians* (Edinburgh: T. & T. Clark, 1912), p. 88.

37. D. Edmond Hiebert, *The Thessalonian Epistles* (Chicago: Moody Press, 1971), p. 205.

38. Leon Morris, *The First and Second Epistles to the Thessalonians* (Grand Rapids: Wm. B. Eerdmans Publishing Co., 1959), p. 256.

39. *Ibid*.

40. James Everett Frame, *A Critical and Exegetical Commentary on the Epistles of St. Paul to the Thessalonians*, p. 307.

41. D. Edmond Hiebert, *The Thessalonian Letters* (Chicago: Moody Bible Institute Correspondence School, 1973), p. 150.

42. Walter Grundmann, "prosdechomai," *Theological Dictionary of the New Testament*, Vol. II, ed. by Gerhard Kittel, trans. and ed. by Geoffrey W. Bromiley (Grand Rapids: Wm. B. Eerdmans Publishing Company, 1964), p. 58.

43. Donald Guthrie, *The Pastoral Epistles* (Grand Rapids: Wm. B. Eerdmans Publishing Company, 1957), p. 199.

44. F. Hauck, "makarios," *Theological Dictionary of the New Testament*, Vol. IV, ed. by Gerhard Kittel, trans. and ed. by Geoffrey W. Bromiley (Grand Rapids: Wm. B. Eerdmans Publishing Company, 1967), p. 367.

45. Marvin R. Vincent, *Word Studies in the New Testament*, Vol. IV (Grand Rapids: Wm. B. Eerdmans Publishing Company, 1946), p. 345.

46. *Ibid.*

47. *Ibid.*, p. 344.

48. Newport J. D. White, "The Epistle to Titus," *The Expositor's Greek Testament*, Vol. 4 (Grand Rapids: Wm. B. Eerdmans Publishing Company, n.d.), p. 195.

49. William Barclay, *The Letters to Timothy, Titus, and Philemon*, rev. ed. (Philadelphia: The Westminster Press, 1975), p. 257.

50. Everett F. Harrison, *Introduction to the New Testament* (Grand Rapids: Wm. B. Eerdmans Publishing Company, 1964), p. 362.

51. D. Edmond Hiebert, *An Introduction to the Non-Pauline Epistles* (Chicago: Moody Press, 1962), p. 50.

52. Robert G. Gromacki, *New Testament Survey* (Grand Rapids: Baker Book House, 1974), p. 338.

53. H. E. Dana and Julius R. Mantey, *A Manual Grammar of the Greek New Testament* (New York: The Macmillan Company, 1927), p. 200.

54. Herbert Preisker, "engus," *Theological Dictionary of the New Testament*, Vol. II, ed. by Gerhard Kittel, trans. and ed. by Geoffrey W. Bromiley (Grand Rapids: Wm. B. Eerdmans Publishing Company, 1964), p. 331.

55. *Ibid.*, p. 332.

56. Robert G. Bratcher, *A Translator's Guide to the Letters from James, Peter, and Jude* (New York: United Bible Societies, 1984), p. 55.

57. M. F. Sadler, *The General Epistles of SS. James, Peter, John and Jude*, sec. ed. (London: George Bell and Sons, 1895), pp. 68-69.

58. James B. Adamson, *The Epistle of James* (Grand Rapids: Wm. B. Eerdmans Publishing Company, 1976), p. 191.

59. *Ibid.*, p. 192.

60. Frank E. Gaebelein, *The Practical Epistle of James* (Great Neck, NY: Doniger & Raughley, Inc., 1955), p. 112.

61. Vernon D. Doerksen, *James* (Chicago: Moody Press, 1983). p. 123.

62. *Ibid.*

63. E. C. Blackman *The Epistle of James* (Naperville, IL: Allenson, 1957), p. 146.

64. J. A. Motyer, *The Tests of Faith* (London: Inter-Varsity Press, 1970), p. 107.

65. C. Leslie Mitton, *The Epistle of James* (London: Marshall, Morgan, & Scott, 1966), p. 186.

66. Spiros Zodhiates, *The Patience of Hope* (Grand Rapids: Wm. B. Eerdmans Publishing Company, 1960), p. 90.

67. David P. Scaer, *James the Apostle of Faith* (St. Louis: Concordia Publishing House, 1983), p. 126.

68. Douglas J. Moo, *The Letter of James* (Grand Rapids: William B. Eerdmans Publishing Company, 1985), p. 169.

69. Homer A. Kent, Jr., *Faith that Works* (Grand Rapids: Baker Book House, 1986), p. 176.

70. Harold T. Bryson, *How Faith Works* (Nashville: Broadman Press, 1985). pp. 116-17.

71. *Ibid.*, p. 119.

72. Peter H. Davids, *The Epistle of James* (Grand Rapids: Wm. B. Eerdmans Publishing Company, 1982), p. 185.

73. Simon J. Kistemaker, *Exposition of the Epistle of James and the Epistles of John* (Grand Rapids: Baker Book House, 1986), p. 103.

74. David Smith, "The Epistles of John" in *The Expositor's Greek Testament*, Vol. V, ed. by W. Robertson Nicoll (Grand Rapids: Wm. B. Eerdmans Publishing Company, n.d.), p. 181.

75. William F. Arndt and F. Wilbur Gingrich, *A Greek-English Lexicon of the New Testament*, 4th rev. ed. (Chicago: The University of Chicago Press, 1957), p. 505.

76. David Smith, "The Epistles of John" in *The Expositor's Greek Testament*, Vol. V, p. 182.

77. Brooke Foss Westcott, *The Epistles of St John* (Grand Rapids: Wm. B. Eerdmans Publishing Company, 1957), p. 81.

78. A. E. Brooke, *A Critical and Exegetical Commentary on the Johannine Epistles* (Edinburgh: T. & T. Clark, 1912), p. 65.

79. Charles H. Spurgeon, *12 Sermons on the Second Coming of Christ* (Grand Rapids: Baker Book House, 1976), p. 134.

80. George G. Findlay *Fellowship in the Life Eternal* (Grand Rapids: Wm. B. Eerdmans Publishing Company, 1955), p. 232.

81. *Ibid.*, p. 233.

82. *Ibid.*

83. Robert S. Candlish, *The First Epistle of John* (Grand Rapids: Zondervan Publishing House, n.d.), p. 213.

84. J. Barton Payne, *The Imminent Appearing of Christ* (Grand Rapids: Wm. B. Eerdmans Publishing Company, 1962), p. 86.

85. Archibald Thomas Robertson, *The General Epistles and the Apocalypse* in *Word Pictures in the New Testament*, Vol. VI (New York: Harper & Brothers Publishers, 1933), p. 306.

86. Eduard Schick, *The Revelation of St. John* (New York: Herder and Herder, 1971), p. 119.

87. W. Lincoln, *Lectures on the Book of the Revelation* (New York: Fleming H. Revell Company, n.d.), p. 241.

88. Leon Morris, *The Revelation of St. John* (Grand Rapids: William B. Eerdmans Publishing Company, 1969), p. 258.

89. J. B. Smith, *A Revelation of Jesus Christ* (Scottdale, PA: Herald Press, 1961), p. 301.

90. *Ibid.*, p. 302.

91. Merrill C. Tenney, *Interpreting Revelation* (Grand Rapids: Wm. B. Eerdmans Publishing Company, 1957), p. 150.

92. J. A. Seiss, *The Apocalypse* (Grand Rapids: Zondervan Publishing House, 1957), p. 523.

93. William F. Arndt and F. Wilbur Gingrich, *A Greek-English Lexicon of the New Testament*, p. 371.

94. *Ibid.*, p. 535.

95. Henry Barclay Swete, *The Apocalypse of St John* (Grand Rapids: Wm. B. Eerdmans Publishing Company, n.d.), p. 310.

96. Archibald Thomas Robertson, *The General Epistles and the Apocalypse*, p. 486.

97. Johannes Schneider, "erchomai," *Theological Dictionary of the New Testament*, Vol. II, p. 674.

98. *Ibid.*

99. Leon Morris, *The Revelation of St. John*, pp. 262-63.

100. J. Barton Payne, *The Imminent Appearing of Christ*, p. 88.

101. A. L. Moore, *The Parousia in the New Testament*, p. 80.

102. *Ibid.*, p. 173.

103. "Parousia," *The Oxford Dictionary of the Christian Church*, sec. ed., ed. by F. L. Cross and E. A. Livingstone (New York: Oxford University Press, 1988), p. 1034.

104. Albrecht Oepke, "parousia," *Theological Dictionary of the New Testament*, Vol. V, ed. by Gerhard Friedrich, trans. and ed. by Geoffrey W. Bromiley (Grand Rapids: Wm. B. Eerdmans Publishing Company, 1967), p. 865.

105. J. Barton Payne, *The Imminent Appearing of Christ*, p. 102.

106. *Ibid.*, p. 85.

107. Quoted from J. Barton Payne, *The Imminent Appearing of Christ*, p. 13.

108. *Ibid.*

109. *Ibid.*

110. *Ibid.*

111. *Ibid.*, p. 14.

112. *Ibid.*

113. *Ibid.*, p. 12.

114. Robert G. Clouse, "SECOND COMING," *The New International Dictionary of the Christian Church*, Rev. Ed., ed. by J. D. Douglas (Grand Rapids: Zondervan Publishing House, 1978), p. 893.

115. J. L. Neve, *A History of Christian Thought*, Vol. 1 (Philadelphia: The Muhlenberg Press, 1946), p. 43.

116. G. Roger Huddleston, "Monasticism," *The Catholic Encyclopedia*, Vol. X (New York: The Encyclopedia Press, Inc., 1913), pp. 459-60.

117. J. Barton Payne, *The Imminent Appearing of Christ*, p. 102.

118. *Ibid.*, p. 19.

119. G. Roger Huddleston, "Monasticism," *The Catholic Encyclopedia*, Vol. X, p. 460.

120. J. Barton Payne, *The Imminent Appearing of Christ*, pp. 22-23, 85.

121. *Ibid.*, p. 24.

122. Heinrich Quistorp, *Calvin's Doctrine of The Last Things*, trans. by Harold Knight (Richmond, VA: John Knox Press, 1955), p. 110.

123. *Ibid.*, p. 111.

124. John Calvin, *Commentary on the First Epistle to the Thessalonians* in *Calvin's Commentaries*, Vol. XXI (Grand Rapids: Baker Book House, 1989), p. 282.

125. John Calvin, *Commentary on a Harmony of the Evangelists* (volume third) in *Calvin's Commentaries*, Vol. XVII (Grand Rapids: Baker Book House, 1989), p. 163.

126. *Ibid.*, p. 156.

127. Quoted from Jesse Forrest Silver, *The Lord's Return*, 5th edition (New York: Fleming H. Revell Company, 1914), p. 122.

128. J. Barton Payne, *The Imminent Appearing of Christ*, p. 25.

129. Williston Walker and Richard A. Norris, David W. Lotz, Robert T. Handy, *A History of the Christian Church*, Fourth Edition (New York: Charles Scribner's Sons, 1965), pp. 554-55.

130. Quoted from J. Barton Payne, *The Imminent Appearing of Christ*, p. 25.

131. *Ibid.*, pp. 26-27.

132. *Ibid.*, p. 27.

133. Quoted from Jesse Forrest Silver, *The Lord's Return*, p. 168.

134. *Ibid.*, p. 161.

135. *Ibid.*, p. 155.

136. Statements from Spurgeon's sermon "Watching for Christ's Coming," quoted from *12 Sermons on the Second Coming of Christ*, pp. 137-38.

137. *Ibid.*, p. 140.

138. *Ibid.*, p. 141.

139. H. A. A. Kennedy, *St Paul's Conceptions of the Last Things* (London: Hodder and Stoughton, 1904), p. 221.

140. A. L. Moore, *The Parousia in the New Testament*, pp. 5-6.

141. James Montgomery Boice, *Philippians*, p. 249.

142. F. W. Beare, *A Commentary on the Epistle to the Philippians*, p. 146.

CHAPTER EIGHT

BEHOLD, THE BRIDEGROOM COMES!

A SIGNIFICANT PROMISE

A second inference for the Pretribulation Rapture of the church is the significant promise of John 14:2-3, which Jesus delivered while gathered with His apostles in an upper room on the night before His crucifixion (Lk. 22:7-14). Through this promise, Jesus purposed to calm the troubled hearts of His closest followers (Jn. 14:1).

Why were they disturbed? On the one hand, these men had committed themselves to the belief that Jesus was the promised Messiah, the one who would crush Satan's forces and restore God's theocratic kingdom to the earth (Mt. 16:16). Because of this commitment, they had left their means of livelihood to follow Jesus (Mt. 4:18-22; 9:9) and had obeyed His commission to announce to Israel that God's kingdom was at hand (Mt. 10:1-7; Lk. 9:1-2. They were convinced that Jesus would restore God's kingdom during their lifetime (Acts 1:6) and that He would remain on the earth as God's representative to administer His rule over that kingdom.

On the other hand, Jesus had already intimated that He would ascend to heaven in "a little while" (Jn. 6:62; 12:35). In addition, immediately before He delivered this promise to the apostles, He issued a specific warning to them: "Little children, yet a little while I am with you. Ye shall seek me; and as I said unto the Jews, Where I go, ye cannot come; so now I say to you" (Jn. 13:33). This prompted Peter to ask Jesus where He was going, and He answered, "Where I go, thou canst not follow me now; but thou shalt follow me afterwards" (Jn. 13:36). Peter asked why he couldn't follow Jesus then (v. 37).

Peter's responses indicate that Jesus' statements aroused disturbing questions within the apostles. If Jesus would be with them for just a little while longer and then would depart to a place to which they could not come for an undisclosed period of time, did this mean that He would not restore God's theocratic kingdom during their lifetime? What implications would Jesus' departure have regarding His remaining on the earth to administer God's rule? Indeed, what effect would His departure have on the whole kingdom program? Why would He leave them? What impact would His departure have on them?

THE INTRODUCTION TO THE PROMISE

Jesus made several preliminary statements to introduce His promise. They are recorded in John 14:2.

"In my Father's house are many mansions." H. E. Dana said, "The word rendered 'mansions' really means abiding places . . . It was the word used for the lodging which the traveler secured at the end of a day's journey."[1]

The Scriptures indicate that God's unique dwelling is in heaven (Dt. 26:15; Ps. 33:13-14; Isa. 63:15; Mt. 5:16, 45; 6:1, 9). In light of this, Ernst Wilhelm Hengstenberg concluded that in John 14:2 "The Father's house is His heavenly abode."[2]

In like manner, F. F. Bruce wrote, "Here, however, 'my Father's house' (oikia) is plainly not on earth: it is the heavenly home to which Jesus is going and in which his people are also promised a place."[3]

The fact that Jesus stated that there are "many" dwelling places in the Father's house in heaven indicates that the apostles were not to "think of the heavenly temple as a sanctuary where none could dwell but the Divine Majesty, but rather as a vast palace which could give shelter and rest to as many as the Lord willed."[4] Thus, there would be room for the entire church to dwell in the Father's house in heaven at the end of its present earthly journey.

"If it were not so, I would have told you." Jesus stated this to emphasize or confirm the truthfulness of His claim that there are many dwelling places in the Father's house.

"I go to prepare a place for you." Through this statement Jesus indicated that He would leave the apostles and go somewhere. Just before the evening in which Jesus made this statement, He "knew that his hour was come that he should depart out of this world unto the Father" (Jn. 13:1). Later that evening in the same discourse, He stated where He would go: to His Father (Jn. 14:12; 16:28). In John 14:28 Jesus clearly indicated what He meant by His statements in verses 2 and 3: "Ye have heard how I said unto you, I go away, and come again unto you. If ye loved me, ye would rejoice, because I said, I go unto the Father." Thus, we can conclude that when Jesus said, "I go to prepare a place for you," He was referring to His ascension to the Father in heaven. It is interesting to note that the verb translated "go" in Christ's statement "I go" is used for His ascension in Acts 1:10-11 and 1 Peter 3:22.

Jesus was careful to assure His apostles that His going to the Father's house had a purpose—namely, to prepare a place for them. F. F. Bruce explained the significance of this purpose as follows: "They had been dismayed when he spoke of going away; now they are assured that his going away is for their advantage. He is going to get a place ready for them and, having done that, he will come back and take them there."[5]

Melanchthon W. Jacobus pointed out an implication of Christ's purpose: "His going to prepare a place, implied His return to take them thither for its occupancy."[6] Thus, His statement was an indirect promise that the apostles would live in the Father's house in heaven in the future.[7]

THE PROMISE

Jesus' promise is recorded in John 14:3: "I will come again, and receive you unto myself."

"And if I go and prepare a place for you." Having already indicated that He would go to the Father's house and prepare a place for them there, Jesus stated a conditional clause to stress the certainty of His coming to receive them, which would be the inescapable result of His going to prepare a place for them. Thus, His departure would not involve a permanent separation from them but would be a "necessary step for a glorious and eternal reunion."[8]

"I will come again." The context of this part of Jesus' promise makes it obvious that He was referring to a future coming. In light of that, we would expect Him to use the future tense of the verb translated "will come." Instead, He used the present tense. F. Blass and A. Debrunner explained the significance of this in their Greek grammar. When discussing the uses of the present tense, they wrote, "In confident assertions regarding the future, a vivid, realistic present may be used for the future."[9] They cited the verb translated "will come" in John 14:3 as an example of this futuristic use of the present tense and stated that that particular verb "figures strongly" in this use.[10]

James H. Moulton indicated the same significance for this use of the present tense when he declared, "We may define the futural present as differing from the future tense mainly in the tone of assurance which is imparted."[11]

In light of this, we can conclude that Jesus purposely used the present tense of the verb to make the promise of His future coming a confident assertion—an assurance or guarantee to the apostles that His future coming was certain. Thus, Leon Morris asserted that this coming of Christ "is so certain that Jesus can speak of it as present. Let there be no doubt: it will certainly come about."[12]

Frederick L. Godet[13], Thomas Whitelaw[14], and Henry Barclay Swete[15] recognized another significance in Christ's use of the present tense for His future coming: It indicated the imminency of that coming. Swete wrote, "The present tense 'I come' is used rather than the future, for the Return is regarded not as a distant event, but as one ever imminent and at hand."[16]

William F. Arndt and F. Wilbur Gingrich wrote that the adverb translated "again" means *"again, once more, anew* when someone repeats something he has already done . . . or an event takes place in the same (or a similar) manner as before, or a state of being recurs in the same (or nearly the same) way as at first."[17] Through this term, Jesus indicated that His future coming would be similar to His first coming. Just as His first coming involved one specific coming, not repeated comings, so this future coming would involve one specific coming.

"And receive you unto myself." Concerning this second part of Jesus' promise, R. C. H. Lenski asserted that Christ's acts of coming again and receiving the apostles unto Himself "go together and occur at the same time."[18]

Arndt and Gingrich stated that the verb translated "receive" means *"take (to oneself), take with* or *along."*[19] They concluded that Jesus was saying, *"I will take you to myself* J 14:3 . . . *with me to my home."*[20]

William Hendriksen claimed that the "root idea" of the verb translated "receive" is "to take over *from* another."[21] This is significant in light of Jesus' promise to the apostles that after He went to the Father, another comforter, the Holy Spirit, would be sent to minister to them (Jn. 14:16-17; 16:7-15). While Christ is in the Father's house in heaven, the Holy Spirit cares for His believers on the earth; but when Christ returns for His believers, He will take over their care from the Holy Spirit.

Arthur W. Pink expressed this concept as follows: "The Holy Spirit has charge of us during the time of our absence from the Saviour; but when the mystical body of Christ is complete then is *His* work done here, and He hands us over to the One who died to save us."[22]

The preposition translated "unto" "denotes movement 'towards.' "[23] This indicates that in Christ's coming to receive His believers, in conjunction with His descent from heaven toward the earth, He will not be the only one involved in movement. His believers will be moved from the earth toward Christ to meet Him.

In His promise, Jesus made it clear that He, not someone else, would come and receive His believers and that He would receive them unto Himself. This implies that this coming to receive believers is so significant to Him personally that He will not entrust this activity to another. In light of this, Pink wrote, "The Lord will not *send* for us, but come in person to conduct us into the Father's House. How precious we must be to Him! . . . To have us with Himself is His heart's desire."[24]

This coming will be significant to Christ personally because it will involve receiving His beloved one, His bride, the church. Concerning Jesus' promise in John 14:3, George Hutcheson stated, "For as bridegrooms used to fetch their brides, so he will not decline to do that duty to his bride."[25] It is interesting to note that the verb translated "receive" in Jesus' promise is used in the New Testament for the action of a bridegroom taking his betrothed wife unto himself (Mt. 1:20, 24). It would appear, then, that in His John 14:3 promise, Jesus was implying an analogy between Jewish marriage customs in Bible times and His coming to receive His bride, the church. That analogy will be developed later in this chapter.

"That where I am, there ye may be also." This is a purpose clause in the Greek text and presents the purpose of Jesus' coming to receive His believers unto Himself. Arndt and Gingrich believed the word translated "where" denotes "place" and was "used in connection w. a designation of place."[26]

In light of this and the fact that in the immediate context Jesus talked about going to prepare a "place" for His believers in the Father's house, we must conclude that the word "where" refers to that designated place in the Father's house in heaven.

R. C. H. Lenski, commenting on the word "where" in John 14:3, expressed this same conclusion when he wrote, " 'Where,' *hopou*, reverts to everything said about the 'place.' "[27] Indeed, the immediate context requires this conclusion. Any other conclusion would rob Jesus' statement about going to prepare a place in the Father's house of any meaningful connection with the rest of the context. That statement would have no contextual purpose. For that reason, Henry B. Swete declared, "What would it avail to prepare the place if He did not come back, and Himself fetch them to fill it?"[28]

In conjunction with this conclusion, it is important to note that Jesus did not say that the purpose of this future coming to receive believers is so that He can be where they are—on the earth. Instead, He said that the purpose is so that they can be where He is—in heaven. In line with this, Leon Morris stated, "The construction emphasizes purpose . . . He is speaking about a firm divine purpose. It is God's plan that Jesus will come back in due course in order that he and his followers may be together in heaven."[29]

If the purpose were so that He could be where the believers are, they would receive Him unto themselves, and they would not move from the earth. But, as noted earlier, Jesus said that He will receive them unto Himself, and His coming to receive them will involve their movement from the earth. Thus, the John 14:3 coming of Christ will not have the purpose of His coming to the earth to dwell here but Christ and His believers dwelling together in the Father's house in heaven.

The Greek text of the purpose clause indicates that Jesus strongly emphasized the pronouns "I" and "ye."[30] A very literal translation of the clause would be, "That where I myself am, there ye yourselves may be also." He did this to emphasize that the purpose of His future coming would be so that He and His believers could be together in the same place. Thus, His separation from them would only be temporary. What a comfort this must have been to His apostles, who were greatly troubled over the possible implications of His going away!

Conclusion. This exegesis of John 14:2-3 leads to the conclusion that in this passage, Jesus indicated that He would ascend to the Father's house in heaven to prepare a dwelling place for His believers there. Then He promised a later, personal coming in which He would receive His believers unto Himself and take them from the earth to dwell with Him in their prepared place in the Father's house. He clearly stated that the purpose of this coming was so that His believers could be where He is. In its context, this purpose rules out Christ and His believers living on the earth as a result of this coming. Instead, they will dwell together in the Father's house in heaven because of this coming.

In line with this conclusion, Swete asserted the following concerning Jesus' John 14:2-3 teaching:

> Further, He would have His disciples connect His coming with the fulfillment of the purpose which He went to accomplish. He comes to take to Himself those for whom He has prepared a place . . . at His return He will take with Him . . . all the Eleven, all the faithful, to the Father's House, to the many mansions prepared for them, that they may be with Him there.[31]

Arno C. Gaebelein pointed out the significance of this coming of Christ in conjunction with its stated purpose when he wrote,

> But here in John xiv the Lord gives a new and unique revelation; He speaks of something which no prophet had promised, or even could promise. Where is it written that this Messiah would come and instead of gathering His saints into an earthly Jerusalem, would take them to the Father's house, to the very place where He is? It is something new . . . He speaks then of a coming which is not for the deliverance of the Jewish remnant, not of a coming to establish His kingdom over the earth, not of a coming to judge the nations, but a coming which concerns only His own.[32]

DIFFERENT VIEWS OF THE JOHN 14:3 COMING

Several views of the future coming of Christ promised in John 14:3 have been advocated.

The Death-of-the-Believer View. Some have proposed that John 14:3 refers to Christ's coming each time a believer dies. Henry Cowles wrote, "This must refer to Christ's coming *in the death* of his saints. At and in their death he comes to receive their souls to himself, to bear them up to his Father's mansions where he has prepared a place for them."[33]

There are problems with this view. It involves many comings of Christ (every time a believer dies); but, as noted above, the coming of John 14:3 involves one specific coming. In addition, the Lord's teaching in Luke 16:22 indicates that it is angels, not Jesus, who come to transport the souls of believers at death.

The Resurrection-of-Christ View. Some believe that Christ's John 14:3 coming refers to His return to His disciples when He rose from the dead.[34]

This view also has problems. First, in verse 3 Jesus clearly indicated that He would come again after He went away. Since, as noted earlier, His going away refers to His ascension to heaven, He thereby indicated that He would come again after His ascension. By contrast, since the resurrection view equates His coming again with His resurrection, and since His resurrection took place before His ascension, the resurrection view places His coming again before His ascension rather than after.

Second, as noted earlier, when Jesus promised that He would come again, He thereby indicated that this future coming would be similar to His first coming. Just as in His first coming He came from heaven, so in this future coming He will come from heaven. By contrast, Jesus did not come from heaven when He rose from the dead.

Third, as noted earlier, the John 14:3 coming of Christ will involve a movement of believers from the earth. By contrast, Jesus' resurrection did not involve such a movement.

The Coming-of-the-Holy Spirit View. Some have asserted that the John 14:3 coming refers to a spiritual coming of Christ in the person of the Holy Spirit on the day of Pentecost.[35]

There are problems with this view. First, the coming of the Holy Spirit on the day of Pentecost did not involve a movement of believers from the earth, but the John 14:3 coming will involve such a movement.

Second, Lenski rightfully concluded that in John 14:2-3 "the coming again is the counterpart of the going away."[36] Just as in the going away Jesus ascended physically to heaven, so in the coming again He will descend physically from heaven. By contrast, Jesus did not descend physically from heaven on the day of Pentecost. Indeed, the Scriptures indicate that Christ remained physically in heaven after the Holy Spirit came on Pentecost (Acts 7:55-56; Rom. 8:34; Col. 3:1; 1 Pet. 3:21-22).

Third, in Christ's John 14:3 coming He will receive the believers. By contrast, when the Holy Spirit comes, He does not receive the believers. Instead, they receive Him (Jn. 20:22; Acts 2:38; 8:15-17; 10:47).

When referring to the John 14:3 coming, John Calvin wrote, "This *return* must not be understood as referring to the Holy Spirit, as if Christ has manifested to the disciples some new presence of himself by the Spirit."[37]

The Future-Coming View. A good number of scholars believe that the John 14:3 coming of Christ refers to a specific event of the future end times. According to this view, at one specific point in the future, Christ Himself will descend from heaven and take His believers as one group together from the earth to the Father's house in heaven to dwell with Him there. Concerning Jesus' John 14:3 coming, J. H. Bernard wrote, "This is an explicit announcement of the Parousia, or Second Advent."[38]

C. K. Barrett stated, "Jesus promises to return to bring his disciples to the heavenly dwelling-places which he is about to prepare; the primary reference of *erchomai* therefore is to the eschatological advent of Jesus."[39] (*"Erchomai"* is the verb translated "I will come" in John 14:3).

J. Ramsey Michaels asserted, "The reference is to Jesus' future coming (cf. 1 John 2:28) and to the resurrection of those who believe in Jesus (cf. 6:39-40, 44, 54)."[40]

Pheme Perkins claimed that Jesus' statement about coming again "refers to the parousia."[41]

Otto Michel wrote, "According to Schlatter Jesus is referring to the ascension when He speaks of going away to prepare a place for them, but the conducting of the disciples into God's house will take place only at the *parousia*."[42]

This author is convinced that these and other scholars have rightly concluded that the future-coming view is the correct view of Jesus' John 14:3 coming. Evidences for this view will now be examined.

EVIDENCES FOR THE FUTURE-COMING VIEW

The First Evidence: The Exegesis of John 14:2-3. The exegesis of John 14:2-3 already examined in this chapter induces this view. The future-coming view is the only view that agrees with every aspect of that exegesis. For example, as noted earlier, the resurrection-of-Christ view and the coming-of-the-Holy Spirit view do not agree with the exegetical aspect, which indicates that at Christ's coming believers will move from the earth and go with Him to heaven. The death-of-the-believer view does have the souls of believers moving from the earth to heaven, but, as noted earlier, that view has problems that rule out its being the correct view.

The Second Evidence: The Relationship of John 14:2-3 to 1 Thessalonians 4:13-18. A comparison of John 14:2-3 with 1 Thessalonians 4:13-18 reveals that they are equivalent to each other in several significant points. First, as noted earlier, the Lord's coming again (Jn. 14:3) involves a descent from heaven by Christ Himself. This corresponds with "the Lord himself shall descend from heaven" (1 Th. 4:16). Thus, both passages present a coming in which Christ Himself will descend from heaven.

Second, in conjunction with His John 14:3 coming, the Lord will receive His believers unto Himself. The exegesis of 14:3 indicates that in conjunction with Christ's descent from heaven toward the earth, believers will be moved from the earth to meet Him. In harmony with this, 1 Thessalonians 4:17 indicates that in conjunction with Christ's descent from heaven (v. 16) believers "shall be caught up together . . . in the clouds, to meet the Lord in the air." Thus, both passages present a coming of Christ that involves a movement of believers from the earth to meet Him.

Third, the purpose of the John 14:3 coming is so that believers can be with Him where He is. Corresponding to this, 1 Thessalonians 4:17 says that the result of His descent from heaven will be "and so shall we ever be with the Lord." Thus, both passages present a coming of Christ involving all believers being with Him.

Fourth, the teaching of John 14:2-3 was presented to calm troubled hearts (v. 1). In like manner, the teaching of 1 Thessalonians 4:13-18 was given to comfort sorrowing hearts (vv. 13, 18). Thus, both passages present a coming of Christ involving truths that should ease the disturbed hearts of believers.

These parallels of John 14:2-3 and 1 Thessalonians 4:13-18 prompt the conclusion that both passages refer to the same coming of Christ. A number of scholars have drawn this conclusion. For example, J. H. Bernard, when commenting on Christ's receiving believers unto Himself (Jn. 14), wrote, "For this meeting of Master and disciples, cf. I Thess. 4:17."[43]

Concerning John 14:3, James Montgomery Boice stated,

> In this verse, Jesus receives the believer so that the believer may be with Him in heaven. Clearly, this is what Paul describes so vividly when he says, "For the Lord himself shall descend from heaven with a shout, with the voice of the archangel, and with the trump of God: and the dead in Christ shall rise first: then we which are alive and remain shall be caught up together with them in the clouds, to meet the Lord in the air: so shall we ever be with the Lord" (1 Thess. 4:16-17).[44]

After Arno C. Gaebelein had written about Jesus' promise to come and receive believers (Jn. 14), he said, "But the full meaning of the promise of our Lord to His eleven disciples was revealed through the Apostle Paul."[45] Later he asserted that that full meaning "is found in 1 Thess. iv:15-18."[46]

Arthur Pink indicated that Jesus' promise to come again and Paul's 1 Thessalonians 4:16-17 statements refer to the same coming.[47] Then, commenting on the former, Pink said, "To the Church it is promised that we shall 'ever be *with the Lord*' (1 Thess. 4:17)."[48]

Rudolf Schnackenburg pointed out several parallels between John 14:3 and 1 Thessalonians 4:16-17[49], and F. F. Bruce hinted at a possible relationship between the two passages.[50]

Regarding the Lord's promised coming, R. V. G. Tasker wrote, "This was a very precious promise to the early Church, and Paul may well be echoing it when he informs the Thessalonians 'by the word of the Lord' that Jesus will descend from heaven and gather believers unto Himself to be with Him for ever (see I Thes. iv.15-17)."[51]

Referring to John 14:3, W. E. Vine stated,

> This is more than a reception to meet Him in the air (1 Thess. 4:17). That will be so, but He takes us, surely, from the place of meeting in the air, into the Father's House, to be with Him. He says, "Where I am;" this is "within the

veil, whither as Forerunner Jesus entered for" (Heb. 6.20). That place is "the Father's House."[52]

It is apparent that the relationship of John 14:2-3 to 1 Thessalonians 4:13-18 produces the conclusion that both passages refer to the same coming of Christ.

The Coming of 1 Thessalonians 4. Several things indicate that Christ's coming in 1 Thessalonians 4 is to rapture the church from the earth. First, as noted in the Introduction, the word translated "caught up" in 1 Thessalonians 4:17 is the same word translated "caught up" for Jesus' ascension or rapture to heaven (Rev. 12:5) and for the rapture of the man who was transported to the third heaven (2 Cor. 12:2-4). In light of the language used in 1 Thessalonians 4:17, Erik Peterson asserted that at the 1 Thessalonians 4 coming of Christ "there will be a rapture."[53]

Second, because Paul wrote 1 Thessalonians as an apostle of the church to members of the church, and since he included them and himself in the Rapture of 1 Thessalonians 4:17 by using the pronoun "we," we can conclude that he was referring to the Rapture of the church from the earth.

Further Conclusions. First, since John 14:2-3 and 1 Thessalonians 4:13-18 refer to the same coming of Christ, and since Christ's coming in 1 Thessalonians 4 is the coming to rapture the church from the earth, His coming in John 14:2-3 is also the coming to rapture the church from the earth. Vine stated the same conclusion when, commenting on Christ's coming in John 14:3, he wrote, "The Lord is not referring to the falling asleep of the individual believer. He is speaking of the time of the Rapture of all believers at the completion of the Church."[54]

Second, since the John 14:2-3 coming of Christ is the coming to rapture the church from the earth, and since the purpose of that coming is that His believers may be with Him in heaven, we can conclude that when Christ raptures the church from the earth, He will return with it to heaven and dwell with it there for a significant period of time. In this coming, after the church meets Him in the air, He and the church will not come directly to the earth to dwell. That would violate the John 14:2-3 concept that in this coming He will take believers to live in the prepared dwellings in the Father's house in heaven. In addition, it would violate the biblical concept of rapture, because, as noted in the Introduction, all the other raptures in the Bible take people from the earth to heaven. In line with this, commenting on 1 Thessalonians 4:17, James Everett Frame wrote, "It is, however, probable that after the meeting of the Lord in the air, the Lord with his saints go not to earth but to heaven."[55]

In addition, in this coming Christ will not take the church to the Father's house, drop it off there, and immediately descend by Himself to dwell on the earth. That would violate the purpose of His John 14:3 coming—that His believers may be where He is, no longer separated from Him.

It is important to note that John 14:2-3 presents a coming of Christ that does not bring Him to the earth. Instead, the combined concepts of John 14 and 1 Thessalonians 4 indicate that in this coming Christ will descend from heaven to the air above the earth, receive believers unto Himself by catching them up from the earth to meet Him in the air, and then return with them to heaven to dwell together there.

Third, since John 14 and 1 Thessalonians 4 both refer to the coming of Christ to rapture the church from the earth, and since, according to 1 Thessalonians 4:17, this coming will result in the church ever being with the Lord, we can conclude that the result of the John 14 coming will be the permanent physical presence of the Lord with the church. The adverb translated "ever" in 1 Thessalonians 4:17 means *"always, at all times."*[56] Once the church meets the Lord in the air at the Rapture, it will never be separated physically from Him again. From that time, wherever Christ goes, the church will go with Him.

Fourth, since John 14 and 1 Thessalonians 4 both refer to the coming of Christ to rapture the church from the earth, and since the church has not yet been raptured from the earth, we can conclude that the John 14 coming of Christ has not yet happened. It is a future event. Thus, the relationship of John 14:2-3 to 1 Thessalonians 4:13-18 is a second evidence for the future-coming view of John 14:2-3.

The Third Evidence: The Jewish Marriage Analogy. Earlier in this chapter we indicated that in His John 14:3 promise, Jesus implied an analogy between Jewish marriage customs in Bible times and His coming to receive His bride, the church. This analogy is a third evidence for the future-coming view.

THE JEWISH MARRIAGE ANALOGY

Jewish Marriage Customs in Bible Times. The first major step in a Jewish marriage in Bible times was betrothal[57], the establishment of a marriage covenant. By Jesus' time, such a covenant was usually established when the prospective bridegroom took the initiative.[58] He would travel from his father's house to the home of the prospective bride, where he would negotiate with the father of the young woman to determine the price (*mohar*) he must pay to purchase her.[59]

Once the bridegroom paid the purchase price, the marriage covenant was established, and the young man and woman were regarded as husband and wife (cp. Mal. 2:14; Mt. 1:18-19).[60] From that moment on, the bride was declared to be consecrated or sanctified, set apart exclusively for her bridegroom.[61] As a symbol of the covenant relationship that had been established, the groom and bride drank from a cup of wine over which a betrothal benediction had been pronounced.[62]

After the marriage covenant was established, the groom left his bride at her home and returned to his father's house, where he remained separated from his bride for approximately 12 months.[63] This afforded the bride time to gather her trousseau and prepare for married life.[64] During this period of separation, the groom prepared a dwelling place in his father's house to which he could bring his bride later.

At the end of the period of separation, the groom came usually at night to take his bride to live with him. The groom, best man, and other male escorts left the groom's father's house and conducted a torch-light procession to the home of the bride.[65] Although the bride was expecting her groom to come for her, she did not know the time of his coming.[66] As a result, the groom's arrival was preceded by a shout[67], which forewarned the bride to be prepared for his coming.

After the groom received his bride, together with her female attendants, the enlarged wedding party returned from the bride's home to the groom's father's house[68], where the wedding guests had assembled.

Shortly after their arrival, the bride and groom were escorted by the other members of the wedding party to the bridal chamber (*huppah*). Prior to entering the chamber, the bride remained veiled so that no one could see her face.[69] While the groomsmen and bridesmaids waited outside, the bride and groom entered the bridal chamber alone. There, in the privacy of that place, they entered into physical union for the first time, thereby consummating the marriage that had been covenanted approximately one year earlier.[70]

After the marriage was consummated, the groom came out of the bridal chamber and announced the consummation of the marriage to the members of the wedding party waiting outside (Ps. 19:5; Jn. 3:29). Then, as the groom went back to his bride in the chamber, the members of the wedding party returned to the wedding guests and announced the consummation of the marriage.[71] Upon receiving this good news, the wedding guests remained in the groom's father's house for the next seven days, celebrating with a great wedding feast.[72]

During the seven days of the wedding feast, the bride and groom remained hidden in the bridal chamber (Gen. 29:21-23, 27-28)[73] for "the seven days of the *huppah*."[74]. Afterwards, the groom came out of hiding, bringing his bride with him, but with her veil removed so that everyone could see who she was.

This is the way that the Jews normally conducted marriages in Jesus' time.

Introduction to the Analogy. Earlier we stated that in His John 14:3 promise, Jesus implied an analogy between Jewish marriage customs in

Bible times and His coming to receive His bride, the church. Now that the
Jewish marriage customs have been considered, the analogy will be introduced and examined.

First, we should note that the New Testament draws an analogy between
human marriage and Christ's relationship to the church and thereby portrays the church as the bride of Christ (Eph. 5:22-33).

Concerning Paul's reference to Genesis 2:24 in Ephesians 5:31, J. Jeremias wrote, "The saying in Gn. 2:24 concerning the union of man and wife
is referred in v. 31 f. to the union (at the *parousia*) of Christ the Bridegroom,
who leaves heaven and comes for His bride, and the community."[75] Here
Jeremias substituted the word "community" for the word "church" in
Ephesians 5, thus saying that the union of Christ the bridegroom and the
church will take place at the *parousia*. In line with this, Jeremias also
asserted that "Eph. 5:31 f. is to be taken eschatologically"[76] but that
mysticism stripped "it of its eschatological content" in the post-New Testament period.[77]

In addition to the Ephesians 5 portrayal, Paul talked about the spiritual
marriage of Christians to Christ in Romans 7:4. Further, in 2 Corinthians
11:2 Paul indicated that through his gospel ministry in Corinth, he had
"espoused" (another word for betrothal) the Corinthian Christians to one
husband (Christ). In that same passage he expressed concern that the
Christians keep themselves spiritually pure during their separation from
Christ so that Paul could present them to Christ as a chaste virgin when He
comes for His bride. Jeremias stated that in this 2 Corinthians passage "Paul
compares the community with a bride, Christ with the bridegroom, and
himself with the best man who has won the bride, who watches over her
virginity, and who will lead her to the bridegroom at the wedding."[78]

In the same vein, James accused Christians who prostitute their spiritual
purity through friendship with the godless world system of being guilty of
spiritual adultery (Jas. 4:4).

These introductory items indicate that the New Testament recognizes a
valid analogy between human marriage and Christ's relationship with the
church and, even more specifically, between human marriage and Christ's
future coming as bridegroom to receive His bride, the church.[79]

Examination of the Analogy. Jesus' John 14:3 coming to receive the
church is analogous with the Jewish marriage customs presented earlier in
several ways. Just as the Jewish bridegroom took the initiative in marriage
by leaving his father's house and traveling to the home of the prospective
bride, so Jesus left His Father's house in heaven and traveled to the earth,
the home of His prospective church, approximately two thousand years ago.

In the same manner as the Jewish bridegroom came to the bride's home
to obtain her by establishing a marriage covenant, so Jesus came to the earth
to obtain the church by establishing a covenant. On the same night in which

Jesus made His John 14:3 promise, He instituted communion. As He passed the communion cup to the apostles, Jesus said, "This cup is the new testament [lit., new covenant] in my blood" (1 Cor. 11:25). By shedding His blood on the cross the next day, He established a new covenant though which He obtained His church.

Parallel to the custom of the Jewish groom paying a purchase price by which he established the marriage covenant and through which he obtained his bride, Jesus paid a purchase price by which He established the new covenant and through which He obtained the church. The price He paid was the shedding of His own life blood. Because of this purchase price, Paul wrote to members of the church, "Know ye not that . . . ye are not your own? For ye are bought with a price; therefore, glorify God in your own body and in your spirit, which are God's" (1 Cor. 6:19-20).

Just as the Jewish bride was declared sanctified or set apart exclusively for her groom once the marriage covenant was established, so the church has been declared sanctified or set apart exclusively for Christ (Eph. 5:25-27; 1 Cor. 1:2; 6:11; Heb. 10:10; 13:12).

In the same way that the Jewish groom and bride drank from a cup of wine as a symbol of the marriage covenant that united them as husband and wife, so Christ has given the cup of communion to the church to drink from periodically as a recurring symbol of the new covenant that has united Him and the church spiritually as husband and wife (1 Cor. 11:25-26).

Just as the Jewish groom left the home of his bride and returned to his father's house after the marriage covenant had been established, so on the day of His ascension Jesus left the earth, the home of the church, and returned to His Father's house in heaven after He had established the new covenant and risen from the dead (Jn. 6:62; Acts 1:9-11).

As the Jewish groom remained separated from his bride in his father's house for a period of time after he left her home, so Christ has remained separated from the church in heaven for almost two thousand years since His ascension from the earth. The church is now living in that period of separation between the time of His departure and the time of His return.

Parallel to the custom of the Jewish groom's preparing a dwelling place for his bride in his father's house during the time of separation, Christ has been preparing a dwelling place for the church in His Father's house in heaven during this period of separation. As noted earlier in John 14:2, Jesus stated that was why He would ascend to heaven.

In the same manner as the Jewish groom came to take his bride to live with him at the end of the period of separation, so Christ will come to take the church to live with Him at the end of His present period of separation from it (Jn. 14:3).

Just as a procession of the groom and male escorts from the groom's father's house came to fetch the bride from her home, so a procession of

Christ and an angelic escort descending from Christ's Father's house in heaven will fetch the church from the earth (1 Th. 4:16-17).

The Jewish bride did not know the time when the groom would come for her. Likewise, the church does not know the time when Christ will come for it. As noted in the chapter on imminency, Christ's coming for the church is an imminent event. It could happen at any moment.

In the same way that the Jewish groom's arrival was preceded by a shout, so Christ's arrival to take the church will be preceded by a shout (1 Th. 4:16).

As the Jewish bride returned with the groom to his father's house after her departure from her home, the church will return with Christ to His Father's house in heaven after it is caught up from the earth to meet Him in the air (Jn. 14:2-3; 1 Th. 4:17).

In the same manner as the Jewish wedding party found wedding guests assembled in the groom's father's house when they arrived, so Christ and the church will find the souls of Old Testament saints (those who were saved in Old Testament times before the church began and who, therefore, are not part of the church) assembled in His Father's house in heaven when they arrive. These souls will serve as the wedding guests for Christ and the church.

Just as the Jewish bride and groom remained hidden for a period of seven days after they arrived at the groom's father's house, so Christ and the church will remain hidden for a period of seven years after they arrive in heaven. While the seven years of the 70th week of Daniel 9 are taking place on the earth, Christ and the church will be in heaven, totally hidden from the view of those living on the earth.

In the same way that the Jewish bride and groom came out of hiding after seven days, now with the bride's veil removed so that all could see who she was, so Christ and the church will come out of hiding from heaven after the seven years of the 70th week, in full view of all who are still alive on the earth, so that everyone can see who the true church is. Paul wrote to members of the church, "When Christ, who is our life, shall appear, then shall ye also appear with him in glory" (Col. 3:4).

Significance of the Analogy. The Jewish marriage analogy indicates the following concerning the John 14:3 coming of Christ: That coming will take place after the ascension of Christ and a period of physical separation from the church, thus ruling out the resurrection-of-Christ view, which places His coming before His ascension. After the period of separation, Christ Himself will descend physically from heaven, ruling out the coming-of-the-Holy Spirit view, which refers to a spiritual coming of Christ in the person of the Holy Spirit on the day of Pentecost. In this coming, Christ will take the entire church—as one body and at the same time—from the earth to heaven, ruling out the death-of-the-believer view, which has Christ coming many times (every time another believer dies) to transport believers' souls to heaven.

The only view of the John 14:3 coming of Christ that fits the Jewish marriage analogy implied by Christ in that passage is the future-coming view. As a result, the Jewish marriage analogy is a significant evidence for that view.

JOHN 14:2-3 AND
THE DIFFERENT RAPTURE VIEWS

The introduction to this book presented a description of various views relative to the time of the church's Rapture: The pretribulation view, the midtribulation view, its pre-wrath derivative position, and the posttribulation view. Which of these views corresponds fully with what has been observed concerning Jesus' promised John 14 coming?

The Midtribulation View. The Midtribulation Rapture view teaches that the church will remain on the earth through the first three and one-half years of the seven-year Tribulation period, and then Christ will come to rapture the church and take it to heaven in the middle of that seven-year period.

This view does not correspond fully with what has been observed concerning His promised John 14 coming. It does not agree with one point of the analogy that Jesus implied between Jewish marriage customs in Bible times and His coming to receive His bride, the church. That analogy indicated that after Christ has raptured the church, He and the church will be in heaven throughout all seven years of the Tribulation period. By contrast, the midtribulation view has the church in heaven only during the second three and one-half years of that seven-year period.

The Pre-Wrath Derivative Position. The pre-wrath position, a derivative of the Midtribulation Rapture view, teaches that the church will remain on the earth until sometime between the middle and end of the 70th week. Thus, Christ will not come and rapture the church from the earth until perhaps three-fourths of the way through that seven-year period.

The pre-wrath position does not correspond in more than one way with what has been observed concerning the Lord's promised John 14 coming. First, this position disagrees with the same point of the analogy as does the midtribulation view. In contrast with the analogy, which indicates that Christ and the church will be in heaven throughout all seven years of the 70th week, the pre-wrath position has the church in heaven during perhaps the last fourth of that seven-year period plus an additional 75 days after the end of the 70th week.[80] Thus, after the Rapture, the church will be in heaven for considerably less than three and one-half years.

Second, the pre-wrath position asserts that there will be only one Second Coming or *parousia* of Christ, but within the boundaries of that one Second Coming Christ will come and go several times.[81] It teaches that there will be four future comings of Christ within the boundaries of the one Second Coming. The first of these comings will take place between the sixth and seventh seals immediately after the Great Tribulation has ended. At this coming, Christ will rapture His bride (which will include the church) from the earth and take it to heaven. Christ will remain in heaven for the remainder of the 70th week.[82]

The second of these comings will take place immediately after the end of the 70th week and at the beginning of a 30-day reclamation period. Christ will descend physically from heaven to the earth to bring the salvation of Israel (the Israelite survivors of the 70th week) and to reclaim the rule of the earth for God.[83] Sometime after the sixth day of the 30-day reclamation period, Christ will return to heaven, where He will remain for approximately 24 days.[84]

The third of these comings will take place after the seventh bowl judgment at the end of the 30-day reclamation period. Christ will come back physically to the earth with His holy angels to defeat the Antichrist and his forces at Armageddon.[85] Then there will be a 45-day restoration period.[86] At the close of those 45 days, Christ will return to heaven to deliver the physical kingdom of earth to God and to receive the rule of the whole earth from God.[87]

The fourth future coming will take place several days after Christ receives the rule of the whole earth from God. He will descend permanently to the earth with His bride (which will include the church) to rule His worldwide Millennial Kingdom.[88]

The pre-wrath position therefore has the bride of Christ (including the church) remaining in heaven from the time it is raptured at the first of these comings of Christ (approximately three-fourths of the way through the 70th week) until the fourth of these comings (when Christ returns with His bride a little more than 75 days after the end of the 70th week to rule the entire world).

It is important to note that the pre-wrath position indicates that Christ will leave heaven and return to the earth twice while His bride remains in heaven. During the first of these times (immediately after the end of the 70th week and at the beginning of a 30-day reclamation period), Christ will be separated from His bride for approximately six days. During the second of these times (after the seventh bowl judgment at the end of the 30-day reclamation period), Christ will be separated from His bride for the 45 days of the restoration period.

Earlier in this chapter we noted that John 14 and 1 Thessalonians 4 refer to the same coming of Christ to rapture His bride, the church, from the earth and take it to heaven to dwell with Him in His Father's house. In addition, we noted that the result of the John 14 coming will be the same result of the rapture as stated in 1 Thessalonians 4:17: "And so shall we ever be with the Lord." Thus, the result of the John 14:3 coming will be the permanent physical presence of the Lord with His bride, the church. Once His bride is raptured to meet Christ in the air, it will never be separated physically from Him. From that time on, wherever Christ goes, His bride will go with Him.

Since the pre-wrath position teaches that there will be two physical separations of Christ from His bride (including the church) *after* He has raptured it and taken it to heaven, we must conclude that it does not correspond with what has been observed concerning Jesus' promised John 14 coming.

The Posttribulation Rapture View. The Posttribulation Rapture view teaches that the church will remain on the earth throughout the entire seven-year Tribulation but will be raptured from the earth to meet Christ in the air immediately after that period, when Christ returns in His glorious Second Coming.

Posttribulationists who are also premillennial believe that after the church meets Christ in the air, it will return immediately to the earth with Him as He continues His descent from heaven and will remain with Him on the earth throughout the Millennium. Posttribulationists who are not premillennial believe that after the church meets Christ in the air, it will be taken by Him to heaven for eternity.

The Posttribulation Rapture view teaches that the church will remain on the earth throughout the entire seven-year Tribulation period but then will be raptured from the earth immediately after that period. It therefore disagrees with the Jewish marriage analogy associated with Jesus' John 14 coming, which indicates that after Christ has raptured the church, He and the church will be in heaven throughout all seven years of the Tribulation period.

Posttribulationists who are premillennial believe that after the church is raptured to meet Christ in the air, it will return immediately to the earth with Him as He continues His descent from heaven and will remain with Him on the earth throughout the Millennium. Their view conflicts with the point noted earlier that in His John 14:3 coming Jesus will receive the church from the earth and take it to His Father's house in heaven to dwell with Him there. In His John 14:3 coming, neither Jesus nor the church will come directly to the earth.

Should some premillennial posttribulationists believe that after the church has been raptured to meet Christ in the air, He will take it to heaven but then leave it there and return to the earth by Himself for the Millennium, that view would be contrary to the point noted earlier that in Jesus'

John 14:3 coming, once the church has been raptured to meet Christ in the air, it will never be separated from Him.

Posttribulationists who are not premillennial believe that after the Church has been raptured to meet Christ in the air, He will take it directly to heaven for eternity. Their view disagrees with the Jewish marriage analogy, which indicates that after Christ raptures the church from the earth and takes it to heaven, He and the church will not remain in heaven from that point on for eternity. Instead, Christ and the church will remain in heaven during the seven years of the Tribulation but then will come out of heaven.

The Pretribulation Rapture View. The Pretribulation Rapture view teaches that the church will be raptured from the earth before the seven-year Tribulation period begins. As a result, the church will not enter or go through any part of the Tribulation period. Instead, after Christ raptures the church to meet Him in the air, He will take it to heaven to live with Him in His Father's house during the seven years of the Tribulation period. At the end of the Tribulation, when Christ returns to the earth in His glorious coming with His angels, He will bring the church to remain with Him on the earth throughout the Millennium.

In contrast with the other rapture views, the pretribulation view corresponds fully with what has been observed in this chapter concerning Jesus' promised John 14 coming. In light of this, His promise in John 14:2-3 is a significant inference in favor of the Pretribulation Rapture of the church.

ENDNOTES

1. H. E. Dana, *The Heavenly Guest* (Nashville: Broadman Press, 1943), p. 108.

2. Ernst Wilhelm Hengstenberg, *Commentary on the Gospel of St. John*, Vol. II, in *Clark's Foreign Theological Library* (Edinburgh: T. & T. Clark, 1865), p. 185.

3. F. F. Bruce, *The Gospel of John* (Grand Rapids: William B. Eerdmans Publishing Company, 1983), p. 297.

4. Henry Barclay Swete, *The Last Discourse and Prayer of Our Lord* (Macmillan and Co., Limited, 1913), p. 6.

5. F. F. Bruce, *The Gospel of John*, p. 297.

6. Melanchthon W. Jacobus, *John* (New York: Robert Carter & Brothers, 1857), p. 248.

7. R. C. H. Lenski, *The Interpretation of St. John's Gospel* (Columbus, OH: Lutheran Book Concern, 1931), p. 946.

8. *Ibid.*, p. 948.

9. F. Blass and A. Debrunner, *A Greek Grammar of the New Testament and Other Early Christian Literature*, trans. and rev. by Robert W. Funk (Chicago: The University of Chicago Press, 1961), p. 168.

10. *Ibid.*

11. James Hope Moulton, *A Grammar of New Testmament Greek*, Vol. I, third edition (Edinburgh: T. & T. Clark, 1908), p. 120.

12. Leon Morris, *Expository Reflections on the Gospel of John* (Grand Rapids: Baker Book House, 1988), p. 492.

13. Frederick Louis Godet, *Commentary on the Gospel of John*, Vol. II, trans. by Timothy Dwight (New York: Funk & Wagnalls Company, 1893), p. 270.

14. Thomas Whitelaw, *The Gospel of St. John* (Glasgow: James Maclehose & Sons, 1888), p. 302.

15. Henry Barclay Swete, *The Last Discourse and Prayer of Our Lord*, p. 8.

16. *Ibid.*

17. William F. Arndt and F. Wilbur Gingrich, *A Greek-English Lexicon of the New Testament*, 4th rev. ed. (Chicago: The University of Chicago Press, 1957), p. 611.

18. R. C. H. Lenski, *The Interpretation of St. John's Gospel*, p. 950.

19. William F. Arndt and F. Wilbur Gingrich, *A Greek-English Lexicon of the New Testament*, p. 624.

20. *Ibid*, p. 625.

21. William Hendriksen, *Exposition of the Gospel According to John*, Vol. II (Grand Rapids: Baker Book House, 1954), p. 266.

22. Arthur W. Pink, *Exposition of the Gospel of John*, Vol. II (Grand Rapids: Zondervan Publishing House, 1976), p. 352.

23. Bo Reicke, "pros," *Theological Dictionary of the New Testament*, Vol. VI, ed. by Gerhard Friedrich, trans. and ed. by Geoffrey W. Bromiley (Grand Rapids: Wm. B. Eerdmans Publishing Company, 1968), p. 721.

24. Arthur W. Pink, *Exposition of the Gospel of John*, p. 352.

25. George Hutcheson, *The Gospel of John*, reprint of a book first published in 1657 (London: The Banner of Truth Trust, 1972), p. 294.

26. William F. Arndt and F. Wilbur Gingrich, *A Greek-English Lexicon of the New Testament*, p. 579.

27. R. C. H. Lenski, *The Interpretation of St. John's Gospel*, p. 951.

28. Henry Barclay Swete, *The Last Discourse and Prayer of Our Lord*, p. 8.

29. Leon Morris, *Expository Reflections on the Gospel of John*, p. 492.

30. R. C. H. Lenski, *The Interpretation of St. John's Gospel*, p. 951.

31. Henry Barclay Swete, *The Last Discourse and Prayer of Our Lord*, p. 9.

32. Arno Clemens Gaebelein, *The Gospel of John* (New York: "Our Hope," 1925), p. 268.

33. Henry Cowles, *The Gospel and Epistles of John* (New York: D. Appleton & Co., 1876), p. 211.

34. Thomas E. Crane, *The Message of Saint John* (New York: Alba House, 1980), p. 96.

35. Frederick Louis Godet, *Commentary on the Gospel of John*, Vol. II, p. 270.

36. R. C. H. Lenski, *The Interpretation of St. John's Gospel*, p. 950.

37. John Calvin, *Commentary on the Gospel According to John*, Vol. II, trans. by William Pringle (Grand Rapids: Wm. B. Eerdmans Publishing Company, 1949), p. 83.

38. J. H. Bernard, *A Critical and Exegetical Commentary on the Gospel According to St. John*, Vol. II (New York: Charles Scribner's Sons, 1929), p. 535.

39. C. K. Barrett, *The Gospel According to St John* (London: S.P.C.K., 1960), pp. 381-82.

40. J. Ramsey Michaels, *John* (San Francisco: Harper & Row, Publishers, 1984), p. 244.

41. Pheme Perkins, *The Gospel According to St. John* (Chicago: Franciscan Herald Press, 1978), p. 158.

42. Otto Michel, "oikia," *Theological Dictionary of the New Testament*, Vol. V, ed. by Gerhard Friedrich, trans. and ed. by Geoffrey W. Bromiley (Grand Rapids: Wm. B. Eerdmans Publishing Company, 1967), p. 132.

43. J. H. Bernard, *A Critical and Exegetical Commentary on the Gospel According to St. John*, Vol. II, p. 535.

44. James Montgomery Boice, *The Gospel of John* (Grand Rapids: Zondervan Publishing House, 1985), p. 927.

45. Arno Clemens Gaebelein, *The Gospel of John*, p. 268.

46. *Ibid.*, p. 269.

47. Arthur W. Pink, *Exposition of the Gospel of John*, Vol. II, p. 352.

48. *Ibid.*

49. Rudolph Schnackenburg, *The Gospel According to St John*, Vol. III (New York: Crossroad Publishing Co., Inc., 1982), p. 62.

50. F. F. Bruce, *The Gospel of John*, pp. 297-98.

51. R. V. G. Tasker, *The Gospel According to St John* (London: The Tyndale Press, 1960), p. 164.

52. W. E. Vine, *John* (Grand Rapids: Zondervan Publishing House, 1957), p. 128.

53. Erik Peterson, "apantesis," *Theological Dictionary of the New Testament*, Vol. I, ed. by Gerhard Kittel, trans. and ed. by Geoffrey W. Bromiley (Grand Rapids: Wm. B. Eerdmans Publishing Company, 1964), p. 380.

54. W. E Vine, *John*, p. 128.

55. James Everett Frame, *A Critical and Exegetical Commentary on the Epistles of St. Paul to the Thessalonians* (Edinburgh: T. & T. Clark, 1960), p. 178.

56. William F. Arndt and F. Wilbur Gingrich, *A Greek-English Lexicon of the New Testament*, p. 614.

57. "Marriage," *The Universal Jewish Encyclopedia*, ed. Isaac Landman (New York: Universal Jewish Encyclopedia Co., Inc., 1948), 7, 372.

58. David R. Mace, *Hebrew Marriage* (New York: Philosophical Library, 1953), p. 167.

59. "Marriage," *The Universal Jewish Encyclopedia*, p. 372.

60. "Betrothal," *The Jewish Encyclopedia*, ed. Isidore Singer (New York: Funk and Wagnalls Company, 1907), III, pp. 126-27.

61. George F. Moore, *Judaism* (Cambridge, MA: Harvard University Press, 1946), II, p. 121.

62. "Marriage," *The Universal Jewish Encyclopedia*, p. 373.

63. *Ibid.*, p. 372.

64. *Ibid.*

65. George B. Eager, "Marriage," *The International Standard Bible Encyclopedia*, ed. James Orr (Grand Rapids: Wm. B. Eerdmans Publishing Company, 1957), III, p. 1998.

66. Emma Williams Gill, *Home Life in the Bible* (Nashville: Broadman Press, 1936), p. 20.

67. James Neil, *Everyday Life in the Holy Land* (New York: Cassell and Company, Limited, 1913). p. 251.

68. J. Jeremias, "numphe," *Theological Dictionary of the New Testament*, Vol. IV, ed. by Gerhard Kittel, trans. and ed. by Geoffrey W. Bromiley (Grand Rapids: Wm. B. Eerdmans Publishing Company, 1967), p. 1100.

69. "Veiling of the Bride," *The Universal Jewish Encyclopedia*, ed. Isaac Landman (New York: Universal Jewish Encyclopedia Co., Inc., 1948), 10, 399.

70. "Marriage," *The Universal Jewish Encyclopedia*, p. 373.

71. "Huppah," *The Universal Jewish Encyclopedia*, 5, 504.

72. *Ibid.*

73. *Ibid.*

74. *Ibid.*

75. J. Jeremias, "numphe," *Theological Dictionary of the New Testament*, Vol. IV, pp. 1104-05.

76. *Ibid.*, p. 1105, footnote 50.

77. *Ibid.*, p. 1106.

78. *Ibid.*, p. 1104.

79. See *Ibid.*, pp. 1104-06.

80. Robert Van Kampen, *The Sign* (Wheaton, IL: Crossway Books, 1992), p. 423 and chart at end of book.

81. *Ibid.*, p. 286.

82. *Ibid.*, pp. 304, 423, and chart at end of book.

83. *Ibid.*, pp. 331, 423, and chart at end of book.

84. *Ibid.*, p. 344 and chart at end of book.

85. *Ibid.*, pp. 344, 360, 369, 423, and chart at end of book.

86. *Ibid.*, pp. 370-377 and chart at end of book.

87. *Ibid.*, pp. 377-379.

88. *Ibid.*, pp. 378, 423.

CHAPTER NINE

THE RAPTURE AND THE COMING OF CHRIST WITH HIS HOLY ANGELS

A third inference for the Pretribulation Rapture of the church is that there are reasons for concluding that the Rapture will take place at a different time than the coming of Christ with His holy angels at the end of the age immediately after the Great Tribulation (i.e., the Second Coming). Thus, the Rapture and the coming of Christ with His angels will be two separate events.

THE EVIDENCE FROM 1 THESSALONIANS 5

We discussed the first reason for the above conclusion in the earlier chapter entitled "The End and Beginning of the Beginning Judgment Phase of the Future Day of the Lord." There we noted three things from 1 Thessalonians 5 indicating that the future broad Day of the Lord is a different subject from the Rapture of the church. We can therefore conclude two things: First, the broad Day of the Lord will not include the Rapture of the church. Second, since the broad Day will not include the Rapture but will include the coming of Christ with His angels immediately after the Great Tribulation, the Rapture must be a separate event from that coming and must take place at a different time than that coming.

The Midtribulation and Posttribulation Rapture views and the pre-wrath position conflict with this, because these views include the Rapture within the broad Day of the Lord. By contrast, the Pretribulation Rapture view agrees with the conclusions noted here.

THE REVERSE ORDER

The second reason for concluding that the Rapture of the church and the coming of Christ with His angels will be two separate events at different times is the fact that the Scriptures teach that the order of things at the Rapture will be the reverse of the order of things at the coming of Christ with His angels. As we noted in the previous chapter, John 14:2-3 and

1 Thessalonians 4:17 indicate that the Rapture will involve the removal of believers from the earth, but the unbelievers will be left on the earth to enter the next period of history. By contrast, several things in the Scriptures indicate that at the coming of Christ with His angels, all unbelievers will be removed from the earth in judgment, but the believers will be left on the earth to enter the Millennial Kingdom. The indications of this order will be examined now.

The Parable of the Wheat and the Tares. In Matthew 13:24-30 Jesus taught the following parable concerning the kingdom of heaven: A farmer sowed good seed in his field, but later his enemy sowed tares in the same field. After the wheat and tares began to grow together, the farmer's servants asked if he wanted them to root out the tares from among the wheat during the growing season. The farmer told them to let the wheat and tares grow together until the harvest, at which time the reapers would *first* gather together the tares and burn them, then gather the wheat into the barn.

In His interpretation of the parable (vv. 36-43), Jesus gave the following identifications: The farmer is the Son of man (Christ); the field is the world; the wheat are the children of the kingdom (believers who belong to God's kingdom); the enemy is Satan; the tares are the children of Satan (the unsaved); the harvest is the end of the world (lit., "the end of the age"); and the reapers are Christ's holy angels (vv. 37-39).

After giving these identifications, Jesus indicated that the order of things when He sends forth His holy angels at the end of the age will be the same as in the parable (vv. 40-43). "First" the tares will be gathered together and burned; then the wheat will be gathered into the barn (v. 30). According to Arndt and Gingrich, the meaning of the word translated "first" in verse 30 is as follows: "of time *first, in the first place, before, earlier, to begin with.*"[1] The tares will be taken away and destroyed first, and the wheat will be left to be gathered into the barn.

In line with this order, Jesus taught that when He sends forth His holy angels at the end of the age, they will gather out of His kingdom "all" unbelievers and cast them into a furnace of fire (vv. 41-42 [the word translated "out of" in v. 41 denotes "separation"[2]]). "Then" the righteous (the believers) will function in God's kingdom (v. 43). In light of the meaning of the word translated "first" in verse 30, we can conclude that the word translated "then" in verse 43 must introduce what "follows in time."[3]

On the basis of what has been seen, we can conclude that Jesus taught the following in the parable of the wheat and the tares: When Christ sends forth His holy angels at the end of the age, they will separate all unbelievers from association with His kingdom by removing them from the earth in judgment. After that has been accomplished, the believers will be left on the earth to function in His kingdom. In conjunction with this, we should note in Daniel 7:27 that Christ's future kingdom (7:13-14) will be "under the whole heaven" (on the earth) and will be given to the saints. Thus, the believers alive when Christ sends forth His holy angels will have to be left on the earth to function within His kingdom.

The Parable of the Dragnet. In Matthew 13:47-50 Jesus taught the following parable concerning the kingdom of heaven: After fishermen had cast their net into the sea and it was filled with fish, they drew it to shore and then separated the fish by gathering the good fish into vessels and casting the bad fish away.

In His interpretation of this parable, Jesus indicated the order of things when His holy angels come forth at the end of the age. The angels will "sever the wicked from among the righteous, And shall cast them into the furnace of fire" (vv. 49-50). Arndt and Gingrich said that the word translated "sever" has the general meaning of "separate, take away" and specifically means "take out" in verse 49.[4]

We should note three things from Jesus' interpretation. First, when the holy angels come forth at the end of the age, the wicked, not the just, will be taken out or removed. Second, when the wicked are taken out, they will be removed "from among" the just. These two things indicate that the just will be left when the wicked are removed. Third, when the wicked are taken out, they will be cast into a horrible place of torment. Thus, their taking out will result in judgment.

On the basis of what has been observed, we can conclude that through the parable of the dragnet Jesus taught that when His holy angels come forth, they will take out the unsaved from among the saved by removing them from the earth in judgment, and the saved will be left on the earth to enter Christ's kingdom.

Matthew 24:37-41. This passage draws a comparison between the days of Noah and Jesus' coming with His angels immediately after the Great Tribulation (see 24:21, 29-31). Twice in the comparison Jesus indicated that the order of things when He comes with His angels will be the same as the order of things in the days of Noah. First, in verse 37 He said, "But as the days of Noah were, so shall also the coming of the Son of man be." Second, He concluded verse 39 with the assertion, "so shall also the coming of the Son of man be."

Jesus' explanation of the comparison (vv. 38-41) indicates four ways in which the order of things at His coming will be the same as the order of things in the days of Noah.

First, in spite of the forewarnings of coming judgment that Noah gave in the days before the flood, the unsaved devoted their full attention to the normal activities of life until the day Noah entered the ark. As a result, they did not prepare for the coming judgment by getting saved. In the same manner, in spite of the Tribulation period's forewarning signs of Christ's coming with His angels in judgment (vv. 32-35), many of the unsaved of that period will devote their full attention to the normal activities of life until the day Christ comes. As a result, they will not prepare for the coming judgment by getting saved.

Second, since the unsaved in Noah's time did not know the precise day on which the judgment would begin, they did not know the specific time deadline by which they must be prepared. As a result, the beginning day of judgment came so suddenly that they had no time to prepare for it and were caught totally unprepared to escape God's judgment. In the same manner, since no one knows the precise day or hour of Christ's coming with His angels in judgment (v. 36), the unsaved of the Tribulation period will not know the specific time deadline by which they must be prepared. As a result, Christ will come so suddenly that there will be no time for the unsaved to prepare, and they will be caught totally unprepared to escape the judgment at that coming.

Third, just as when the flood occurred all the unsaved were taken away from the earth in judgment, so at Jesus' coming with His angels all the unsaved will be taken from the earth in judgment. In verse 39, after Jesus asserted that the unsaved of Noah's day "knew not until the flood came, and took them all away," He said, "so shall also the coming of the Son of man be."

Fourth, when the flood removed all the unsaved from the earth in judgment, the saved (Noah and his family) were left on the earth (through means of the ark) to enter the next age of world history. Likewise, when all the unsaved are removed from the earth in judgment in conjunction with Jesus' coming with His angels, the saved will be left on the earth to enter the next age of world history, the Millennium.

In verses 40-41 Jesus gave two specific examples of the order of things at His coming with His angels. The word "Then" at the beginning of verse 40 goes back to the end of verse 39, where Jesus talked about this future coming. It indicates that verses 40-41 give examples of what will happen when Jesus comes. One person will be taken from a field, but another will be left in the same field. One person will be taken from a mill, but another will be left at that mill.

Jesus gave these two examples of the order of things at His coming with His angels and indicated that the order of things at that coming will be the same as the order of things in the days of Noah. Since the order of things in the days of Noah involved the taking away of all the unsaved from the earth in judgment and leaving the saved on the earth to enter the next period of history, we can conclude that at Christ's coming the people who will be taken from the field and the mill are unsaved who will be taken from the earth in judgment. The people left in the field and at the mill are saved who will be left on the earth to enter the Millennium.

Thus, in Matthew 24 Jesus taught that at His coming with His angels, all the unsaved will be removed from the earth in judgment, and all the saved will be left on the earth to enter the Millennial Kingdom.

Jesus was not referring to the Rapture of the church in Matthew 24. When that event takes place, all the saved will be removed from the earth to meet Christ in the air, and all the unsaved will be left on the earth. Thus, the Rapture will occur in reverse of the order of things in the days of Noah and, therefore, the reverse of the order at Jesus' coming immediately after the Great Tribulation.

A Potential Problem. Several things may be potential problems for the understanding of the Matthew 24 passage just presented. First, the verb *paralambano*, used for taking away people from the field and mill at Christ's coming with His angels, is a different word from *airo*, used for taking away the unsaved in judgment by the flood.

Arndt and Gingrich taught that although in some passages the verb *airo* is used for lifting up and taking a person or thing along in a positive sense (Mt. 4:6; 11:29), in Matthew 24:39, where it is used for taking away the unsaved by the flood, it contains "no suggestion of lifting up" and has the negative sense of removal "by force, even by killing."[5] Arndt and Gingrich asserted that in Matthew 24:40-41, where *paralambano* refers to taking away people from the field and mill at Christ's coming, that verb means to "take (to oneself), take with or along."[6] It is the same verb used in a positive sense in John 14:3 for Jesus' taking up or receiving believers to Himself in the Rapture of the Church.

Since the verb *paralambano*, used for taking away people from the field and mill at Christ's coming, is a different verb from *airo*, used in a negative sense for taking away the unsaved in judgment by the flood, and since the verb *paralambano* is also used in a positive sense in John 14:3 for Jesus' taking up or receiving believers to Himself in the Rapture, are we required to conclude that in Matthew 24:40-41 Jesus was referring to the Rapture when He talked about taking away people from the field and mill when He comes with His angels?

Several things indicate that we are not required to draw that conclusion. First, the fact that the verb *paralambano* is used in a positive sense in John 14:3 does not mean that it is always used in a positive sense. We should note that this verb is used in a negative sense several times in the New Testament. For example, it was used for the Devil's taking Jesus up into Jerusalem on a high mountain to tempt Him (Mt. 4:5, 8); for an evil spirit's taking seven other evil spirits with him to dwell inside a man (Mt. 12:45); for soldiers' taking Jesus into the common hall to be mocked and physically abused by the whole band of soldiers (Mt. 27:27); and for Jesus' being taken to be crucified (Jn. 19:16).

Second, the fact that two different verbs are used in Matthew 24—one for taking away the unsaved in judgment by the flood and the other for taking people from the field and mill at Christ's coming—does not automatically mean that those verbs have two different senses or refer to two different kinds of events. The Scriptures sometimes use two different verbs to refer to the same event. For example, in 2 Kings 2 both the Hebrew words *alah* (v. 1) and *laqach* (vv. 3, 5) are used for the same event—the taking up of Elijah into heaven.

In addition, it is important to note that the verbs *airo* and *paralambano*, which are used in Matthew 24:39 and 40-41 for taking away the unsaved in judgment by the flood and for taking people from the field and mill at the Christ's coming, are used in John 19:15-16 to refer to the same event—the taking of Jesus for crucifixion. In the cry of the crowd, "Away with him, away with him, crucify him" (v. 15), the word translated "away" is the verb *airo*. Thus, the crowd literally shouted, "Take, take, crucify him." Verse 16 indicates that "they took" (*paralambano*) Jesus to crucify Him. Since these two verbs are used for the same negative event in John 19:15-16, we are not required to conclude that they are used for two different kinds of events in Matthew 24.

Third, we should note that Matthew 24:40-41 does not say that the people taken from the field and mill will be taken by Jesus. In His interpretation of the Matthew 13 parables, examined earlier, Jesus said that angels will take away the unsaved and cast them into a furnace of fire.

Fourth, there is a specific reason for the two different verbs in Matthew 24. When God judged the unsaved of Noah's time, He used an impersonal agency (flood waters) to administer that judgment. He did not use personal agents to take the unsaved away with them to their place of judgment. In light of that fact, the Scriptures used the verb *airo*, which did not involve the idea of a personal being or beings taking other persons along with them. (v. 39).

By contrast, in Jesus' teaching and interpretation of the Matthew 13 parables examined earlier, He indicated that at His coming at the end of the age He will send forth His holy angels to gather to themselves all the living unsaved so that they can take them with them to their place of judgment and administer judgment to them (Mt. 13:24-30, 37-42, 47-50). Because personal agents will be used to take away the unsaved to their place of judgment, the Scriptures used the verb *paralambano*, which involves the idea of a personal being or beings taking other persons with them (Mt. 24:40-41).

Another Potential Problem. In the context of Matthew 24:37-41, Jesus declared that when he comes immediately after the Great Tribulation, He "shall send his angels with a great sound of a trumpet, and they shall gather together his elect from the four winds, from one end of heaven to the other" (Mt. 24:31).

Must we conclude that this refers to the gathering of church saints in the Rapture to meet Christ in the air and that therefore, in light of this context, the taking of people from the field and mill is a reference to church saints being taken from the earth in the Rapture?

Several things indicate that there is good reason for concluding that the gathering of the elect in Matthew 24:31 refers, not to the Rapture, but to the gathering of the believing remnant of Israel alive on the earth at Jesus' coming after the Great Tribulation.

First, the term "elect" is not used exclusively for church saints in the Bible. Many passages teach that God made national Israel His elect or chosen people in contrast with all other nations. For example, in Deuteronomy 7:6 Moses said to the people of Israel, "For thou art an holy people unto the LORD thy God; the LORD thy God hath chosen thee to be a special people unto himself, above all people who are upon the face of the earth." In light of this and other similar statements in Deuteronomy, G. Quell wrote that Deuteronomy "established the concept of election in the sense of the designation of Israel as the people of God."[7] He further asserted that with regard to election, "the nations did not experience what Israel experienced."[8]

With reference to Israel's relationship to God, 1 Chronicles 16:13 states, "O ye seed of Israel, his servant, ye children of Jacob, his chosen ones." In Isaiah 45:4 God called the nation "Israel mine elect." G. Schrenk pointed out that in the New Testament (Rom. 11:28) Paul also referred to God's election of the whole nation of Israel.[9]

Second, the Bible also uses the concept of election in a second, more limited sense with regard to Israel. The elect are the faithful, believing Israelite remnant in contrast with the unbelieving sinners within the nation. In Isaiah 65:7-16 God drew a contrast between these two groups and their destinies. In verse 9 He called the believing remnant "mine Elect," and in verses 17-25 He indicated that in the future Millennium His elect remnant of the nation will be blessed greatly on the earth.[10]

Third, in Matthew 24:31 Jesus talked about His elect being gathered "from the four winds, from one end of heaven to the other." Arndt and Gingrich stated that in Matthew 24:31 this expression concerning the winds refers to "the four directions or cardinal points."[11] Thus, the elect will be gathered from all over the world at Christ's coming with His angels.

In light of this, three things should be noted from the Old Testament. First, because of Israel's persistent rebellion against God, He declared that He would scatter the Jews "into all the winds" (Ezek. 5:10, 12) or "toward all winds" (Ezek. 17:21). In Zechariah 2:6 God stated that He did scatter them abroad "as the four winds of the heavens." Concerning the expression "the four winds" in the Old Testament, J. Barton Payne wrote, "The 'four winds,' *ruhot*, describe the four quarters or four directions of the world (Jer. 49:36; Ezk. 37:9)."[12] Thus, in the Old Testament it had the same meaning as that noted above in Matthew 24:31. God did scatter the Jews all over the world.

Next, God also declared that in the future Israel would be gathered from the east, west, north, and south, "from the ends of the earth" (Isa. 43:5-7). We should note that in the context of this promise, God called Israel His "chosen" (vv. 10, 20).

Following is the final thing to note from the Old Testament. Just as Jesus indicated that the gathering of His elect from the four directions of the world will take place in conjunction with "a great trumpet" (literal translation of the Greek text of Mt. 24:31), so Isaiah 27:13 teaches that the scattered children of Israel will be gathered to their homeland in conjunction with the blowing of "a great trumpet" (literal translation of the Hebrew).

Franz Delitzsch stated that this teaching in Isaiah refers to "the still living *diaspora*" being "gathered together by the signal of God."[13] He also indicated that Assyria and Egypt, referred to in this passage, represent all the lands of exile.[14]

Gerhard Friedrich wrote that in that future eschatological day "a great horn shall be blown (Is. 27:13)" and the exiled will be brought back by that signal.[15] Again, he asserted that in conjunction with the blowing of the great trumpet of Isaiah 27:13, "There follows the gathering of Israel and the return of the dispersed to Zion."[16]

It is significant to note that Isaiah 27:13, which foretells this future regathering of Israel, is the only specific reference in the Old Testament to a "great" trumpet.[17]

Although Isaiah 11:11-12 does not refer to a great trumpet, it is parallel to Isaiah 27:13 because it refers to the same regathering of Israel.[18] In its context, this passage indicates that when the Messiah (a root of Jesse, vv. 1, 10) comes to rule and transform the world as an "ensign" (a banner), He will gather together the scattered remnant of His people Israel "from the four corners of the earth."

In light of the fact that Isaiah 27:13 and 11:11-12 refer to the same regathering of Israel, T. Francis Glasson wrote,

> In the O.T. and also in later Jewish writings two things are associated with the gathering of the dispersed: the trumpet and the ensign (or standard). The following prayer still appears in the Jewish Daily Prayer Book: Sound the *great trumpet* for our freedom; lift up the *ensign* to gather our exiles, and gather us from the four corners of the earth. Blessed art thou, O Lord, who gatherest the banished ones of thy people Israel. (Quoted from *Authorized Daily Prayer Book of the United Hebrew Congregations of the British Empire* [S. Singer], p. 48).[19]

In their New Year service, in which they pray almost identically this same prayer, Jews quote Isaiah 27:13 and 11:12.[20]

In *The Apocalypse of Abraham*, an ancient piece of Jewish literature written sometime between 200 B.C. and 200 A.D., the following statement was made: "Then will I blow the trumpet from the winds and send forth mine elect . . . he then summons my despised people out of all nations."[21] In this statement, "mine elect" refers to God's Messiah, who will gather together God's scattered people.[22]

Fourth, another reason for believing that Matthew 24:31 refers to the gathering of the believing remnant of Israel is the fact that the context of Matthew 24:31 is Jewish in nature. It refers to the destruction of Herod's Temple in Jerusalem (vv. 1-2), the abomination of desolation that will take place in the future Temple in Jerusalem in the middle of the 70th week (v. 15; cp. Dan. 9:27), the urgency of the inhabitants of Judea fleeing to the mountains when the abomination of desolation takes place (v. 16), and the sabbath day (v. 20).

Fifth, Matthew 25:31-32 refers to another gathering of people at Jesus' coming with His angels. This will involve Gentiles, not Jews (the words translated "nations" mean "Gentiles"[23]). The context makes it clear that all Gentiles (saved and unsaved) who are alive on the earth at the time will be gathered. Since this gathering will involve all Gentiles (saved and unsaved), and since the Bible never calls all Gentiles God's "elect," this gathering cannot be the gathering of the Lord's "elect" referred to in Matthew 24:31. It must be totally separate from that gathering, even though both gatherings will take place in conjunction with Jesus' coming with His angels.

In addition, since this gathering of all Gentiles is separate from the gathering of the Lord's "elect" in Matthew 24:31, and since it will include saved (or "elect") Gentiles, then the gathering of the Lord's "elect" in Matthew 24:31 cannot include even the saved (or "elect") Gentiles. If it were to include them, it would not be separate from the gathering of all Gentiles.

Since the gathering of the Lord's "elect" in Matthew 24:31 is separate from the gathering of all Gentiles in Matthew 25:32 and cannot include even the saved Gentiles, the Lord's "elect" who are gathered in Matthew 24:31 must be the believing remnant of Israel who will be alive at Jesus' coming with His angels. In light of this, Matthew 24:31 does not prompt the conclusion that taking people from the field and mill refers to church saints being taken from the earth in the Rapture. When the Rapture takes place, *all* church saints—Jews and Gentiles—will be taken from the earth. It will not be limited just to the saved of Israel.

Luke 17:26-37. This passage presents Luke's account of the same teaching of Jesus recorded in Matthew 24:37-41. In Luke, Jesus indicated that just as God's judgment came upon the unsaved of Noah's time on the day Noah entered the ark, and just as it came upon the unsaved of Lot's time on the day Lot went out of Sodom, so God's judgment will come upon the unsaved on the earth "in the day when the Son of man is revealed" (v. 30).

We should note that the text does not say God's judgment will come upon the unsaved on the day the church is raptured. In addition, Noah and Lot were not raptured from the earth on the day judgment came upon the unsaved. Instead, they remained on the earth while the unsaved were taken away through judgment, and they continued on the earth into the next period of history.

Jesus gave examples of the order of things on the day He will be revealed. At that time one person will be taken from a bed, but another will be left in the same bed. One person will be taken from a place of grinding, but another will be left at that place. One person will be taken from a field, but another will be left in that same field (vv. 34-36).

In verse 37 Luke recorded something Matthew omitted. After Jesus gave the examples of people being taken and left, His disciples asked, "Where, Lord?" It was not necessary for the disciples to ask for the location of the people who will be left, for obviously they will be left in the same bed, place of grinding, and field where they were before the other people were taken away. We must conclude that the disciples were asking where those who are to be removed will be taken when Jesus comes.

In light of the disciples' question, Jesus' answer is very significant because it identifies those who will be taken when He comes. He answered, "Wherever the body is, there will the eagles be gathered together" (v. 37). Arndt and Gingrich indicated that the word translated "eagles" refers to vultures[24], which eat dead, decaying flesh. In line with this, Arndt and Gingrich stated that in Luke 17:37 the verb translated "will be gathered together" refers to the gathering "of birds of prey around a dead body."[25]

Jesus' answer indicates that those people who will be removed from the bed, place of grinding, and field when He comes will be taken into the realm of death. Death will be God's judgment upon them, and their dead bodies will be eaten by vultures (cp. Rev. 19:17-18, 21). The fact that the bodies of those taken away will be eaten by vultures indicates that those taken away in Luke 17 are not church saints taken away in the Rapture. When the Rapture takes place, the bodies of church saints will not be eaten by vultures but will be changed into immortal resurrection type bodies and transported from the earth to meet Jesus in the air (1 Cor. 15:51-53; 1 Th. 4:13-17). Thus, in Luke 17 those taken away from the earth when Jesus comes will be the unsaved, removed in judgment. Those left on the earth will be the saved.

We can conclude that in Luke 17, just as in Matthew 24, Jesus taught that at His coming with His angels immediately after the Great Tribulation the order of things will be as follows: All the living unsaved will be taken from the earth in judgment, and all the living saved will be left on the earth to enter the millennial age.

Matthew 25:31-46. In this passage Jesus declared that when He comes in His glory with His angels, all living Gentiles (saved and unsaved) will be gathered before Him and separated into two groups—the sheep (the saved) and the goats (the unsaved) [vv. 31-33]. The saved will be granted entrance into the Millennial Kingdom on the earth (vv. 34-40), and the unsaved will be taken away from the earth to a place of fiery judgment (vv. 41-46; cp. Mt. 13:41-43, 49-50).

Once again Jesus taught that at His coming with His angels the unsaved will be taken from the earth in judgment, and the saved will be left on the earth to enter the Millennium.

Conclusions. The Matthew 13; 24; 25; and Luke 17 passages examined in this chapter consistently teach the same order of things for the coming of Christ with His angels immediately after the Great Tribulation. All the living unsaved will be taken from the earth in judgment, and all the living saved will be left on the earth to enter the next period of history. By contrast, at the Rapture of the church all the saved will be taken from the earth to meet Jesus in the air, and all the unsaved will be left on the earth to enter the next period of history. Thus, the order of things at the Rapture will be the reverse of the order of things at Christ's coming immediately after the Great Tribulation.

This reverse order prompts the following conclusions: The Rapture of the church and the coming of Christ with His angels must be two separate events, and they must take place at two different times.

How do these conclusions compare with those of the various Rapture views? They conflict with those of the Posttribulation Rapture view and the pre-wrath position, which conclude that the Rapture of the church will take place at the same time as the coming of Christ immediately after the Great Tribulation and that, therefore, the Rapture will be part of that coming. In addition, the pre-wrath position claims that Matthew 13; 24; and Luke 17 teach that when Christ comes immediately after the Great Tribulation, all the saved will be taken from the earth in the Rapture, and all the living unsaved will be left on the earth to enter the Day of the Lord to suffer God's wrath. Thus, it advocates an order that conflicts with that observed in this chapter.

By contrast, the conclusions prompted by the reverse order studied in this chapter agree with those of the Pretribulation and Midtribulation Rapture views, because both of these views conclude that the Rapture and the coming of Christ with His angels will take place at totally different times and therefore the Rapture will be a separate event from that coming.

In light of the problems noted elsewhere in this book that militate against the Midtribulation Rapture view, we can conclude that the scriptural teaching that the order of things at the Rapture of the church will be the reverse of the order at the coming of Christ with His angels leads to an inference in favor of the Pretribulation Rapture view.

THE IMPOSSIBILITY OF PROPHETIC FULFILLMENT

The third reason for concluding that the Rapture of the church and the coming of Christ with His angels will be two separate events at different times is as follows: If the Rapture and the coming of Christ with His angels were both to take place at the same time, immediately after the 70th week (which would be immediately after the Great Tribulation), certain biblical prophecies could not be fulfilled. This reason is a problem specifically for the Posttribulation Rapture view.

Background. To understand the problem, we must observe several background matters. First, as noted above, the Posttribulation Rapture view teaches that the Rapture of the church will take place when Christ comes with His angels immediately after the Great Tribulation or 70th week, and therefore the Rapture of the church will be part of that coming.

Second, the Bible teaches that when the Rapture takes place, all church saints, including all the saved alive on the earth at that time, will take part in it (1 Th. 4:17) and will receive immortal resurrection type bodies (1 Cor. 15:51-53) that will not participate in marriage (Mk. 12:25) and will not die (Lk. 20:36).

Third, when the Rapture takes place, every believer alive on the earth will be made sinlessly perfect like Christ (1 Jn. 3:2).

Fourth, since, as studied earlier in this chapter, all the living unsaved will be taken from the earth in judgment when Christ comes with His angels, no unsaved will be on the earth to enter the Millennial Kingdom when it is established after Christ comes.

Fifth, the Scriptures prophesy the birth of children during the Millennial Kingdom (Jer. 30:19-20; Ezek. 47:22), indicating that there will be marriage in that age of history.

Sixth, the Scriptures prophesy that Christ will put to death the wicked during His millennial reign (Isa. 11:4). G. Herbert Livingston wrote that the word translated "wicked" indicates people who are violators "of the social rights of others, . . . violent, oppressive, greedy, engaged in plotting against and trapping poor people, . . . quite willing to murder to gain their ends," threats to the community, "dishonest in business and in the courtroom" and haters of the Lord.[26] This prophecy indicates that there will be death for some people during the Millennium.

Seventh, the Scriptures prophesy that a large host of earthly unsaved rebels will follow Satan in a massive revolt against the rule of Christ and the saints after the end of the Millennium (Rev. 20:7-9).

The Problem for the Posttribulation-Premillennial Rapture View. Posttribulationists who are premillennial believe that after the church is raptured to meet Christ in the air after the 70th week of Daniel 9, it will return immediately to the earth with Him as He continues His descent from heaven and will remain with Him on the earth throughout the Millennium. In light of the second and third points noted immediately above, if this posttribulation belief were correct, all the saved would enter the Millennium in a sinlessly perfect state with immortal resurrection type bodies that will not participate in marriage or die.

As noted in the fourth point above, the Bible teaches that all the living unsaved will be taken from the earth in judgment when Christ comes with His angels, and therefore no unsaved will be on the earth to enter the Millennial Kingdom. In light of this biblical teaching, if the Rapture of the church were to take place when Christ comes after the 70th week, as the Posttribulation-Premillennial Rapture view claims, the only people who would enter the Millennial Kingdom would be the saved, all of whom would be sinlessly perfect and would have immortal resurrection type bodies.

This would mean that throughout the Millennium there would be no sin, marriage, birth, death, or unsaved rebels. If this were true, it would be impossible for the biblical prophecies noted in the fifth through seventh points above to be fulfilled, such as the birth of children (which implies marriage), the putting to death of the wicked (which implies the presence of unsaved wicked, sin, and death), and a large host of earthly, unsaved rebels following Satan in a massive revolt against the rule of Christ and the saints after the end of the Millennium. If all those who enter the Millennium are sinlessly perfect, and if there are no births during the Millennium, where would the wicked of the Millennium come from, and where would the large host of earthly unsaved rebels who follow Satan after the Millennium come from?

Any premillennial posttribulationists, who believe that when Christ comes after the 70th week He will rapture the church to meet Him in the air, take it to heaven, leave it there, and return to the earth by Himself for the Millennium, force the conclusion that all the saved will be taken from the earth at Christ's coming, and therefore no saved will enter the earthly Millennial Kingdom. This is contrary to the biblical teaching that when Christ comes with His angels, all the living saved will be left on the earth to enter the Millennial Kingdom.

In addition, in light of the biblical teaching that no unsaved will be on the earth to enter the Millennial Kingdom when it is established, if a view that has no saved entering that kingdom were correct, then no people (unsaved or saved) would be on the earth for Christ to rule over during the Millennium. This again would make it impossible to fulfill the prophecies noted above.

The Problem for the Other Posttribulation Rapture View. Those posttribulationists who are either amillennial or postmillennial, instead of premillennial, believe that the church will be raptured from the earth on the very last day of this earth's history, when Christ comes to put an end to this present earth. According to this view, all the saved will be taken permanently from the earth, and the earth will be destroyed on the same day that Christ comes. Thus, there will be no Millennial Kingdom on this earth after the day of Christ's coming.

This view is contrary to the biblical teaching that when Christ comes with His angels, all the living saved will be left on the earth to enter the Millennial Kingdom. Since it rejects the idea of a Millennial Kingdom on the earth after Christ comes, this view would make it impossible to fulfill the prophecies noted above.

Conclusions. The issue of the fulfillment of the biblical prophecies noted above, which is a problem for the Posttribulation Rapture view, is not a problem for the Pretribulation and Midtribulation Rapture views, and seemingly is not a problem for the pre-wrath position, since the latter views teach that the Rapture of the church will take place before the end of the 70th week. However, in light of the other problems noted elsewhere in this book, which militate against the Midtribulation Rapture View and the pre-wrath position, it can be concluded that the issue of the fulfillment of the biblical prophecies noted above leads to an inference in favor of the Pretribulation Rapture view.

THE HARMONY OF THE PRETRIBULATION RAPTURE VIEW

The Pretribulation Rapture view harmonizes with the conclusions, the order of things, and the fulfillment of prophecies examined in this chapter. It thereby avoids the problems that the Posttribulation Rapture view and the pre-wrath position have in conjunction with these examined matters.

Because the Pretribulation Rapture view teaches that the church will be raptured from the earth *before* the seven-year 70th week of Daniel 9 begins and that Christ will come with His angels *after* the 70th week ends, it agrees with the following conclusions noted earlier: The Rapture of the church and the coming of Christ with His angels must be two separate events, and they must take place at two different times.

In addition, because the Pretribulation Rapture view teaches that the church will be raptured from the earth more than seven years before Christ's coming with His angels, it does not require that coming of Christ to have the same order of things as the Rapture of the church. Instead, it teaches that the order of things at Christ's coming with His angels will be the reverse of the order at the Rapture. Thus, the Pretribulation Rapture view agrees with the order of things observed in this chapter's examination of Matthew 13; 24; 25; and Luke 17.

Finally, the Pretribulation Rapture view teaches that the prophecies noted earlier—concerning sin, marriage, birth, death, and unsaved rebels in relationship to the Millennium—will be fulfilled. The Pretribulation Rapture view says that after the church has been raptured from the earth before the 70th week (Tribulation period) begins, the following scenario of events will transpire: During the Tribulation many people will be saved (Rev. 7). Many of those Tribulation saints will be martyred (Rev. 6:9-11; 13:7; 20:4), but a good number of them will survive the Tribulation alive.

At Christ's coming with His angels (after the Tribulation), all the living unsaved will be taken from the earth in judgment, and all the Tribulation saints who are still alive will be left on the earth to enter the Millennial Kingdom (Mt. 13:24-30, 36-43, 47-50; 24:37-41; 25:31-46; Lk. 17:26-37).

Because these living Tribulation saints never experienced death, they will enter the kingdom with mortal bodies and their sin natures. As a result, they will be able to participate in marriage and give birth to children during the Millennium (Jer. 30:19-20; Ezek. 47:22), and those children will be born in an unsaved state with sin natures. Thus, although no unsaved will enter the Millennial Kingdom at its beginning, after a while, through birth, unsaved people will be present on the earth again.

Many of those born during the Millennium will never get saved. Some of them will become so incorrigibly wicked that Christ will put them to death during His reign (Isa. 11:4). Many will be greatly annoyed and irritated by the absolute, righteous rule of Christ and the saints, which will be administered worldwide. They will hope for someone supernatural to appear and lead them in a revolt to overthrow this rule. As a result, these unsaved rebels will flock to Satan when he appears on the earth after the Millennium to lead such a revolt (Rev. 20:7-9).

ENDNOTES

1. William F. Arndt and F. Wilbur Gingrich, *A Greek-English Lexicon of the New Testament*, 4th rev. ed. (Chicago: The University of Chicago Press, 1957), p. 733.

2. *Ibid.*, p. 233.

3. *Ibid.*, p. 831.

4. *Ibid.*, p. 126.

5. *Ibid.*, p. 24.

6. *Ibid.*, pp. 624-25.

7. G. Quell, "eklegomai," *Theological Dictionary of the New Testament*, Vol. IV, ed. by Gerhard Kittel, trans. and ed. by Geoffrey W. Bromiley (Grand Rapids: Wm. B. Eerdmans Publishing Company, 1967), p. 163.

8. *Ibid.*, p. 164.

9. G. Schrenk, "ekloge," *Theological Dictionary of the New Testament*, Vol. IV, ed. by Gerhard Kittel, trans. and ed. by Geoffrey W. Bromiley (Grand Rapids: Wm. B. Eerdmans Publishing Company, 1967), p. 179.

10. *Ibid.*, p. 183.

11. William F. Arndt and F. Wilbur Gingrich, *A Greek-English Lexicon of the New Testament*, p. 64.

12. J. Barton Payne, "riah," *Theological Wordbook of the Old Testament*, Vol. II, ed. by R. Laird Harris, Gleason L. Archer, Jr., and Bruce K. Waltke (Chicago: Moody Press, 1980), p. 836.

13. Franz Delitzsch, *Biblical Commentary on the Prophecies of Isaiah*, trans. by James Martin (Grand Rapids: Wm. B. Eerdmans Publishing Company, 1960), Vol. I, p. 461.

14. *Ibid.*

15. Gerhard Friedrich, "salpigx," *Theological Dictionary of the New Testament*, Vol. VII, ed. by Gerhard Friedrich, trans. and ed. by Geoffrey W. Bromiley (Grand Rapids: Wm. B. Eerdmans Publishing Company, 1971), p. 84.

16. *Ibid.*, p. 80.

17. T. Francis Glasson, *The Second Advent* (London: The Epworth Press, 1963), p. 199.

18. *Ibid.* and Delitzsch, *Biblical Commentary on the Prophecies of Isaiah*, Vol. I, p. 461.

19. Glasson, *The Second Advent*, pp. 198-99.

20. *Ibid.*, p. 199.

21. *Apocalypse of Abraham*, 31:1 f., quoted by Gerhard Friedrich, "salpigx," *Theological Dictionary of the New Testament*, Vol. VII, p. 84.

22. *The Catholic Encyclopedia*, Vol. I (New York: The Encyclopedia Press, Inc., 1907), p. 604.

23. William F. Arndt and F. Wilbur Gingrich, *A Greek-English Lexicon of the New Testament*, p. 217.

24. *Ibid.*, p. 19.

25. *Ibid.*, p. 301.

26. G. Herbert Livingston, "rasha," *Theological Wordbook of the Old Testament*, Vol. II, ed. by R. Laird Harris, Gleason L. Archer, Jr., and Bruce K. Waltke (Chicago: Moody Press, 1980), pp. 863-64.

CHAPTER TEN

THE RELATIONSHIP OF CHURCH SAINTS TO THE WRATH OF GOD

 fourth inference for the Pretribulation Rapture of the church is the biblical teaching concerning the relationship of church saints to the wrath of God. Several passages present that teaching.

1 THESSALONIANS 1:10

In 1 Thessalonians 1:10 Paul declared that the Thessalonian Christians had turned to God "to wait for his Son from heaven, whom he raised from the dead, even Jesus, who delivered us from the wrath to come." Several things should be noted concerning this.

The Thessalonians' Expectation. The infinitive (*anamenein*), which is translated "to wait for," consists of two parts. The first part (*ana*) means "up" in this word.[1] The second part (*meno*) means "wait for, await" and is used of people who *"wait for* someone who is arriving."[2] Thus, the word literally refers to the activity of people who "wait up for" someone who is arriving. They do not go to bed at their normal time because they are expecting someone to arrive at any moment. Their understanding is that no time period must elapse before that person can come.

W. E. Vine asserted that the word Paul used carries "the suggestion of waiting with patience and confident expectancy,"[3] referring to the activity of people who wait patiently for others to arrive because they are confident that they could come at any moment.

Paul used the present tense form of the infinitive. A. T. Robertson indicated that the present tense of this specific infinitive gives it the sense of "to keep on waiting for."[4] It refers to the continuous action of waiting for someone.

The combination of the meaning and present tense of the infinitive translated "to wait for" in 1 Thessalonians 1:10 prompts us to conclude that Paul was teaching that the Thessalonian Christians were continuously and patiently expecting or waiting up for Christ to return from heaven, because they were confident that He could come at any moment.

In line with this conclusion, D. Edmond Hiebert wrote,

> The infinitive rendered "to wait for" (*ananenein*) means "to await, expect, wait up for" and pictures them as people who are eagerly and expectantly looking forward to the coming of one whose arrival is anticipated at any time; the present tense gives this as their continuing attitude. Clearly the Thessalonians held the hope of the imminent return of Christ.[5]

I. Howard Marshall stated, "The hope (1:3) of the coming of Jesus was an integral part of the Thessalonians' religion; it was something that they anticipated as a real possibility in their own lifetimes (4:15, 17; 5:4). This hoped-for imminence of the *parousia* made it a vital part of their Christian belief."[6]

This continuous waiting up for the Lord to come prompts the question, From whom or what did the Thessalonian believers derive this concept of the imminent return of Christ? In light of the fact that Paul had been their teacher when he was with them prior to writing 1 Thessalonians (Acts 17; 1 Th. 2:13; 2 Th. 2:5), it seems apparent that he was the one who taught them to expect the Lord to return at any moment.

Further, it should be noted that Paul did not tell the Thessalonians that they were wrong to have this expectancy. Instead, he referred to their waiting up for the Lord in an approving manner. John Lillie concurred in the following entry:

> Observe that there was nothing in this attitude of the model church of Macedonia, that Paul thought it necessary to reprove or correct. So far from that, he mentions it as the legitimate and immediate fruit of conversion—as something that the brethren were everywhere talking of with joy, and to the honour of Thessalonica . . . Wherever the grace of God then appeared, it taught men, as one grand motive to all sober, and righteous, and godly living, to "look for that blessed hope, and the glorious appearing of our great God and Saviour Jesus Christ"; yea, to look for it as near—as a thing to be loved, and hastened, and waited for at all seasons, whether of sorrow or of joy.[7]

D. Edmond Hiebert made this significant observation:

> If they had been taught that the Great Tribulation, in whole or in part, must first run its course, it is difficult to see how they could be described as expectantly awaiting Christ's return. Then they should rather have been described as bracing themselves for the Great Tribulation and the painful events connected with it.[8]

The Identification of the Awaited Person. Paul clearly identified the person for whom the Thessalonians were continuously waiting to come from heaven as the Lord Jesus, whom God had already raised from the dead. It was fitting that Paul referred to Him as Jesus, because that name means "Savior" (Mt. 1:21), and in 1 Thessalonians 1:10 Paul indicated that He is the one who delivers or saves church saints from wrath.[9]

In addition, it is significant that Paul identified Him as the one whom God had raised from the dead, because in this context Paul declared that Jesus delivers church saints from future wrath. If Jesus were still dead, He would not be able to deliver them from future wrath. Thus, Paul's "mention of the resurrection here is probably motivated by the desire to give a basis for the future hope" of deliverance from wrath.[10]

The Delivering Ministry of Christ. Paul asserted that Christ delivers church saints from wrath. His use of the pronoun "us" indicates that Christ delivers the group to which Paul belonged. Since Paul was an apostle and member of the church, he belonged to the group of church saints.

The word translated "delivered" is a present tense participle derived from the verb *rhuomai*. Hermann Cremer quoted Winer's statement that this verb means "to draw or snatch out to oneself, to rescue, to save, to preserve."[11] Marvin R. Vincent stated that the verb literally means "to draw to one's self" and "almost invariably" refers to deliverance from "some evil or danger or enemy."[12]

D. Edmond Hiebert indicated that in addition to its meaning, this verb "places the emphasis upon the greatness of the peril from which deliverance is given by a mighty act of power."[13] Concerning such an act of power, George Milligan wrote that in the Bible "the thought of deliverance by *power*" is "apparently always associated with" the verb *rhuomai*.[14]

It would appear, then, that Paul was referring to Christ's delivering church saints from future wrath through a mighty act of power—the act of drawing or snatching them out to Himself.

The preposition translated "from" in the expression "delivered us from" is the word *ek*. According to Arndt and Gingrich, *ek* is used "to denote separation" and, more specifically, "to introduce the place fr. which the separation takes place."[15] They indicate that, in that sense, it is used especially with "verbs of motion," such as *rhuomai*, the verb Paul used in participial form for Christ's ministry of delivering church saints from future wrath.[16] Thus, Paul indicated that Christ delivers church saints from future wrath by separating them from it, not by sheltering or protecting them from the wrath while they are in its midst.

In what sense will Christ separate church saints from the future wrath? Will it be by removing them from the wrath after they have been in it for a period of time, or will it be by preventing them from ever entering the future wrath? Several things indicate that it is the latter sense of separation.

First, the present tense of the participle translated "delivered" indicates that the church saints' deliverance or separation from the future wrath was already a present reality when Paul wrote 1 Thessalonians 1:10.[17] In Romans 5:9-10, Paul clearly taught that Jesus had already obtained deliverance from wrath for them through His death. Gustav Stahlin declared, "It is certainly an inalienable part of the New Testament message that deliverance from the wrath to come was achieved in the death of Christ."[18]. Again he wrote, "Why is deliverance from wrath bound up with Jesus? Because we are justified by His blood, reconciled by His death (R. 5:9f.)" and therefore "are no longer enemies (R. 5:10)."[19]

God's resurrection of Jesus from the dead guaranteed that the already obtained deliverance of church saints from future wrath would never cease to be a present reality. It meant that Jesus would always be available to execute that deliverance through a mighty act of power—drawing or snatching them out to Himself before the future wrath comes. As noted earlier, the fact that God had already resurrected Jesus after His death was the basis for their hope or assurance of deliverance from wrath.

In line with this, Gustav Stahlin stated that the apostolic message "relates deliverance from God's wrath inseparably to Jesus. Jesus is the One who already saves, 1 Th. 1:10. Jesus it is who will then deliver us from the wrath to come, R. 5:9. Only through Him can we have assurance that we are not destined for wrath, 1 Th. 5:9f."[20] Stahlin went on to indicate that through Jesus church saints are already saved, because Jesus is already the deliverer.[21]

The fact that the church saints' deliverance or separation from the future wrath is already a present reality before the future wrath begins, and the fact that God's resurrection of Jesus from the dead guaranteed that the already obtained deliverance will never cease to be a present reality prompt us to conclude that Christ will separate the church saints from the future wrath by preventing them from ever entering that wrath. If they were to enter the future wrath, there would be a genuine sense in which their deliverance from it would not be an already obtained deliverance or present reality.

The second thing indicating that Christ will separate the church saints from the future wrath by preventing them from ever entering it is Paul's use of the preposition *ek* translated "from" in the expression "delivered us from the wrath to come." Frederic Henry Chase concluded that in 1 Thessalonians 1:10, where special reference is made to the Thessalonians' waiting up for Christ's return, "*ek* may most naturally be taken to point to the completeness of the deliverance. 'He brings us clean out of the reach of future judgment.' "[22]

George Milligan came to the same conclusion. He indicated that with "the thought of deliverance by *power*" associated with the verb translated "delivered" in 1 Thessalonians 1:10, the *ek*, which follows immediately after that verb, emphasizes the completeness of the deliverance. He therefore suggested that the force of Paul's statement concerning Jesus' delivering ministry is that "He brings us altogether out of the reach of future judgment."[23]

In the same vein, Thomas L. Constable wrote,

> The word translated "from" means that Christians are kept from, not taken
> out of it. The same verb (rescues) and preposition (from) are used in 2
> Corinthians 1:10 where Paul said he was delivered from a deadly peril.
> Obviously this does not mean Paul died and was resurrected. Christians will
> be kept away from God's wrath, not kept safe through it.[24]

The third indication that Christ will separate church saints from the
future wrath by preventing them from ever entering it is Paul's declaration
in 1 Thessalonians 5:9 that God has not appointed them to wrath. The
context of Paul's declaration indicates that he was referring to the future
Day of the Lord wrath (5:2-3). When discussing the meaning of the preposition *ek* in 1 Thessalonians 1:10, W. E. Vine emphasized the significance
of Paul's declaration in 1 Thessalonians 5:9 by stating,

> The question whether *ek* here means "out of the midst of" or "away from,"
> is to be determined by some statement of Scripture where the subject is
> specifically mentioned; this is provided, e.g., in 5:9, the context of which
> makes clear that believers are to be delivered from (not "out of") the Divine
> wrath to be executed on the nations at the end of the present age.[25]

The fact that God has not appointed church saints to the Day of the Lord
wrath indicates that they will never enter that wrath. If they were to enter
it, they would be appointed to at least some of it.

The Wrath to Come. Paul described the wrath from which Christ delivers
church saints in the following literal manner: "The wrath the coming." The
fact that he used the definite article "the" twice and the descriptive term
"coming" prompts the conclusion that he was referring to a specific future
time of God's wrath, unique or distinct in contrast with all past expressions
of His wrath. Many scholars, in agreement with this conclusion, are convinced that Paul's designation "the wrath to come" refers to God's future
or eschatological wrath. For example, George Milligan asserted that the
repeated article "the" draws attention to "coming" as the "essential feature" of this wrath.[26] He further stated that "the wrath to come" is "used
absolutely of the Divine wrath, and in accordance with the context" (wait
for his Son from heaven) "and the general N.T. usage, having here the
definite eschatological reference for which the language of the prophetic
writings has prepared us, cf. e.g. Isa. 2:10-12; Zeph. 3:8ff."[27] These Isaiah
and Zephaniah passages describe future Day of the Lord wrath from God.

Concerning the wrath in 1 Thessalonians 1:10, D. Edmond Hiebert
wrote, "Its eschatological character is stressed by the added definition as
the wrath which is 'to come.' "[28]

James Everett Frame declared that Paul referred to "the eschatological
judgment," as is indicated by "the day of wrath" of Romans 2:5.[29]

A. T. Robertson stated, "It is eschatological language, this coming wrath of God for sin."[30]

Gustav Stahlin observed that wrath (*orge*) is eschatological or future when combined with the word for "coming" (*erchomai*), and that, since Paul combined these terms in the expression "the wrath to come" in 1 Thessalonians 1:10, he was referring to eschatological wrath.[31] Therefore, the following statement by Stahlin is most significant: "There are two points in the future where eschatological *orge* has a place, first, in the tribulation before the end, then in the final judgment itself."[32] He further stated that the term *orge* is one of several technical terms "for the eschatological tribulation."[33]

In light of what has been seen, it appears that Paul meant that the wrath to come, from which Christ delivers the church saints, is the future eschatological wrath that begins with the future Day of the Lord or Tribulation. Earlier chapters in this study demonstrated that a uniquely intense outpouring of God's wrath will start with the broad Day of the Lord.

Conclusion. This examination of 1 Thessalonians 1:10 has produced several observations. First, the Thessalonian church saints were continuously waiting up for Christ to come from heaven, because they were confident that He could come at any moment.

Second, Christ delivers church saints from the future wrath of God.

Third, Christ's deliverance of church saints from that wrath of God is an already obtained deliverance, and it will never cease to be a present reality.

Fourth, Christ will execute that already obtained deliverance by separating church saints from the future wrath of God in the sense of preventing them from ever entering it.

Fifth, Christ will separate or prevent church saints from entering the future wrath of God through a mighty act of power—drawing or snatching them out to Himself before the wrath begins.

Sixth, the wrath to come is the future eschatological wrath of God that will begin with the broad Day of the Lord or Tribulation.

The last five of these observations, when taken together, prompt the conclusion that Christ will draw or snatch out church saints to Himself before God's wrath of the broad Day of the Lord or Tribulation begins, thereby preventing them from entering that period of wrath.

The fact that Paul introduced the subject of Christ's deliverance of church saints from the wrath to come in conjunction with his reference to the Thessalonians' continuous waiting up for Christ to come from heaven strongly implies that Christ's drawing or snatching out the church saints to Himself will take place before the Tribulation begins and in conjunction with a coming of Christ from heaven. This concept corresponds to that found in John 14:2-3 and 1 Thessalonians 4:13-18, which, as noted earlier, refer to the future event of Christ's drawing or snatching out church saints from the earth to Himself when He comes from heaven to rapture the church. Thus, Paul's declaration in 1 Thessalonians 1:10 is a strong inference for the Pretribulation Rapture view.

In light of what has been seen, the following statement by Thomas L. Constable concerning 1 Thessalonians 1:10 is significant:

> Paul, the Thessalonian believers, and Christians today will escape all aspects of God's wrath, general and specific, including the Tribulation period. The clear implication of this verse is that Paul hoped in the Lord's imminent return. Otherwise Paul would have told his readers to prepare for the Tribulation.[34]

1 THESSALONIANS 4:13-18

First Thessalonians 4:13-18 is the most extensive New Testament passage dealing with the Rapture of the church. Two things from this passage should be noted in association with the issue of the church saints' relationship to the future wrath of God.

The Sorrow of the Thessalonian Saints. In verse 13 Paul wrote, "But I would not have you to be ignorant, brethren, concerning them who are asleep, that ye sorrow not, even as others who have no hope." The word translated "sorrow" means "be sad, be distressed, grieve."[35] Paul's statement indicates that the Thessalonian believers were distressed over the fact that some of their fellow saints had died.

We should note two things concerning this distress and Paul's response to it. First, if these church saints had been taught that the church must go through all or any part of the broad Day of the Lord or Tribulation, with its intense outpouring of God's wrath, "the logical reaction for them would have been to rejoice that these loved ones had escaped that great period of suffering" through death (cp. Job 3:11-26; Eccl. 4:1-2; 2 Cor. 5:8; Phil. 1:23).[36] There is, however, no indication that they found any reason to rejoice over the deaths of their fellow saints. This at least implies that they had not been taught that the church must go through all or any part of the Tribulation.

Second, the only means Paul used to relieve their distress over the deaths of their fellow saints was the truth of the future Rapture of the church. If these distressed saints had been taught that the church must go through all or any part of the Tribulation, why didn't Paul comfort them further with the additional fact that through their deaths, their fellow saints had escaped that future time of God's wrath?

The Catching Up of the Church Saints. In verses 16 and 17 Paul taught that when Christ comes from heaven to rapture the church, the dead church saints will be resurrected and then caught up together with the living church saints to meet Christ in the air.

Three things should be noted concerning the verb translated "shall be caught up." First, the verb means to "*snatch* or *take away*."[37] In this instance, Paul used it for Christ's snatching up or taking away of church saints from the earth to Himself in the air (v. 17). Second, sometimes it was used "of rescue from a threatening danger" (for example, Jude 23).[38] Third, whenever it was used for divine activity, it was "always expressing the mighty operation of God."[39] On this occasion Paul used it for Christ's mighty act of catching up all church saints from the earth to the air.

In all three of these details, this verb is basically parallel with the verb form translated "delivered" in 1 Thessalonians 1:10. As we noted earlier, that verb form means "to draw or snatch out to oneself"; it normally referred to deliverance from some evil, danger, or enemy and indicated deliverance by a mighty act of power.

Conclusion. The threefold parallelism just observed, together with the two things noted in conjunction with the sorrow of the Thessalonian saints, prompts the conclusion that 1 Thessalonians 4:13-18 and 1:10 refer to the same future event—Christ's coming from heaven to snatch out the church saints from the earth to Himself, thereby preventing them from entering the threatening danger of the Tribulation with its intense outpouring of God's wrath. Thus, both passages refer to the Rapture of the church before God's wrath of the Tribulation begins. Therefore, 1 Thessalonians 4:13-18 indicates that church saints will have no relationship to this future wrath of God.

1 THESSALONIANS 5:9

In 1 Thessalonians 5:9 Paul declared, "For God hath not appointed us to wrath but to obtain salvation by our Lord Jesus Christ." To understand Paul's declaration, we must examine the background and context (5:1-11) of this passage.

The Background

The background of 1 Thessalonians 5:9 consists of two things. First, as noted in an earlier chapter, the major subject of 1 Thessalonians 5:1-11 is the broad Day of the Lord, a significant future span of time that will include a major turning point of history (the destruction of the rule of Satan and rebellious mankind over the world system and the restoration of God's theocratic kingdom rule over the world system) and has been determined by God for the accomplishment of His purpose for history.

Second, as demonstrated in another earlier chapter, the broad Day of the Lord will have a twofold nature and thus will have two phases. The first phase, during the 70th week of Daniel 9, will be characterized by darkness and a tremendous outpouring of divine wrath on the world. The second phase, during the Millennium, will be characterized by light, an outpouring of divine blessing, and the administration of God's rule over the whole world.

The Context

In the context of 1 Thessalonians 5:9, Paul drew a sharp contrast between two distinct groups of people—church saints and the unsaved. This contrast consists of several parts.

The Contrast of Pronouns. Paul used the pronouns "ye," "yourselves," "you," "we," "us," and "our" to refer to the church saints. By contrast, he used "they" and "them" to refer to the unsaved. This contrast is especially prominent in verses 3-4 and 7-8. After presenting the Day of the Lord destruction to come upon "them" (v. 3), Paul began verse 4 with "But ye, brethren." Certainly the word "But" indicates a contrast; in addition, as D. Edmond Hiebert pointed out, the "ye" is "emphatic, sharpening the contrast. The renewed direct address, *brethren*, further underlines the contrast."[40]

After describing the lifestyle that "they" practiced (v. 7), Paul exhorted, "But let us" (v. 8).

The Contrast of Spheres. Paul contrasted two different spheres (v. 4). The church saints are not "in" darkness, implying that the unsaved are in darkness. Commenting on Paul's declaration, Hiebert asserted, "Spiritual darkness is the habitual sphere in which the man of the world lives and moves."[41]

Other Scriptures indicate that the sphere of darkness is ruled by evil angelic beings (Eph. 6:12) and that, as a result of being in that sphere, the understanding of the unsaved is darkened (Eph. 4:18). They do not understand ultimate reality and the true purpose of life and history; therefore, they are oblivious to the judgment that is coming, and they practice the unfruitful works of darkness (Eph. 5:11).

By contrast, church saints are not in the sphere of darkness because they have become rightly related to God—who is light (1 Jn. 1:5)—through His Son—who is the light of the world (Jn. 8:12). In addition, they have been delivered out of the power ("domain")[42] of darkness (Col. 1:13; 1 Pet. 2:9) and are now in the sphere of light.

Many scholars are convinced that the clause Paul wrote in the second half of verse 4 is a result clause. For example, James Everett Frame stated that the clause "is not of purpose but of conceived result."[43] Thus, in that clause Paul was saying that as a result of the church saints being delivered from the sphere of darkness and placed into the sphere of light, the broad Day of the Lord will not overtake them as a thief.

As we noted earlier, the broad Day of the Lord will have two phases. Since the first phase (the judgment phase of the 70th week, characterized by darkness and a tremendous outpouring of God's wrath) will come as a thief (vv. 2-3), it appears that in the second half of verse 4 Paul was saying that as a result of church saints being delivered from the sphere of darkness and placed into the sphere of light, the coming-as-a-thief phase will not overtake them. Since that phase will be characterized by darkness, it is reserved for those who are in the sphere of darkness, not for those who are in the sphere of light. Amos 5:18-20 indicates that darkness will be the total nature of the Day of the Lord for the unsaved. It will bring no divine light or blessing to them. Thus, it is upon "them" (the unsaved in darkness), not "you" (the church saints in light), that the Day of the Lord will come as a thief in the night with sudden destruction. "They" (the unsaved), not "you" (the church saints), will not escape (1 Th. 5:2-3).

The broad Day of the Lord will overtake the church saints, but not the phase that will come as a thief. Since the church saints belong to the sphere of light, the second phase of the Day of the Lord will overtake them (the phase during the Millennium, characterized by light, an outpouring of divine blessing, and the administration of God's rule over the whole world).

The Contrast of Natures. In verse 4 Paul declared that church saints are not "in" darkness, but in verse 5 he asserted that they are not "of" darkness nor "of" night. Instead, they are "of" light and "of" day. This change of prepositions indicates a change of concepts. In verse 4 the preposition "in" refers to the sphere in which a person is located, but in verse 5 the preposition "of" refers to a person's nature.

In the Greek text of verse 5, the word translated "children" is the word for "son." Thus, in that verse Paul said, "ye are all sons of light, and sons of the day; we are not of night, nor of darkness."

In the Scriptures the term "son" signifies that a person has the same nature as his father. One indicator of this is the fact that in the Old Testament and post-biblical Judaism the Hebrew words for "son" were "often used to denote the relationship which determines the nature of a man."[44] Another indicator is the fact that when Jesus claimed to be the Son of God, the Jews recognized that He was thereby claiming absolute deity or the same nature as God the Father for Himself (Jn. 5:17-18; 10:36; cp. Mt. 26:63-66 with Lk. 22:69-71). In line with this, Marvin R. Vincent, commenting on Paul's statement that church saints are not "of darkness," said, "The genitive, *of darkness*, points to nature and origin. To *belong* to darkness is more than *to be in* darkness."[45]

In light of this significance of the term "son," it is evident that in verse 5 Paul was saying that the nature of the church saints is light and day, not night or darkness. By implication, the nature of the unsaved is night and darkness, not light or day (cp. Eph. 2:3).

Paul placed the word meaning "all" in the emphatic position in the Greek text, thereby emphasizing that what he was saying was true of all church saints.[46]

In the Greek text of 1 Thessalonians 5:2, Paul began the verse with the word meaning "for." Thus, in verse 4 he stated the coming-as-a-thief phase of the broad Day of the Lord will not overtake church saints[47], because the nature of all church saints, without exception, is light and day, not night or darkness. The implication is that the wrathful phase of the broad Day of the Lord belongs to those with the nature of night and darkness (the unsaved), not to those with the nature of light and day (the church saints).

The Contrast of Attitudes and Actions. In verses 5:6-8 Paul drew a contrast between the attitudes and actions of the unsaved and the church saints. He began the section with the word "Therefore," indicating that he was drawing this conclusion on the basis of what he had just said: He concluded what the attitudes and actions the church saints should be because they and the unsaved exist in radically different spheres and have radically different natures.

Since the unsaved exist in the sphere of darkness (v. 4) and have the nature of night and darkness (v. 5), Paul used two activities that normally take place in the dark of night to describe their attitude (vv. 6-7): sleeping and getting drunk.[48] When people sleep or are drunk, they are not alert to reality and what is going on around them; thus, they do not respond with appropriate actions.

Paul's point was that because of their sphere and nature of darkness and night, the unsaved are not alert to ultimate reality and the significance of what is going on around them. They are not alert to God, His plan and purpose for history, the conflict of the ages between the kingdom of God and the kingdom of Satan, what is coming in the future, and, therefore, the ultimate significance of day-to-day events in the world. As a result, the unsaved do not have faith in God's Word; they do not love God, His Son, and His way; they are ignorant concerning what will happen to them in the future; and they live and act in ways contrary to ultimate reality.

By contrast, since the church saints exist in the sphere of light (v. 4) and have the nature of light and day (v. 5), Paul exhorted them not to have the attitude of the unsaved but to have contrasting attitudes and perform contrasting actions (vv. 6, 8).

First, Paul exhorted them not to have the unsaved attitude characterized by sleep. Albrecht Oepke indicated this means that church saints were not to have the

> unspiritual attitude which is the direct opposite of the concentration and energy of the life of faith which are to be expected and even demanded of believers, especially in view of the approaching *parousia*. The demand "let us not sleep" (1 Th. 5:6) is not just a piece of general wisdom. Nor is it a mere word of encouragement in face of a particular situation. As the context shows quite plainly, the image is eschatological.[49]

Thus, church saints are to be concerned about ultimate reality, God's plan and purpose for history, and the implications of these things for them.

Then Paul exhorted church saints to have two contrasting attitudes. The first is continuous (present tense) watchfulness (v. 6). The word translated "watch" means to "be on the alert, be watchful."[50] Albrecht Oepke asserted that 1 Thessalonians 5:6 is one of several passages in which this word is used especially "in relation to the *parousia*."[51] Thus, church saints are to be continuously alert or on the watch for Christ to come, because the reality of God's plan and purpose for history and, therefore, for them and their future indicates that He could come at any moment.

Second, church saints are to have an attitude of continuous (present tense) sobriety (vv. 6, 8). Arndt and Gingrich indicated that Paul used the word translated "sober" in a figurative sense, thus meaning to "be free fr. every form of mental and spiritual 'drunkeness', fr. excess. passion, rashness, confusion, etc., *be well-balanced, self-controlled*."[52] In the same vein, Otto Bauernfiend asserted that, in the figurative sense, the word refers to the opposite of "all kinds of mental fuzziness."[53] Bauernfiend also stated that the immediate contexts of the five New Testament passages (1 Th. 5:6, 8; 2 Tim. 4:5; 1 Pet. 1:13; 4:7; 5:8) in which the word is used clearly indicate that sobriety "consists in acknowledgment of the reality given with God's revelation and in discharge of the resultant ministry by worship, hope, love and warfare."[54] Thus, church saints are to be continuously free from all fuzzy thinking or wrong concepts concerning ultimate reality. They are to continuously acknowledge the reality revealed by God and to live and minister in the well-balanced, self-controlled manner required by that reality.

Herbert Preisker summarized this twofold exhortation to watchfulness and sobriety as follows:

> In 1 Th. 5:6 Paul admonishes the community not to live indifferently in all kinds of vices (the stupor of sins), but, with a sense of the imminence of the *parousia*, to be awake in a sanctified life. To fill out the picture he demands sobriety, and issues a special warning against the tension which might be caused by eschatological expectation.[55]

At the beginning of verse 8 Paul again emphasized the contrast between church saints and the unsaved by using the word "but" and placing it and the pronoun referring to church saints in the emphatic position.[56] Paul indicated that in contrast with the unsaved (who do not have faith in God's Word, do not love Him, His Son, and His ways, and are ignorant concerning what will happen to them in the future), church saints should put on two pieces of armor—a breastplate (consisting of faith in God's Word and love of God, His Son, His ways, and fellow saints) and a helmet (consisting of hope of salvation, cp Rom. 13:12, "the armor of light"). Through this language Paul indicated that church saints are to be not only watchmen but also warriors.[57]

It should be noted that Paul did not refer to the helmet of salvation, but to the helmet of the *hope* of salvation. Concerning the New Testament concept of hope, Leon Morris wrote,

> We must remind ourselves that the use of the term "hope" does not imply any uncertainty. The New Testament idea of hope is something which is certain, for it is grounded in the divine action. But it is not realized as yet, and thus is still hope, not sight.[58]

Since hope is always fixed upon something that has not yet been realized but is certain to be realized in the future, when Paul referred, not to salvation but to the *hope* of salvation, he was not referring to eternal salvation from the penalty of sin. His readers had already experienced that when they trusted Christ as Savior in the past. Instead, Paul was referring to a future or eschatological salvation that church saints have not yet experienced but are certain to experience.[59]

Since, as we noted earlier, the major subject of 1 Thessalonians 5:1-11 is the broad Day of the Lord, and since in verses 2-3 Paul specifically emphasized its first phase—that characterized by darkness and a tremendous outpouring of God's wrath on the world—in verse 8 Paul must have been referring to future salvation or deliverance from the first phase of the broad Day of the Lord. In light of this and the fact that a helmet was designed to protect the head, in which the mind resides, we can draw the conclusion that when Paul stated that church saints should put on the helmet of the hope of salvation, he was indicating that they should protect their minds with the certainty of being delivered from the wrathful first phase of the broad Day of the Lord. Their minds should not be tormented by uncertainty as to whether they will or will not be overtaken by that phase.

The Contrast of Destinies. In 1 Thessalonians 5:2-7 Paul clearly indicated that the unsaved will be overtaken by and will experience the destruction of the wrathful first phase of the broad Day of the Lord. By contrast, in verses 9-11 he just as clearly asserted that church saints are appointed to a radically different destiny.

Paul began verse 9 with the causal conjunction that could be translated "because" or "for,"[60] thereby introducing the reason why church saints should protect their minds with the certainty of being delivered from the wrathful first phase of the broad Day of the Lord: "God hath not appointed us to wrath but to obtain salvation by our Lord Jesus Christ." In light of what was seen earlier concerning the major subject of 1 Thessalonians 5:1-11 and the specific emphasis in verses 2-3, Paul must have meant that God has not appointed church saints to the broad Day of the Lord wrath. Instead, He has appointed them to be saved from that wrath through Christ.

The observations and statements of several scholars regarding this reason are significant. James Everett Frame stated that the word translated "appointed" refers to the purpose of God.[61] He also indicated that the salvation mentioned in this verse involves freedom from wrath and is comparable to the deliverance from the wrath to come of 1 Thessalonians 1:10.[62] Thus, Paul was indicating that God did not purpose church saints to experience His wrath, but instead He purposed them to obtain salvation or deliverance from the future period of His wrath that belongs to the unsaved. This is significant because the Scriptures teach that whatever God purposes is certain to happen (Isa. 14:24-27).

Concerning the word translated "appointed," George G. Findlay declared, "It implies the *authority* with which God called the Thessalonians to salvation (comp. 2:12) as well as the fact of His gracious *intention* respecting them."[63]

John Eadie wrote, "God did not appoint us to wrath, to be the victims of it, or to suffer under it."[64]

C. F. Hogg and W. E. Vine pointed out that the word "not" in the expression "God hath not appointed us to wrath" is in the emphatic position[65], indicating that Paul wanted to emphasize the fact that church saints will not experience God's wrath. Hogg and Vine also asserted that the wrath to which church saints have not been appointed is the outpouring of God's wrath that will cause the sudden destruction described in verse 3 (the destruction upon the unsaved in the first phase of the broad Day of the Lord).[66]

D. Edmond Hiebert claimed that the word translated "appointed" refers to the "deliberate purpose of God."[67] He also recognized that the wrath to which church saints have not been appointed is the wrath to come of 1 Thessalonians 1:10. He stated, "As in 1:10 *wrath* here is used in its eschatological sense, the wrath of God upon the sinner in the coming day of judgment."[68] Concerning Paul's declaration, "God hath not appointed us to wrath," Hiebert wrote that God

> has no intention that we should become the subjects of His wrath, fall under its punitive action, when the day of "sudden destruction" (5:3) falls upon the unsaved . . . the divine wrath against sin was diverted from us when by faith we were united with "the Son of his love" (Col. 1:13). Wrath is the destiny of Christ-rejecting souls.[69]

Once again, referring to Paul's assertion that church saints have not been appointed to wrath, Hiebert declared,

> This negative assertion seems clearly to assure that believers will not have part in the coming Great Tribulation, when God's wrath falls upon a Christ-rejecting world (Rev. 6:15-17; 14:10; 19:15). They are looking forward not to the coming of that day when God will display His wrath in divine judgment but to the coming of the Lord Himself.[70]

Commenting on the significance of the word "appointed" in relation to the salvation referred to in verse 9, Leon Morris claimed that "salvation proceeds from God's appointment." He asserted that that appointment "rests our salvation on the divine initiative." He also declared that "Salvation includes the fact that God did not destine His own to experience His wrath."[71]

Thomas L. Constable wrote,

> God's intention for them is not the wrath that will come on the earth in the Day of the Lord, but the full salvation that will be theirs when the Lord returns for them in the clouds. The wrath of God referred to here clearly refers to the Tribulation; the context makes this apparent. Deliverance from that wrath is God's appointment for believers. That temporal salvation comes through the Lord Jesus Christ just as does eternal salvation.[72]

At the end of verse 9 and beginning of verse 10 Paul taught that God appointed church saints to obtain this salvation from the future wrath of God by (lit. through) the Lord Jesus Christ; more specifically, through His death for them. Concerning this teaching, George G. Findlay said, "Christ's death (see ver. 10) is set forth as our ground of hope in this prospect."[73]

D. Edmond Hiebert stated, "The death of Christ 'for us' is the meritorious cause for our deliverance from the wrath of God against sin (2 Cor. 5:21)."[74]

Because Christ's death for church saints caused their salvation from the future wrath of God, and because Christ's death has already been accomplished once for all (Rom. 6:9-10), the salvation of church saints from the future wrath of God has already been obtained. Their future experience of this already obtained deliverance is certain.[75] In line with this, Gustav Stahlin stated, "Liberation from God's wrath is bound up with faith in Christ, Jn. 3:36. In faith in Him we have the eschatological gift of freedom from wrath as a present reality."[76]

In the latter part of verse 10, Paul presented the purpose of Christ's death for the church saints: "that, whether we wake or sleep, we should live together with him." Arndt and Gingrich claim that in this passage Paul used the words "wake" and "sleep" figuratively for "*be alive* and *be dead.*"[77]

The words translated "together with" "denote what belongs together in time and place."[78] The verb translated "should live" was used "of physical life in contrast to death."[79]

In light of the usage of these terms, we can conclude that Paul was saying that the purpose of Christ's death was that all church saints, whether alive or dead, may live together physically with Christ at the same time and in the same place. This purpose implies physical resurrection for the dead church saints.

In summary, Paul taught in verses 9-10 that the reason church saints should protect their minds with the certainty of being delivered from the wrathful first phase of the broad Day of the Lord is because God has appointed them to a radically different destiny from that of the unsaved. The unsaved will be overtaken by and experience the destruction of the wrathful first phase of the broad Day of the Lord. By contrast, God did not purpose church saints to experience His wrath. Instead, He intentionally purposed them to obtain salvation or deliverance from the wrathful first phase of the broad Day, which belongs to the unsaved.

Church saints are delivered from the wrathful phase of the Day of the Lord by the already accomplished death of Christ. Christ died so that all church saints, whether alive or dead, may live together physically with Him at the same time and in the same place.

Thus, Christ died for church saints to cause their destiny of living together with Him instead of experiencing the Day of the Lord wrath. Because this destiny of church saints was purposed by God and caused by the death of Christ, it is absolutely certain to be fulfilled. James Everett Frame stated that in relationship to his exhortation to church saints to put on the hope of salvation, Paul was "encouraging the faint-hearted to be assured that that hope is bound to be fulfilled."[80]

Paul used the word translated "Wherefore" at the beginning of verse 11 to introduce a self-evident inference prompted by his teaching in verses 9 and 10.[81] The fact that church saints have the absolutely certain destiny of living together with Christ instead of experiencing the Day of the Lord wrath infers that they should be continuously comforting and edifying one another with that truth. Paul commanded them to do both continuously (he used the imperative mood and present tense for "comfort" and "edify").

A Significant Parallel. We should note that the language of 1 Thessalonians 5:10-11 is parallel to the Rapture language of 1 Thessalonians 4:16-18 in three points. First, as we saw earlier, the language of 1 Thessalonians 5:10 concerning dead church saints living physically with Christ implies physical resurrection for them, and 1 Thessalonians 4:16 specifically refers to the physical resurrection of dead church saints at the Rapture.

Second, 1 Thessalonians 5:10 indicates that living and dead church saints will live together with Christ at the same time and in the same place, and 1 Thessalonians 4:16-17 teaches that at the Rapture living and dead church saints will be caught up together at the same time to meet Christ in the same place and, as a result, will always be with Him.

Third, in 1 Thessalonians 5:10 church saints are commanded to continuously comfort and edify one another with the truth of their destiny of living with Christ instead of experiencing the Day of the Lord wrath. In 1 Thessalonians 4:18 church saints are commanded to continuously comfort one another with the truth of their destiny of being raptured to be with Christ.

In addition, we should observe that both 1 Thessalonians passages are parallel to John 14:2-3, which, as we noted in an earlier chapter, refers to a future coming of Christ in which He will receive His believers to Himself so that they can be where He is.

Several scholars recognize the parallelism of 1 Thessalonians 5:10-11 to 1 Thessalonians 4:16-18. James Everett Frame indicated that the 1 Thessalonians 5:10 statement "that, whether we wake or sleep, we should live together with him" is to be understood in the light of the related 1 Thessalonians 4:13-18 passage. In conjunction with this he said, "For survivors and dead, salvation comes simultaneously at the *Parousia*, as *will bring with him* (4:14) and *shall we ever be with the Lord* (4:17) prepare us to expect."[82]

Concerning 1 Thessalonians 5:10, George G. Findlay declared, "the 'with Him' of ch. 4:14, 17 is echoed and unfolded in the 'together with Him' of this verse, as it formed the basis of the 'together with *them*' of ch. 4:17." Regarding Paul's 1 Thessalonians 5:11 command to church saints to comfort one another, Findlay said, "he concludes almost in the language of ch. 4:18."[83]

When commenting on Paul's teaching in 1 Thessalonians 5:10, Raymond C. Kelcy called it "This parallel to 4:13-17."[84]

William Hendriksen wrote, "The relation between 5:10 and 11 is a close parallel to that between 4:17 and 18."[85]

Conclusion. In light of the parallelism just observed and the fact that, as we noted earlier in 1 Thessalonians 5:6, Paul exhorted church saints to be continuously alert or on the watch for Christ to come at any moment, it appears that it will be through the Rapture that church saints will experience their destiny of living together with Christ and being saved from the Day of the Lord wrath. They will experience their already obtained deliverance from that wrath by being removed from the earth in the Rapture before the wrathful first phase of the broad Day of the Lord begins.

In line with this conclusion, D. Edmond Hiebert asserted that the salvation referred to in 1 Thessalonians 5:8-9 is "the future eschatological deliverance of believers at the *parousia*. It is the antithesis of the wrath mentioned in" verse 9.[86]

In addition, Thomas L. Constable wrote, "The salvation they look forward to is deliverance from the wrath to come when the Lord returns, as is clear from the context."[87]

Thus, 1 Thessalonians 5:9 indicates that church saints will have no relationship to the Day of the Lord wrath.

REVELATION 3:10

In Revelation 3:10 Christ promised the saints of the church in Philadelphia, "Because thou hast kept the word of my patience, I also will keep thee from the hour of temptation, which shall come upon all the world, to try them that dwell upon the earth." Understanding the significance of this promise requires an examination of its various parts.

The Basis of the Promise. Christ's promise is based on the fact that the Philadelphia church saints had kept the word of Christ's patience (lit., "Because you kept the word of the patience of me"). The major question related to this basis is the meaning of "the word of the patience of me."

The word translated "patience" (*hupomone*) usually meant *"patience, endurance, fortitude, steadfastness, perseverance* esp. as they are shown in the enduring of toil and suffering."[88] The related verb (*hupomeno*) meant *"remain* instead of fleeing, *stand one's ground, hold out, endure* in trouble, affliction, persecution."[89] In light of these meanings, there is the strong possibility that through the expression "the word of the patience of me" Christ was referring to a specific message that had been addressed to church saints exhorting them to follow His model of steadfastly enduring testing or persecution. Such a message is found, for example, in Hebrews 12:1-3.

If this is the intended meaning, then the word translated "patience" refers to Christ's own endurance of testing. In addition, it would mean that the basis of Christ's promise in Revelation 3:10 is the fact that the Philadelphia church saints had obeyed the specific message to follow His model. They themselves had kept the word of His patience by steadfastly enduring severe testing or persecution. In line with this view, J. B. Smith wrote,

> The reference here is to the patience of Christ as in 1:9. Compare also II Thessalonians 3:5 where the literal rendering is: "The Lord direct you . . . into the patience of Christ." The believers at Philadelphia followed the example and teaching of Christ who likewise endured the contradiction of sinners (Hebrews 12:3), and they had the mind of Christ who was obedient unto death, even the death of the cross.[90]

A major factor in favor of this view is that in the great majority of the instances where the word *hupomone* is used in the New Testament, it has the same meaning as that adopted by this first view.

A second possible meaning for the expression "the word of the patience of me" is proposed by several scholars. F. Hauck asserted that the word translated "patience" (*hupomone*) and its related verb (*hupomeno*), when directed toward God, means "to expect, to wait."[91] In light of this, when speaking of the word *hupomone* in the expression "patience of Jesus Christ" in Revelation 1:9, Hauck wrote that it "is to be construed as expectation of Jesus."[92] In addition, he declared that Christ's statement "you kept the word of the patience of me" in Revelation 3:10 "is plainly intended to praise the loyal preservation of faith in the *parousia* in the community. Pious waiting for Jesus is the heart-beat of the faith of the NT community."[93] Again he said, "Waiting for Jesus (1:9; 3:10) is on the one side the attitude which fills the whole soul of believers."[94]

Arndt and Gingrich agreed that the word *hupomone* sometimes meant "(patient) expectation." They indicated that that is its meaning in the expression "patience of Jesus Christ" in Revelation 1:9 and that perhaps that is its meaning in Revelation 3:10.[95]

In the same vein, Richard C. Trench wrote, "Better, however, to take the whole Gospel as 'the word of Christ's patience,' everywhere teaching, as it does, the need of a patient waiting for Christ, till He, the waited-for so long, shall at length appear."[96]

Accordingly, the expression "the word of the patience of me" could be translated "the word of the expectancy of me." Thus, through that expression Christ was referring to a specific message that had been delivered to church saints that He would return from heaven and that His return could take place at any moment. Such a message is found, for example, in John 14:1-3; 1 Thessalonians 4:13-18; 5:6; and James 5:7-9.

If this is the intended meaning, the word translated "patience" refers, not to Christ's own endurance of testing, but to the church saints' enduring expectation of Christ's return. It also would mean that the basis of Christ's promise in Revelation 3:10 is the fact that the Philadelphia church saints steadfastly held the belief that Christ would return from heaven and could return at any moment. As a result, they persistently waited for His coming. The implication may be that they held tenaciously to this belief and expectancy in spite of all the ridicule, opposition, and persecution heaped on them by the unsaved world because of that belief (cp. 3:8).

One thing in favor of this view is Christ's exclamation in 3:11, "Behold, I come quickly; hold that fast which thou hast."

We should note that both of these views involve church saints passing a test. The first view involves a test of obedience to a divine message. According to that view, the church saints kept the message by obeying it. The second view involves a test of faith in a divine message. In that view, the church saints kept the message by tenaciously holding to belief in it. As a result, regardless of which view is correct, the ultimate result is the same—the church saints passed a test.

The Content of the Promise. Because the church saints kept a divine message, Christ promised, "I also will keep thee from the hour of temptation." To discern precisely what Christ promised, we must note several things.

The first is the meaning of the word translated "temptation" (*peirasmos*) and its related verb (*peirazo*). An examination of all New Testament uses of these words reveals that they have two basic meanings. First, they refer to testing or trying people to determine, demonstrate, or expose the kind of people they are. For example, Jesus asked Philip a question "to prove" (*peirazo*) him (Jn. 6:5-6). Paul commanded the Corinthians to "examine" (*peirazo*) themselves to determine if they were believers (2 Cor. 13:5). God "tried" (*peirazo*) Abraham to demonstrate that he was a man of faith who tenaciously held to or kept God's message to him (Heb. 11:17-19). The church saints in Ephesus "tried" (*peirazo*) false apostles to expose the fact that they were liars (Rev. 2:2). In line with this first meaning, Arndt and Gingrich assert that the noun *peirasmos* means "test, trial," and its related verb (*peirazo*) means to "try, make trial of, put to the test, to discover what kind of a pers. someone is."[97]

Second, in the New Testament the noun and its related verb also refer to tempting or enticing to sin. Perhaps the clearest example of this is found in James 1:13-14, which declares that God cannot be "tempted" (a derivative form of *peirasmos*) with evil and that a man is "tempted" (*peirazo*) "when he is drawn away of his own lust, and enticed." Arndt and Gingrich confirm the fact that these words also have this second meaning.[98]

Later, this examination of Revelation 3:10 will present evidence for the conclusion that Christ used *peirasmos* in the sense of the first meaning. Thus, He promised to keep the Philadelphia church saints from the hour of testing that would determine, demonstrate, or expose the kind of people being tested.

The second thing to be noted concerning the meaning of Christ's promise is the fact that He promised to keep the Philadelphia church saints from the *hour* of testing, not just the testing itself. This is an important distinction. The word translated "hour" (*hora*) means "*the time* when someth. took place, is taking place, or will take place."[99] Thus, Christ promised to keep these church saints from the *time period* characterized by the testing Christ had in mind. If the Lord had meant that He would keep them from just the testing itself, He could have made that very clear by omitting the words "the hour" and simply saying, "I will keep you from the testing."

The third thing to be noted is the meaning of the preposition translated "from" (*ek*) in the expression "from the hour." As observed earlier in this chapter, this preposition often carries the sense of separation from a person or thing. Arndt and Gingrich said that is its meaning in Revelation 3:10.[100] Thus, Christ promised to keep the church saints from the hour or time period of testing by separating them from it.

In what sense will He separate them from the period of testing? Three possible answers must be considered. First, Christ will separate them from it in the sense of shielding them from the testing while they live within the period of testing. Thus, their experience will be similar to that of the Israelites who lived in Egypt when God sent the ten plagues on that land. Those Israelites lived within the time period and nation of those plagues, but God prevented the plagues from touching them.

The first answer must be rejected, because it has Christ separating the church saints from the testing itself but not from the time period of the testing. This is contrary to the promise of Christ noted above. If people live within a time period, they are not separated from it.

Added to this is the fact that in the Greek text the next part of Christ's statement, "which shall come upon all the world," modifies the word translated "hour" rather than the word meaning "testing." This indicates that in His promise Christ emphasized the "hour" or time period instead of the testing.[101] By contrast, this first answer emphasizes the testing rather than the time period.

The idea of the saints being shielded from the testing while living within and through its time period also would have been expressed more clearly through the use of another preposition, either *en* (meaning "in") or *dia* (meaning "through") [thus, "I will keep you *in* or *through* the time period of testing"] rather than *ek*.[102]

Finally, even if the church saints were to be shielded from the testing God's wrath will bring on the earth in the period of testing Christ had in mind, the Scriptures (Rev. 6:9-11; 13:7, 15; 20:4) make it clear that many of the saints alive on the earth during that period will be martyred by unbelievers. Thus, even though they will not be put to death by God's wrath, they will still experience violent death as if they had not been shielded from God's wrath. This militates against the answer that Christ will shield or protect the saints in or through that period of testing.[103]

The second answer asserts that Christ will separate the church saints from the period of testing in the sense of removing them from it after they have been in it for some length of time. Thus, they will enter the time period and experience it for awhile but then be removed from it before it ends.

This second answer must also be rejected, because it has Christ separating the church saints from only part of the period of testing. By contrast, Christ promised to separate them from the time period ("the hour"), not just part of it. The language of Christ's promise does not infer that they are removed after part of the period has run its course. If people live within even part of a time period, they are not separated or kept from it.

The third answer maintains that Christ will separate the church saints from the period of testing in the sense of removing them from the earth before that time period begins. This answer has several points in its favor. First, Christ promised to separate the church saints from the period of testing, not from the testing only or part of the time period. The language implies that He will separate or keep them from the entire period of testing. The only way to keep people from an entire time period is to prevent them from entering it. But people will enter it if they are present on the earth when that time period comes. Thus, the only way to prevent people from entering the entire period of testing is to remove them from the earth before the time period begins.

Second, as noted earlier, Christ based His promise on the fact that the church saints had already passed their test. In light of that, it appears that because they had already passed their test, Christ promised that He would not put them into the period that, as will be demonstrated later, will have the purpose of testing a very different group of people. In line with this, W. Robert Cook wrote, "Thus the period of testing for church saints is fulfilled

(Rom. 5:1-5; James 1:2-4, 12; 1 Pet. 1:3-9; 4:12-13) and the hour of testing for the world is about to come."[104]

Third, Christ immediately followed His Revelation 3:10 promise with the exclamation, "Behold, I come quickly" (v. 11). As we noted in an earlier chapter, this exclamation, which appears several times in Revelation, expresses the imminency of Christ's return.

Why would Christ interject this exclamation that He could come at any moment immediately after talking about the period of testing which was "about to come" (lit. trans. of the Greek text)? The fact that He did so implied a connection between His imminent return and the fact that the period of testing was "about to come." Henry Alford indicated that the fact that the period of testing was about to come "is immediately connected with" Christ's exclamation, "I come quickly."[105]

What could that connection be? According to Henry B. Swete, the fact that the period of testing was about to come means that it "was near at hand."[106] In light of that, the connection seems to be that the period of testing was near at hand because Christ could come at any moment. The period of testing would begin shortly after His imminent coming. Thus, until Christ's imminent coming has become a past event, the period of testing is always about to come.

This connection, together with Christ's promise to keep or separate the church saints from the period of testing, and the fact that the possible basis of Christ's promise was that the Philadelphia saints steadfastly held the belief that Christ would return from heaven and could return at any moment and therefore persistently waited for Him to come, strongly implied that it will be through His any-moment coming that He will keep or separate the church saints from the entire period of testing.

The Scriptures indicate that this imminent coming of Christ will involve the removal of the church saints from the earth by rapture (Jn. 14:2-3; 1 Cor. 15:51-52; 1 Th. 4:13-18). Thus, the more specific implication of Christ's exclamation in Revelation 3:11 is that it will be through the Rapture of the church saints from the earth in conjunction with His imminent coming from heaven that Christ will keep or separate them from the entire period of testing.

Since, as we noted earlier, the only way to prevent people from entering the entire period of testing is to remove them from the earth before that period begins, the further implication is that Christ will keep or separate the church saints from the entire period of testing by rapturing them from the earth *before* that period begins.

The Identification of the Hour of Testing. Jesus identified the period of testing by defining it as the hour of testing "which shall come upon all the world" (lit., "the one about to come upon all the inhabited earth"). Several things should be observed regarding this definition. First, this period of testing was yet future when Christ made His promise to the Philadelphia church saints. He said that it was "about to come." Thus, it would not include any testings that they may have experienced already.

Second, the fact that Christ's statement placed the definite article "the" before the words translated "hour" and "about" indicates that He had a specific or definite period of testing in mind. He was not referring to history in general with its sporadic testings. The implication was that there would be something distinctive or unique about this period of testing.

Third, this period of testing would affect, not just Philadelphia or the Roman Empire, but the whole inhabited earth. The word translated "all" means "whole, entire, complete,"[107] and the term translated "world" means "the inhabited earth, the world."[108] Taken together, they refer to "the whole inhabited earth."[109] Arndt and Gingrich place this specific expression in Revelation 3:10 in a different category than that of the Roman Empire, indicating that it refers to more than just the Roman Empire.[110] This same expression was used in Revelation 16:14 to refer to the kings of the whole inhabited earth gathering together to battle at Armageddon in conjunction with the sixth bowl judgment near the end of the 70th week of Daniel 9. In addition, it was used in Jesus' statement concerning the preaching of the gospel of the kingdom in all the inhabited earth to all nations during the future Tribulation period (Mt. 24:14). In both of these passages, it must refer to the entire inhabited earth, not just the Roman Empire.

Jesus thereby was referring to a period of time when the entire inhabited earth will be tested. He was not talking about unrelated incidents of testing, widely separated from each other in time and location and therefore never worldwide in scope, which have been characteristic of history in general (for example, the testing of the church saints in the city of Smyrna, which gave them tribulation for ten days, Rev. 2:10). Instead, He was referring to a distinct future period of time that will be uniquely characterized by its intense, concentrated, worldwide scope of testing.

Fourth, the language in Jesus' reference to this future period of world-wide testing implied that it was well-known to the church saints[111]. It was well-known because both Old and New Testament Scriptures, written years before Revelation, foretold this unique, future period of testing or Tribula-tion, which would take place prior to the coming of the Messiah to rule the world in the Messianic Age or Millennium (Isa. 2:10-21; Dan. 12:1; Zeph. 1:14-18; Mt. 24:4-31). An earlier chapter demonstrated the fact that this future period of testing was well-known to ancient Jews, that they taught that the time period would consist of the last seven years prior to the Messiah's coming to reign, and that they called the time period "the birth-pangs of the Messiah" or "the Messianic woes."

These four defining items indicate that the period of testing to which Jesus referred in Revelation 3:10 is to be identified as the Tribulation, the first or judgment phase of the broad Day of the Lord, or the 70th week of Daniel 9, covering the last seven years prior to Christ's Second Coming to rule the world.

The comments of several scholars concerning the identification of this period of testing demonstrate basic agreement with this conclusion. Heinrich Seesemann indicated that Christ's terminology in Revelation 3:10 referred to "the total eschatological terror and tribulation of the last time."[112]

Referring to the teaching in various passages of Revelation, Johannes Schneider stated, "The Messianic Age of joy in all the glory of its consummation (19:7)" will be "preceded by the Messianic tribulation (3:10; cf. 7:14)."[113] He also claimed that "early Christian proclamation shared the view of Jewish apocalyptic that the final tribulation would precede entry into the kingdom of God."[114]

Henry Alford claimed that the period of testing mentioned in Revelation 3:10 was foretold in Matthew 24 and is "the great time of trouble which shall be before the Lord's second coming."[115]

Robert L. Thomas wrote, "It is to be a time of distress on the world before the coming of Christ, one known as the Day of the Lord, the Tribulation, or the Great Tribulation (cf. Dan. 12:1; Joel 2:31; Mark 13:14; 2 Thess. 2:1-12; Rev. 7:14; 14:7)."[116]

The Purpose of the Hour of Testing. In the final part of Revelation 3:10, Christ stated that the purpose of the future period of testing to come upon the whole inhabited earth would be "to try them that dwell upon the earth." The word translated "to try" is an infinitive of purpose derived from the verb *peirazo*, which, as noted earlier, refers either to the testing or trying of people to determine, demonstrate, or expose the kind of people they are, *or* to the tempting of people to sin.

To determine which of these two meanings Christ had in mind, we must discern who will do the trying in the future. According to Gerhard Delling, the word translated "hour" (*hora*) in Christ's promise, "I also will keep thee from the hour of temptation," refers in general to " 'the divinely appointed time' for the actualisation of apocalyptic happenings."[117] This indicates that God appointed or purposed the future period of testing; therefore, He is the one who will do the trying.

Since, according to James 1:13, God does not tempt people to sin, we must conclude that the purpose infinitive in Revelation 3:10 refers to God's *testing* people, not to His *tempting* them to sin. Thus, Christ was declaring that the purpose of the future period of testing will be for God to test "them that dwell upon the earth" to demonstrate or expose the kind of people they are.

What is the identification of "them that dwell upon the earth"? A study of all the references to them in Revelation clearly indicates that they will be the people who, during the Tribulation, will kill God's saints (6:10); thus, they will be haters of the saints. They will be tormented by God's two witnesses and will rejoice over and celebrate the deaths of these two men (11:10), implying that they will despise the two witnesses. It is interesting to note that the word translated "tormented" means "to test the genuineness of,"[118] indicating that the tormenting activities of the two witnesses will be one aspect of God's testing of those dwelling on the earth during the 70th week.

The earth-dwellers will wonder or be astonished when they see the beast (17:8), and they will worship him (13:8, 12). They will be deceived by the second beast through miracles and will be persuaded by him to make an image to the first beast (13:14-15). Three woes will be pronounced upon them in conjunction with the last three trumpet judgments (8:13). They will be made drunk with the wine of the great whore's illicit unions (17:2). The names of those dwelling on the earth were never written in the book of life from the foundation of the world (13:8; 17:8).

All of these Revelation references to "them that dwell upon the earth" clearly indicate that they will be unsaved people of the future period of testing who will never get saved. Revelation 14:9-11 teaches with certainty that those who worship the beast will never experience salvation. Instead, they will suffer the full strength of God's wrath and will be tormented continuously throughout eternity.

By way of contrast with these people dwelling on the earth, those who get saved during the future period of testing will be redeemed "from the earth" (Rev. 14:3). In addition, unlike those who are concerned only about "earthly things" and who will end in destruction, present-day church saints have their "conversation" (lit., "commonwealth, state")[119] in heaven. Therefore, they should be waiting eagerly for Christ to come from heaven and take them there (Phil. 3:19-20) and should be setting their minds on things "above," not on things "on the earth" (Col. 3:2). In line with this contrast, Henry Alford said that the expression "to try them that dwell upon the earth" in Revelation 3:10 "applies to those who are not of the church of Christ."[120]

In light of what has been seen concerning the identification of those in Revelation 3:10 who are dwelling on the earth, we can draw the following conclusion: The purpose of the future period of testing will be for God to test those dwelling on the earth to expose them as the kind of people who are so adamantly opposed to Him that they will never repent, no matter what is done to them. Through that exposure, God will demonstrate that these people deserve His eternal judgment.

Several things in Revelation clearly indicate that the future period of testing will accomplish that purpose. When God causes the cosmic distur-bances of the sixth seal, although the earth-dwellers will be terrified and will recognize that these are expressions of God's wrath, instead of repenting they will cry for the mountains and rocks to fall on them and hide them from God and the wrath of Christ (6:12-17). In spite of the devastating horrors of the sixth trumpet, which will kill one-third of mankind, the earth-dwellers will not repent of their wicked deeds (9:20-21). The fourth bowl will cause people to be scorched with great heat; the fifth bowl will cause excruciating pain; and the sixth bowl will cause hailstones weighing approximately 94 pounds each to bombard people.[121] Although they will recognize that these are God's wrath judgments, the earth-dwellers will blaspheme Him rather than repent (16:1, 7, 8-11, 21).

Concerning the purpose of this future period of testing, Richard C. Trench wrote,

> God is then putting *"them that dwell upon the earth"* to proof, . . . such times of Great Tribulation are trials or *"temptations,"* because they bring out the unbelief, hardness of heart, blasphemy against God, which were before latent in these children of this world; hidden from others, hidden from themselves, till that "hour of temptation" came and revealed them (Rev. 9:20, 21; 16:9, 11, 21).[122]

In light of what has been seen regarding the purpose of this future period of testing, two things can be concluded. First, God purposed this period of testing for those who are so irreversibly ungodly that they will never get saved. He did not purpose it for church saints. Second, the means of God's testing will be an intense, concentrated, worldwide outpouring of His wrath. Since, as we noted earlier, the future period of testing is to be identified with the first or judgment phase of the broad Day of the Lord, this testing will be the outpouring of His broad Day of the Lord wrath.

Conclusion. This study of Revelation 3:10 has prompted several conclusions. First, because the Philadelphia church saints had already passed their test, Christ promised to keep or separate them from the future period of testing that God has purposed for the testing of an altogether different kind of people—those who are so irreversibly ungodly that they will never repent, no matter what is done to them.

Second, that future period of testing is to be identified as the Tribulation, the first or judgment phase of the broad Day of the Lord, or the 70th week of Daniel and will cover the last seven years prior to Christ's coming to rule the earth during the Millennium.

Third, God's means of testing those dwelling on the earth during the future period of testing will be the worldwide outpouring of His broad Day of the Lord wrath.

Fourth, Christ will keep or separate the Philadelphia church saints from the period of testing by rapturing them from the earth at His imminent coming before the period of testing begins.

Revelation 3:13 indicates that the Holy Spirit intends Christ's message to the Philadelphia church to be applicable to all churches; therefore,

Christ's promise to the Philadelphia church saints is a promise to all church saints. Christ will keep or separate all church saints from the future period of testing by rapturing them from the earth at His imminent coming before the period of testing begins.

This, together with the four conclusions, leads to a fifth conclusion: Revelation 3:10 indicates that church saints will have no relationship to the broad Day of the Lord wrath.

CONCLUSION

All four passages examined in this chapter have prompted the same conclusion: Church saints will have no relationship with the broad Day of the Lord wrath. Christ will remove them from the earth by rapture before the broad Day of the Lord begins.

Earlier chapters have presented evidence to the effect that the broad Day of the Lord will begin at the start of the Tribulation or 70th week. In light of this, we can conclude that the biblical teaching of 1 Thessalonians 1:10; 4:13-18; 5:9; and Revelation 3:10 concerning the relationship of church saints to the wrath of God infers a Pretribulation Rapture of the church.

ENDNOTES

1. W. E. Vine, *An Expository Dictionary of New Testament Words* (London: Oliphants Ltd., 1940), Vol. IV, p. 194.

2. William F. Arndt and F. Wilbur Gingrich, *A Greek-English Lexicon of the New Testament*, 4th rev. ed. (Chicago: The University of Chicago Press, 1957), p. 505.

3. Vine, *An Expository Dictionary of New Testament Words*, Vol. IV, p. 194.

4. A. T. Robertson, *Word Pictures in the New Testament*, Vol. IV, (New York: Richard R. Smith, Inc., 1931), p. 14.

5. D. Edmond Hiebert, *The Thessalonian Epistles* (Chicago: Moody Press, 1971), p. 70.

6. I. Howard Marshall, *1 and 2 Thessalonians* in *The New Century Bible Commentary* (Grand Rapids: Wm. B. Eerdmans Publishing Company, 1983), p. 58.

7. John Lillie, *Lectures on the Epistles of Paul to the Thessalonians* (New York: Robert Carter and Brothers, 1860), pp. 75-76.

8. Hiebert, *The Thessalonian Epistles*, p. 205.

9. Robertson, *Word Pictures in the New Testament*, Vol. IV, p. 14.

10. Marshall, *1 and 2 Thessalonians*, p. 59.

11. Hermann Cremer, *Biblico-Theological Lexicon of New Testament Greek*, fourth English edition (Edinburgh: T. & T. Clark, 1895), p. 516.

12. Marvin R. Vincent, *Word Studies in the New Testament*, Vol. IV (New York: Charles Scribner's Sons, 1900), p. 20.

13. Hiebert, *The Thessalonian Epistles*, p. 72.

14. George Milligan, *St Paul's Epistles to the Thessalonians* (London: Macmillan and Co., Limited, 1908), p. 15.

15. Arndt and Gingrich, *A Greek-English Lexicon of the New Testament*, p. 233.

16. *Ibid.*

17. Frederic Henry Chase, "The Lord's Prayer in the Early Church," *Texts and Studies*, ed. by J. Armitage Robinson (Cambridge: The University Press, 1891), p. 79.

18. Gustav Stahlin, "orge," *Theological Dictionary of the New Testament*, Vol. V., ed. by Gerhard Friedrich, trans. and ed. by Geoffrey W. Bromiley (Grand Rapids: Wm. B. Eerdmans Publishing Company, 1967), p. 446.

19. *Ibid.*, p. 445.

20. *Ibid.*

21. *Ibid.*

22. Chase, "The Lord's Prayer in the Early Church," p. 79.

23. Milligan, *St Paul's Epistles to the Thessalonians*, p. 15.

24. Thomas L. Constable, *1 Thessalonians* in *The Bible Knowledge Commentary*, New Testament edition, ed. by John F. Walvoord and Roy B. Zuck (Wheaton, IL: Victor Books, 1983), p. 693.

25. Vine, *An Expository Dictionary of New Testament Words*, Vol. III, p. 149.

26. Milligan, *St Paul's Epistles to the Thessalonians*, p. 15.

27. *Ibid.*

28. Hiebert, *The Thessalonian Epistles*, p. 73.

29. James Everett Frame, *A Critical and Exegetical Commentary on the Epistles of St. Paul to the Thessalonians* in *The International Critical Commentary* (Edinburgh: T. & T. Clark, 1912), p. 90.

30. Robertson, *Word Pictures in the New Testament*, Vol. IV, p. 14.

31. Stahlin, *Theological Dictionary of the New Testament*, Vol. V., p. 430.

32. *Ibid.*

33. *Ibid.*

34. Constable, *1 Thessalonians*, p. 693.

35. Arndt and Gingrich, *A Greek-English Lexicon of the New Testament*, p. 483.

36. Hiebert, *The Thessalonian Epistles*, p. 205.

37. Arndt and Gingrich, *A Greek-English Lexicon of the New Testament*, p. 108.

38. *Ibid.*

39. Werner Foerster, "harpazo," *Theological Dictionary of the New Testament*, Vol. I, ed. by Gerhard Kittel, trans. and ed. by Geoffrey W. Bromiley (Grand Rapids: Wm. B. Eerdmans Publishing Company, 1964), p. 472.

40. Hiebert, *The Thessalonian Epistles*, p. 214.

41. *Ibid.*, p. 215.

42. Arndt and Gingrich, *A Greek-English Lexicon of the New Testament*, p. 278.

43. Frame, *A Critical and Exegetical Commentary on the Epistles of St. Paul to the Thessalonians*, p. 183.

44. Eduard Lohse, "huios," *Theological Dictionary of the New Testament*, Vol. VIII, ed. by Gerhard Friedrich, trans. and ed. by Geoffrey W. Bromiley (Grand Rapids: Wm. B. Eerdmans Publishing Company, 1972), p. 358.

45. Vincent, *Word Studies in the New Testament*, Vol. IV, p. 45.

46. C. F. Hogg and W. E. Vine, *The Epistles to the Thessalonians* (London: Pickering & Inglis, Ltd., 1959), p. 158.

47. *Ibid.*

48. John Eadie, *A Commentary on the Greek Text of the Epistles of Paul to the Thessalonians* (London: Macmillan and Co., 1877), p. 185.

49. Albrecht Oepke, "katheudo," *Theological Dictionary of the New Testament*, Vol. III, ed. by Gerhard Kittel, trans. and ed. by Geoffrey W. Bromiley (Grand Rapids: Wm. B. Eerdmans Publishing Company, 1965), p. 436.

50. Arndt and Gingrich, *A Greek-English Lexicon of the New Testament*, p. 166.

51. Oepke, "gregoreo," *Theological Dictionary of the New Testament*, Vol. II, ed. by Gerhard Kittel, trans. and ed. by Geoffrey W. Bromiley (Grand Rapids: Wm. B. Eerdmans Publishing Company, 1964), p. 338.

52. Arndt and Gingrich, *A Greek-English Lexicon of the New Testament*, p. 540.

53. O. Bauernfiend, "nepho," *Theological Dictionary of the New Testament*, Vol. IV, ed. by Gerhard Kittel, trans. and ed. by Geoffrey W. Bromiley (Grand Rapids: Wm. B. Eerdmans Publishing Company, 1967), p. 937.

54. *Ibid.*, p. 939.

55. H. Preisker, "methuo," *Theological Dictionary of the New Testament*, Vol. IV, ed. by Gerhard kittel, trans. and ed. by Geoffrey W. Bromiley (Grand Rapids: Wm. B. Eerdmans Publishing Company, 1967), p. 547.

56. Hogg and Vine, *The Epistles to the Thessalonians*, p. 163.

57. Hiebert, *The Thessalonian Epistles*, p. 221.

58. Leon Morris, *The First and Second Epistles to the Thessalonians* (Grand Rapids: Wm. B. Eerdmans Publishing Company, 1959), pp. 159-60.

59. Frame, *A Critical and Exegetical Commentary on the Epistles of St. Paul to the Thessalonians*, p. 187.

60. Hiebert, *The Thessalonian Epistles*, p. 222.

61. Frame, *A Critical and Exegetical Commentary on the Epistles of St. Paul to the Thessalonians*, p. 188.

62. *Ibid.*, p. 187.

63. George G. Findlay, *The Epistles to the Thessalonians* in *The Cambridge Bible for Schools and Colleges* (Cambridge: The University Press, 1891), p. 113.

64. Eadie, *A Commentary on the Greek Text of the Epistles of Paul to the Thessalonians*, p. 189.

65. Hogg and Vine, *The Epistles to the Thessalonians*, p. 166.

66. *Ibid.*

67. Hiebert, *The Thessalonian Epistles*, p. 222.

68. *Ibid., p. 223.*

69. *Ibid.*

70. *Ibid.*

71. Morris, *The First and Second Epistles to the Thessalonians*, p. 160.

72. Constable, *1 Thessalonians*, p. 706.

73. Findlay, *The Epistles to the Thessalonians*, p. 113.

74. Hiebert, *The Thessalonian Epistles*, p. 225.

75. Eadie, *A Commentary on the Greek Text of the Epistles of Paul to the Thessalonians*, p. 190.

76. Stahlin, "orge," *Theological Dictionary of the New Testament*, Vol. V, ed. by Gerhard Friedrich, trans. and ed. by Geoffrey W. Bromiley (Grand Rapids: Wm. B. Eerdmans Publishing Company, 1967), p. 446.

77. Arndt and Gingrich, *A Greek-English Lexicon of the New Testament*, p. 166.

78. *Ibid.*, p. 41.

79. *Ibid.*, p. 336.

80. Frame, *A Critical and Exegetical Commentary on the Epistles of St. Paul to the Thessalonians*, p. 188.

81. Arndt and Gingrich, *A Greek-English Lexicon of the New Testament*, p. 197.

82. Frame, *A Critical and Exegetical Commentary on the Epistles of St. Paul to the Thessalonians*, p. 189.

83. Findlay, *The Epistles to the Thessalonians*, p. 115.

84. Raymond C. Kelcy, *The Letters of Paul to the Thessalonians* (Austin, TX: R. B. Sweet Co., Inc., 1968), p. 113.

85. William Hendriksen, *New Testament Commentary: Exposition of I and II Thessalonians* (Grand Rapids: Baker Book House, 1955), p. 128.

86. Hiebert, *The Thessalonian Epistles*, p. 222.

87. Constable, *1 Thessalonians*, p. 706.

88. Arndt and Gingrich, *A Greek-English Lexicon of the New Testament*, p. 854.

89. *Ibid.*, p. 853.

90. J. B. Smith, *A Revelation of Jesus Christ* (Scottdale, PA: Herald Press, 1961), p. 87.

91. F. Hauck, "hupomeno, hupomone," *Theological Dictionary of the New Testament*, Vol. IV, ed. by Gerhard Kittel, trans. and ed. by Geoffrey W. Bromiley (Grand Rapids: Wm. B. Eerdmans Publishing Company, 1967), p. 586.

92. *Ibid.*

93. *Ibid.*

94. *Ibid.*, p. 588.

95. Arndt and Gingrich, *A Greek-English Lexicon of the New Testament*, p. 854.

96. Richard Chenevix Trench, *Commentary on the Epistles to the Seven Churches in Asia* (New York: Charles Scribner, 1861), p. 237.

97. Arndt and Gingrich, *A Greek-English Lexicon of the New Testament*, p. 646.

98. *Ibid.*

99. *Ibid.*

100. *Ibid.*, p. 233.

101. Robert L. Thomas, *Revelation 1-7, An Exegetical Commentary* (Chicago: Moody Press, 1992), p. 288.

102. Henry C. Thiessen, *Will the Church Pass Through the Tribulation?* (New York: Loizeaux Brothers, 1941), p. 24.

103. Thomas, *Revelation 1-7, An Exegetical Commentary*, p. 286.

104. W. Robert Cook, *The Theology of John* (Chicago: Moody Press, 1979), p. 168.

105. Henry Alford, *Revelation* in *The Greek Testament*, Vol. IV (Chicago: Moody Press, 1958), p. 586.

106. Henry Barclay Swete, *The Apocalypse of St. John* (Grand Rapids: Wm. B. Eerdmans Publishing Company, n.d.), p. 56.

107. Arndt and Gingrich, *A Greek-English Lexicon of the New Testament*, p. 567.

108. *Ibid.*, p. 563.

109. *Ibid.*, p. 564.

110. *Ibid.*

111. Alford, *Revelation*, p. 586.

112. Heinrich Seesemann, "peira," *Theological Dictionary of the New Testament*, Vol. VI, ed. by Gerhard Friedrich, trans. and ed. by Geoffrey W. Bromiley (Grand Rapids: Wm. B. Eerdmans Publishing Company, 1968), p. 30.

113. Johannes Schneider, "erchomai," *Theological Dictionary of the New Testament*, Vol. II, ed. by Gerhard Kittel, trans. and ed. by Geoffrey W. Bromiley (Grand Rapids: Wm. B. Eerdmans Publishing Company, 1964), p. 674.

114. *Ibid.*, p. 678.

115. Alford, *Revelation*, p. 586.

116. Thomas, *Revelation 1-7, An Exegetical Commentary*, p. 289.

117. Gerhard Delling, "hora," *Theological Dictionary of the New Testament*, Vol. IX, ed. by Gerhard Friedrich, trans. and ed. by Geoffrey W. Bromiley (Grand Rapids: Wm. B. Eerdmans Publishing Company, 1974), p. 677.

118. Schneider, "basanos," *Theological Dictionary of the New Testament*, Vol. I, ed. by Gerhard Kittel, trans. and ed. by Geoffrey W. Bromiley (Grand Rapids: Wm. B. Eerdmans Publishing Company, 1964), p. 563.

119. Arndt and Gingrich, *A Greek-English Lexicon of the New Testament*, p. 692.

120. Alford, *Revelation*, p. 586.

121. Arndt and Gingrich, *A Greek-English Lexicon of the New Testament*, p. 811.

122. Trench, *Commentary on the Epistles to the Seven Churches in Asia*, pp. 238-39.

CHAPTER ELEVEN

THE REQUEST TO THE TROUBLED THESSALONIANS

I n 2 Thessalonians 2:1-2, Paul and his companions (1:1) made the following request to the Thessalonian saints:

> Now we beseech you, brethren, by the coming of our Lord Jesus Christ, and by our gathering together unto him, That ye be not soon shaken in mind, or be troubled, neither by spirit, nor by word, nor by letter as from us, as that the day of the Lord is present.

This request and the circumstances that prompted it present a fifth inference for the Pretribulation Rapture of the church.

THE CONTENT OF THE REQUEST

The First Part of the Request. Paul and his companions requested the Thessalonian saints to avoid doing two things. First, they were not to be "soon shaken in mind." Arndt and Gingrich claimed that in 2 Thessalonians 2:2 the word translated "soon" is used "in an unfavorable sense *too quickly, too easily, hastily*."[1] The verb form translated "shaken" is in the aorist rather than the present tense. Thus, it does not emphasize continuous action. The fact that it is used together with the word meaning "too quickly, too easily, hastily" indicates that it refers to a sudden, hasty action.

This verb form means "*be shaken, be made to waver* or *totter*."[2] It was especially used to describe the violent motion caused by strong winds or waves and thus for the action of a ship driven from its secure mooring.[3] In light of this meaning, Leon Morris concluded that, when applied to people, this verb refers to those "who lack a secure anchorage, and are readily tossed here and there."[4]

The literal translation of the words "in mind" is "from the mind." J. Behm asserted that in 2 Thessalonians 2:2 the word for "mind" refers "to the sure power of judgment which is always at the command of sober understanding."[5] It refers to the ability to determine whether something is true or false, and that ability is the result of the clear, stable knowledge or understanding of the truth. If people possess a clear, stable knowledge or understanding of the truth, they thereby have a criterion or standard by which to evaluate and determine the truthfulness of every claim or concept presented to them.

In light of what we have seen, we can conclude that in the first part of their request, Paul and his companions asked that the Thessalonian saints not depart hastily from their ability to determine whether a claim presented to them was true or false. They had obtained that ability as a result of the clear, stable knowledge or understanding of the truth imparted to them by Paul and his companions through their ministry at Thessalonica and the first epistle to the Thessalonians. If they departed from that ability, they would lose their secure mooring or anchor and could be "tossed to and fro, and carried about with every wind of doctrine, by the sleight of men, and cunning craftiness, by which they lie in wait to deceive" (Eph. 4:14). Departure from that ability would imply departure from the truth that had given them the ability. It would imply departure from at least some of the teaching Paul and his companions had imparted to them.

The Second Part of the Request. Paul and his companions requested that the Thessalonian saints not "be troubled." By way of contrast with the verb form in the first part of their request, the verb form in the second part is in the present tense and thereby refers to a continuous state.[6] Arndt and Gingrich stated that the verb translated "be troubled" means to *"be inwardly aroused, be disturbed* or *frightened."*[7] James Everett Frame indicated that with its meaning and present tense, this verb form refers to a continuous "state of alarm, agitation, nervous excitement."[8] He also implied that the Thessalonians were into this troubled state as a result of their hasty departure from their ability to determine whether a claim was true or false.[9]

THE IMPLICATION OF THE REQUEST

Paul's request to the Thessalonians implies that these saints were in turmoil. Apparently at least some of them had already departed hastily from their ability to determine whether a claim was true or false and, as a result, had fallen into a constant state of alarm and nervous anxiety.

THE CAUSE OF THE TURMOIL

The last part of verse two discloses the cause of the turmoil. Some person or persons had deceived them (v. 3) by claiming that the Day of the Lord had already begun.

We should note that Paul used the perfect tense of the verb translated "is present." The perfect tense "views action as a finished product" and "signifies action as complete from the point of view of present time."[10] In light of this, Frame asserted that the verb does not mean "is coming," "is at hand," or "is near." Instead, it means "has come," "is on hand," or "is present."[11] Thus, the cause of the Thessalonians' trouble was the erroneous claim that the broad Day of the Lord, about which they had been taught in the past (2 Th. 2:5; 1 Th. 5:1-3), had already come and that they were in it.[12]

The middle of verse two implies that whoever started this claim asserted that it had been communicated originally by Paul and his companions, either through means of a divinely inspired prophetic utterance ("by spirit"), by some oral teaching ("by word"), or by letter.[13] The words translated "as from us" are related to all three of these means of communication.[14] Since the Thessalonians looked to Paul and his companions to be their authoritative teachers, this assertion that they originated the claim that the Day of the Lord had already begun was a very deceptive trick designed to persuade the Thessalonians of the truthfulness of the claim.

Paul made it very clear that he and his companions had nothing to do with the erroneous claim. In the next several verses he completely repudiated it by demonstrating conclusively that the broad Day of the Lord had not come.

THE ISSUE AT STAKE

Introduction. In verse one Paul's language indicated that there was some significant relationship between the request to the Thessalonians and the coming (*parousia*) of Christ and gathering together of church saints to Him. He wrote, "Now we beseech you, brethren, by the coming of our Lord Jesus Christ, and by our gathering together unto him." To understand this relationship, we must observe three things.

Three Observations. First, the preposition *huper*, translated "by," usually means "on behalf of."[15] According to Harald Riesenfeld, this meaning contains the "idea of protection" and thus carries the concept of "in defence of."[16] Concerning the use of *huper* in 2 Thessalonians 2:1, Leon Morris made the following significant comments:

> Here it is more or less equivalent to *peri*, but it has its own particular emphasis. It signifies something like "in the interests of the truth concerning." Lightfoot (on Gal. 1:4) discusses these two prepositions and remarks that *huper* has "a sense of 'interest in,' which is wanting to *peri*." This probably accounts for its use here.[17]

Second, the definite article "the" appears before the expression "coming of our Lord Jesus Christ," but it does not appear before "our gathering together unto him."[18] According to C. F. Hogg and W. E. Vine, this indicates "that these are complementary elements in one event."[19] In line with this, Leon Morris wrote, "The coming of the Lord and the gathering of the saints are regarded as closely connected, as the use of a single article shows. They are two parts of one great event."[20] Wolfgang Schrage claimed the same significance in light of the common article.[21] Thus, Paul was referring to the coming of Christ that would involve the gathering of saints to Him.

Third, regarding the phrase "unto him" in the expression "our gathering together unto him," Leon Morris stated, "Notice the significance of 'unto him.' It is not simply that the saints meet one another: they meet their Lord and remain with Him for ever (cf. 1 Thess. 4:17)."[22] Morris thereby indicated that the gathering together of saints unto Christ in 2 Thessalonians 2:1 is the same event as that in 1 Thessalonians 4:17. Since these are the same event, and since, as noted earlier, the event in 1 Thessalonians 4:17 is the Rapture of the church, the gathering together of church saints unto Christ in 2 Thessalonians 2:1 is also a reference to the Rapture of the church.

James Everett Frame also recognized that 2 Thessalonians 2:1 and 1 Thessalonians 4:17 refer to the same event, namely the Rapture.[23] Hogg and Vine demonstrated the same conclusion. When writing concerning the significance of the 2 Thessalonians 2:1 expression "our gathering together unto him," they said, "Here it refers to the 'rapture' of the saints into the air to meet and to be for ever with the Lord, see 1 Ep. 4:17."[24] Regarding 2 Thessalonians 2:1 Wolfgang Schrage stated that "it is to Him that the" gathering together "of Christians will take place at the Lord's return. This is not active assembling; it is a being assembled and united (cf. *harpagesometha*, 1 Th. 4:17)."[25] *Harpagesometha* is the word translated "shall be caught up" in 1 Thessalonians 4:17. Thus, in 2 Thessalonians 2:1 Paul was referring to the coming of Christ that will involve the Rapture of the church from the earth to be with Him.

The Significance of the Three Observations. These three observations taken together indicate that Paul and his companions wrote their request to the Thessalonians in the interest of the truth concerning the coming of Christ to rapture the church from the earth to be with Him. The purpose of their request was to defend or protect the truth concerning the coming of Christ to rapture the church. This, then, was the significant relationship between their request to the Thessalonians and the coming of Christ and gathering together of church saints unto Him. This fact indicates that the truth pertaining to that doctrine was being threatened by the erroneous claim that the Day of the Lord had already begun and that the church saints were in it; by the assertion that Paul and his companions were the original communicators of that claim; and by the Thessalonians' disturbed reaction to the claim and assertion.

It appears that at least some of the Thessalonians had departed from the earlier teaching of Paul and his companions concerning the coming of Christ to rapture the church (1 Th. 1:10; 4:13-18; 5:4-11). This is implied by the combination of the following three things: the hasty departure of at least some of the Thessalonians from their ability to determine whether the claim concerning the Day of the Lord was true or false; their resultant constant state of alarm and nervous anxiety; and the fact that Paul and his companions, in light of their departure and state, wrote to defend the truth concerning the coming of Christ to rapture the church.

The combination of these three things also implied that the claim that the Day of the Lord had already begun and that the Thessalonians were in it was contrary to the earlier teaching of Paul and his companions concerning two things: the coming of Christ to rapture the church and the relationship of church saints to the broad Day of the Lord. If in their earlier teaching Paul and his companions had taught that Christ's coming to rapture the church would take place *sometime after* the broad Day of the Lord had begun and that the church saints therefore would be in at least part of that Day, several things would have been true. First, the claim that the Day of the Lord had already begun and that the Thessalonians were in it would not have been contrary to the earlier teaching of Paul and his companions. Second, there would have been no need for the Thessalonians to determine whether that claim was true of false, because it would have agreed with the teaching they had already received. Third, none of the Thessalonians would have departed hastily from their ability to determine the truthfulness of that claim. Fourth, it would not have been necessary for Paul and his companions to write to protect or defend their earlier teaching.

By contrast, if in their earlier teaching Paul and his companions had taught the Thessalonians that Christ would come to rapture the church before the broad Day of the Lord begins and that church saints therefore would not enter the judgment phase of the Day of the Lord, several things would have been true. First, the claim that the Day of the Lord had already begun and that the Thessalonians were in it would have been contrary to that earlier teaching. Second, that claim, together with the assertion that it had originated with Paul and his companions, could have caused trouble for the Thessalonians. Third, that set of circumstances would have made it necessary for Paul and his companions to defend their earlier teaching. If earlier they had taught the Thessalonians that Christ would come to rapture the church *before* the broad Day of the Lord begins and that church saints therefore would not enter the judgment phase of the Day of the Lord, the circumstances would have been exactly as found in 2 Thessalonians 2.

Conclusion. In light of what we have seen, we can conclude that the real issue at stake with the Thessalonians was not the *fact* of Christ's coming to rapture the church, but the *time* of that coming and therefore the relationship of church saints to the broad Day of the Lord. The request and circumstances found in 2 Thessalonians 2:1-2 prompt the conclusion that Paul and his companions had taught the Thessalonians that Christ would come to rapture the church *before*, not sometime after, the broad Day of the Lord begins and that church saints therefore would not enter the judgment phase of the Day of the Lord.

This conclusion is supported by Paul's teaching to the Thessalonians in 1 Thessalonians 1:10; 4:13-18; and 5:4-11, which teaching was examined in an earlier chapter.

CONCLUSION

Earlier chapters in this study gave evidence to the effect that the broad Day of the Lord will begin at the beginning of the 70th week of Daniel 9 or the Tribulation period. In light of this, since the request and circumstances found in 2 Thessalonians 2:1-2 prompt the conclusion that Paul and his companions had taught the Thessalonians that Christ would come to rapture the church before, not sometime after, the broad Day of the Lord begins and that church saints therefore would not enter the judgment phase of the Day of the Lord, we can conclude that the request and circumstances found in 2 Thessalonians 2:1-2 present a significant inference for the Pretribulation Rapture of the church.

ENDNOTES

1. William F. Arndt and F. Wilbur Gingrich, *A Greek-English Lexicon of the New Testament*, 4th rev. ed. (Chicago: The University of Chicago Press, 1957), p. 814.

2. *Ibid.*, p. 747.

3. Leon Morris, *The First and Second Epistles to the Thessalonians* (Grand Rapids: Wm. B. Eerdmans Publishing Company, 1959), p. 215.

4. *Ibid.*

5. J. Behm, "nous," *Theological Dictionary of the New Testament*, Vol. IV, ed. by Gerhard Kittel, trans. and ed. by Geoffrey W. Bromiley (Grand Rapids: Wm. B. Eerdmans Publishing Company, 1967), p. 959.

6. Morris, *The First and Second Epistles to the Thessalonians*, p. 215.

7. Arndt and Gingrich, *A Greek-English Lexicon of the New Testament*, p. 364.

8. James Everett Frame, *A Critical and Exegetical Commentary on the Epistles of St. Paul to the Thessalonians* in *The International Critical Commentary* (Edinburgh: T. & T. Clark, 1912), p. 245.

9. *Ibid.*

10. H. E. Dana and Julius R. Mantey, *A Manual Grammar of the Greek New Testament* (New York: The Macmillan Company, 1927), p. 200.

11. Frame, *A Critical and Exegetical Commentary on the Epistles of St. Paul to the Thessalonians*, p. 248.

12. Morris, *The First and Second Epistles to the Thessalonians*, p. 217.

13. *Ibid.*, p. 216.

14. *Ibid.*, footnote 8.

15. *Ibid.*, p. 214, footnote 1.

16. Harald Riesenfeld, "huper," *Theological Dictionary of the New Testament*, Vol. VIII, ed. by Gerhard Friedrich, trans. and ed. by Geoffrey W. Bromiley (Grand Rapids: Wm. B. Eerdmans Publishing Company, 1972), p. 508.

17. Morris, *The First and Second Epistles to the Thessalonians*, p. 214, footnote 1.

18. C. F. Hogg and W. E. Vine, *The Epistles to the Thessalonians* (Fincastle, VA: Bible Study Classics, 1914), p. 242.

19. *Ibid.*

20. Morris, *The First and Second Epistles to the Thessalonians*, p. 214.

21. Wolfgang Schrage, "episunagoge," *Theological Dictionary of the New Testament*, Vol. VII, ed. by Gerhard Friedrich, trans. and ed. by Geoffrey W. Bromiley (Grand Rapids: Wm. B. Eerdmans Publishing Company, 1971), p. 842.

22. Morris, *The First and Second Epistles to the Thessalonians*, p. 214.

23. Frame, *A Critical and Exegetical Commentary on the Epistles of St. Paul to the Thessalonians*, p. 244.

24. Hogg and Vine, *The Epistles to the Thessalonians*, p. 242.

25. Schrage, *Theological Dictionary of the New Testament*, Vol. VII, p. 842.

CHAPTER TWELVE

THE 70-WEEKS PROPHECY OF DANIEL 9

A sixth inference for the Pretribulation Rapture of the church is derived from a study of the 70-weeks prophecy recorded in Daniel 9:24-27. To understand this inference, we must observe two preliminary matters before examining the prophecy.

THE DISTINCTION BETWEEN ISRAEL AND THE CHURCH

Several lines of evidence point to the fact that Israel and the church are not essentially the same.

First, Israel is a nation in the technical sense of the term, but the church is not. Several things illustrate this distinction. Israel has a national language, but the church does not. Israel is an earthly political state with an earthly capital city, an earthly political government, and political rulers, but the church is not. In His Mosaic Covenant relationship with Israel, God established and regulated that nation's earthly political government, but God has not established an earthly political government for the church. Israel has a common, national tradition and history, but the church is comprised of people from many different national traditions and histories. Israel has a national army with which to fight military battles against other nations, but the church does not have such an army.

Second, in spite of the fact that Israel became the people of God through its Mosaic Covenant relationship with Him, it rejected Christ, just as God had forewarned that the nation would (Isa. 53; Jn. 1:11; 12:37-41). By contrast, the church received Christ.

Third, the fact that Israel was the original persecutor of the church indicates that they are not the same.

Fourth, as long as a Gentile remained a Gentile, he was excluded from membership in Israel (Eph. 2:11-12). To become a member, he had to become an Israelite through circumcision and placement under the Law. He had to enter fully into Israel's Mosaic Covenant relationship with God. By contrast, a Gentile can be in full, equal membership in the church as a Gentile. He does not have to become an Israelite to enter that membership (Eph. 2:13-16; 3:1-6). The Holy Spirit led the early church leaders to recognize this distinction that God made between Israel and the church (Acts 15:1-29).

Fifth, Israel had both believers and unbelievers in full Mosaic Covenant relationship with God. When God established the Mosaic Covenant with Israel, He established it fully with the entire membership of that nation, saved and unsaved alike. All Israelites were subject to the regulations of the covenant regardless of their inner spiritual state. Regeneration was not required of those at Mount Sinai in order to enter the Mosaic Covenant relationship with God, and future generations of Israelites entered that covenant relationship by virtue of their physical birth to Israelite parents, not by virtue of a spiritual birth. The unsaved members of Israel were as much the Mosaic Covenant people of God as were the saved members, and Israel's membership consisted of unsaved people as well as saved.

By contrast, the church (not organized Christendom, but the true body of Christ formed by Spirit baptism) consists only of saved or regenerated members. Two things indicate this. First, Luke declared that "the Lord added to the church daily such as should be saved" (Acts 2:47). In addition, Spirit baptism forms the church (1 Cor. 12:13), and Spirit baptism happens only to the saved. On the day of Pentecost, only saved Jews were baptized with the Spirit; unsaved Jews were not (Acts 2). In spite of the fact that Cornelius was a God-fearing Gentile (Acts 10:1-2), he was not baptized with the Spirit until he was saved (Acts 10:44-47; 11:13-18). Since Spirit baptism happens only to the saved, and since Spirit baptism forms the church, the church has only saved people in its membership.

Sixth, the Scriptures never called the saved Jews of Old Testament Israel "the church of God" in contrast with the unsaved Jews; but the Scriptures do call the saved Jews (and the saved Gentiles) of the church "the church of God" in contrast with the unsaved Jews (and the unsaved Gentiles) of the New Testament era (1 Cor. 10:32). The fact that the Scriptures apply the term "the church of God" to the saved Jews of the church but did not apply it to the saved Jews of Old Testament Israel implies three things: There is a distinction between the saved Jews of the church and the saved Jews of Old Testament Israel; the term "the church of God" can be applied legitimately only to the church but not to Old Testament Israel; and Old Testament Israel and the church are not essentially the same.

Seventh, in Romans 11 the Apostle Paul taught that in Old Testament times, as the covenant people of God, Israel was in the place of God's blessing. Because Israel rejected Christ through unbelief, God removed it temporarily from the place of His blessing. During the time that Israel is removed, God has placed the church in the place of blessing. Thus, the church is in the place of God's blessing while Israel is out of it. This leads to the conclusion that Israel and the church are not the same.

These seven lines of evidence indicate that the nation of Israel and the church are separate, distinct entities.

THE TIME WHEN THE CHURCH BEGAN

The second preliminary matter that must be observed is when the church began in history. The New Testament presents several lines of evidence to the effect that the church did not begin until the day of Pentecost recorded in Acts 2.

The First Line of Evidence. The church was not formed apart from the baptism with the Spirit, and Spirit baptism did not begin until the day of Pentecost. In Colossians 1:18 and 24, Paul declared that the body of Christ is the church. In 1 Corinthians 12:13 he indicated that all believers in Christ (Jew and Gentile alike) are placed into the body of Christ through Spirit baptism. Thus, Paul taught the necessity of Spirit baptism for the formation of the church.

John the Baptist clearly indicated that he was not baptizing people with the Spirit in his time. Instead, he stated that Jesus would baptize with the Spirit in the future (Lk. 3:16). On the day of His ascension, Jesus declared that His believers should remain in Jerusalem for a few more days to receive the baptism with the Spirit to which John referred, which the Father had promised and about which Jesus had talked (Acts 1:4-5). The language of Jesus' statement implied that Spirit baptism had not yet begun historically and would not begin until a few days after His ascension. Acts 2 indicates that it began on the day of Pentecost, ten days after the Lord's ascension.

On the basis of these statements by Paul, John the Baptist, and Jesus, we can draw two conclusions. First, since Spirit baptism is necessary for the formation of the church, and since Spirit baptism did not begin historically until the day of Pentecost, the church did not begin historically until the day of Pentecost.

Second, on the day of Pentecost the Holy Spirit began to be related to believers in Jesus Christ in ways in which He was not related to Old Testament believers. Certainly the Holy Spirit was at work in the world in some ways before the day of Pentecost (cp. Gen. 6:3; Ex. 35:30-33; Num. 11:26-30; 24:2), but on Pentecost He came with some new ways of working that had not been present before. Thus, there is something distinctive about the relationship of the Holy Spirit to saints since Pentecost. This is substantiated by other statements in the New Testament. On the last day of the Feast of Tabernacles, Jesus promised that believers would have rivers of living water flowing out of their hearts (Jn. 7:37-38). John explained Jesus' statement as follows: "But this spoke he of the Spirit, whom they that believe on him should receive; for the Holy Spirit was not yet given, because Jesus was not yet glorified" (Jn. 7:39). John indicated that the Spirit would come in a new, distinctive sense after Jesus was glorified through His death, resurrection, and ascension (Jn. 12:16, 23-27; 17:1, 5; Phil. 2:8-9).

The night before Jesus was crucified, He promised that after He returned to the Father in heaven, the Father would send the Holy Spirit to His disciples (Jn. 14:2-4, 16-17, 26; 16:12-16). He declared that the Spirit would not come while He was present on the earth (Jn. 16:7). He also drew a clear distinction between the relationship of the Spirit with His disciples *before* His ascension and *after* His ascension: "For he dwelleth with you, and shall be in you" (Jn. 14:17).

The Second Line of Evidence. The fact that the church did not begin until Pentecost is found in Peter's assertion that something new began when the believers were baptized with the Spirit on Pentecost. Speaking of his experience at Cornelius's house (Acts 10), Peter said, "And as I began to speak, the Holy Spirit fell on them, as on us at the beginning. Then remembered I the word of the Lord, how he said, John indeed baptized with water; but ye shall be baptized with the Holy Spirit" (Acts 11:15-16).

In this statement Peter indicated two things: Jesus' promise concerning Spirit baptism was fulfilled when the Spirit fell on the Jewish believers at Pentecost; and the baptism with the Spirit on Pentecost took place when something new began. The word Peter used for "beginning" "denotes beginning in the exact sense, i.e., 'the place in a temporal sequence at which something new, which is also finite, commences.' "[1]

Since the new thing began on Pentecost when the baptism with the Spirit took place, and since (as we noted earlier) Spirit baptism was necessary for the formation of the church, it would appear that Peter was indicating that the church was the new thing that began on Pentecost.

The Third Line of Evidence. Paul's teaching concerning the "mystery" is another evidence for the church beginning in Acts 2. Concerning the meaning of the term "mystery," Arndt and Gingrich said,

> Our lit. uses it to mean the secret thoughts, plans, and dispensations of God which are hidden fr. the human reason, as well as fr. all other comprehension below the divine level, and hence must be revealed to those for whom they are intended."[2]

In line with this meaning, Paul used the term "mystery" to refer to a body of divine knowledge that was kept completely hidden from mankind in ages past (Rom. 16:25; 1 Cor. 2:7-8; Eph. 3:4-5, 9; Col. 1:26), which mankind could never have discovered through the use of their senses or reason (1 Cor. 2:9), and which God has now revealed to them (Rom. 16:25-26; 1 Cor. 2:10; Eph. 3:3-5; Col. 1:26-27).

We should note several things about the Ephesians 3 "mystery." First, it revealed the fact that there would be a period of time when believing Jews and Gentiles would be untied together as equals in one body. In Ephesians 2:11-19 Paul made it clear that this union did not exist before the death of Christ.

Second, in a parallel passage to Ephesians 3, Paul indicated that this body, which is related to the mystery, is the church (Col. 1:18, 24-27). Thus, in Ephesians 3 Paul was saying that the mystery revealed the fact that there would be a period of time when there would be a body called the church existing in the world.

Third, Paul made it clear that this knowledge concerning the church had been known by God from eternity past. He taught that the church had been part of God's eternal plan (Eph. 3:9, 11).

Fourth, Paul declared that this knowledge concerning the church had been kept hidden from mankind in past ages (Eph. 3:4-5, 9).

Fifth, Paul asserted that God did not reveal this knowledge concerning the church until the time of the apostles and New Testament prophets (Eph. 3:3-5). In Colossians 1:26 he talked about "the mystery which hath been hidden from ages and from generations, but now is made manifest to his saints." Paul's use of the word "now" indicated that knowledge concerning the existence of the church was not revealed to mankind until Paul's lifetime.

Sixth, in Ephesians 3:8-10, Paul stated that one of the purposes of God's revealing the mystery concerning the church during the time of the apostles and prophets was "To the intent that now, unto the principalities and powers in heavenly places, might be known by the church the manifold wisdom of God." This statement of purpose indicates that there were certain aspects of God's wisdom that were totally unknown to the angels before the church came into existence. Nothing prior to the church had required the use of these facets of God's wisdom. The formation of the church demanded the exercise and therefore the display of aspects of divine wisdom that God never before had operated or revealed because only this unique wisdom could bring about the peaceful, equal union of such confirmed, implacable enemies as Jews and Gentiles into one body.

Once again Paul used the word "now," indicating that God intended to wait until the time of the apostles and New Testament prophets to reveal to the angels the facets of His wisdom that the formation of the church demanded. In Ephesians 3:11 Paul stated that God's intention to wait until that time to reveal these aspects of His wisdom was part of His eternal purpose.

Following is a summary of Paul's teaching concerning the mystery in Ephesians 3. As part of His eternal purpose for history, God in eternity past determined that there would be a time in history when He would bring together believing Jews and Gentiles as equals to form one body, the church. Since this was His own plan, God knew about it all along; but He kept this knowledge about the church completely hidden in Himself and from mankind throughout many ages of time. Mankind could not discover this knowledge about the church on their own. God intentionally waited until the time of the apostles and New Testament prophets to reveal to them knowledge concerning the church and to reveal to the angels the facets of

His wisdom that the formation of the church required to be exercised. Paul's teaching concerning the Ephesians 3 mystery leads to several conclusions. First, mankind knew nothing about the church until the time of the apostles and New Testament prophets.

Second, the church did not exist before that time. If it had existed before the time of the apostles and New Testament prophets, certainly mankind would have known about it before then.

Third, the Old Testament contained no revelation concerning the church. It did contain revelation that Gentiles would experience great salvation in the future, but revelation concerning salvation and revelation concerning the church are not the same, because salvation and the church are not the same. Just as a ticket, which is necessary to enter a sports stadium, is not the same thing as the stadium, so salvation, which is necessary to enter the church, is not the same thing as the church. Although the Old Testament contained revelation concerning the salvation of Gentiles, nowhere did it contain revelation that there would be a time when saved Gentiles would be united with saved Jews as equals in one body.

Fourth the church was not formed until the time of the apostles and New Testament prophets. Had it been formed earlier, those aspects of God's wisdom related to the formation of the church would have been known to the angels before the time of the apostles and New Testament prophets.

The Fourth Line of Evidence. The church could not exist until after the death of Christ. In Ephesians 2:13-16 Paul made statements to the effect that Gentiles, who used to be far off, now had been brought near "by the blood of Christ" (v. 13); that Jesus Himself is the peace between Jew and Gentile (v. 14); that He is the one who has made Jew and Gentile one, has broken down the dividing wall between them, has abolished the enmity "in his flesh," has made "one new man" of Jew and Gentile "in himself," and has reconciled both Jew and Gentile unto God "in one body by the cross" (vv. 14-16).

We should note several things concerning these statements. First, they clearly indicate that the uniting of Jew and Gentile together as equals to form one new man, one body, was the result of Jesus' shedding His blood and dying on the cross.

Second, a comparison of these statements with Paul's statements in Ephesians 3:6 and Colossians 1:18, 24 makes it obvious that the one body of Ephesians 2:16 is the church.

Third, the church was formed as the result of Jesus' death.

Fourth, in the statements of Ephesians 2:13-16 Paul emphasized the situation of the Gentiles after the death of Christ in contrast with their situation before His death (vv. 11-12). Before Christ's death, the Gentiles were alienated from the Jews; but after Christ's death, Gentiles were united with Jews in one body. Paul's use of the word "now" (v. 13) indicated that this radical change had taken place during his lifetime, meaning that the one body, the church, was not formed until after Christ's death and during Paul's lifetime.

Fifth, Paul described the union of Jew and Gentile as "one new man" (v. 15). The word translated "new" means "what is new and distinctive as compared with other things," "what is new in nature, different from the usual," and "new in kind."[3] It would appear, then, that this union of Jew and Gentile formed a new body that was different in nature and kind from anything that had existed before. It was not a continuation of something that already had been in existence and was essentially the same in nature.

Since the uniting of Jew and Gentile together as equals to form one body was the result of Christ's death, since that body was formed only after Christ's death, since that body was new and different in nature and kind from anything that had existed before, and since that one body is the church, the church did not and could not exist until after the death of Christ.

A statement Paul made to the Ephesian elders also leads to the conclusion that the church could not have existed until after Christ's death. In that statement Paul referred to "the church of God, which he hath purchased with his own blood" (Acts 20:28). The word translated "purchased" means "acquire, obtain, gain for oneself."[4] Paul therefore was declaring that Jesus acquired or obtained the church through his death, implying that Jesus did not have the church before He shed His blood.

The Fifth Line of Evidence. The church could not exist before the apostles and New Testament prophets. After Paul taught that God had started to do something new during his lifetime by bringing Jews and Gentiles together as equals to form "one new man," "one body" (Eph. 2:11-16), he continued his teaching concerning this new work of God through the use of a metaphor—that of a building (Eph. 2:19-22). He declared that Gentiles are no longer strangers and aliens but are members of the "household of God" (v. 19). In 1 Timothy 3:15 Paul clearly stated that the household of God is the church; therefore, in Ephesians 2:19 he was teaching that Gentiles are members of the church.

Paul began to use the metaphor of a building by asserting that the members of the church "are built upon the foundation of the apostles and prophets" (v. 20). We should note several things concerning this assertion. First, since the church consists of its members, and since the members are built upon the foundation of the apostles and prophets, Paul was indicating that the church itself is built upon the foundation of the apostles and prophets.

Second, continuing his use of the metaphor of a building, Paul pointed out that just as a building has a foundation and superstructure, so the church has a foundation and superstructure. The church's foundation consists of the apostles and prophets, and its superstructure consists of the other church saints.

Third, the prophets who, together with the apostles, make up the foundation of the church are New Testament prophets, not Old Testament prophets. The context indicates that this is so, for in Ephesians 3:5, where Paul referred to the apostles and prophets again, he said, "as it is now revealed unto his holy apostles and prophets." Through the use of the word "now," Paul made it clear that the prophets to whom he referred were living during his lifetime and that of the other apostles.

Fourth, since a building cannot be built without a foundation, and since the church's foundation consists of the apostles and New Testament prophets, the church could not have been built before the time of the apostles and New Testament prophets. According to Arndt and Gingrich, in Ephesians 2:20 the word Paul used for "foundation" has the meaning "of the indispensable prerequisites for someth. to come into being."[5] Thus, the church could not come into being apart from the apostles and New Testament prophets.

The Sixth Line of Evidence. Jesus promised in Matthew 16:18, "I will build my church." The verb translated "will build" is future tense and indicative mood in the text, and "the future indicative expresses anticipation of an event in future time."[6]

The implication of Jesus' statement is that the church was not in existence when He said this. The church would be something new that He would build in the future. Thus, Otto Michel stated that the verb "will build" in Matthew 16:18 "denotes an eschatological act of Christ, a new authorisation by God. The Messiah will build . . . the new community."[7]

Prior to His Matthew 16:18 statement, Jesus had been presenting Himself to Israel as its Messiah, the one who would set up the promised theocratic kingdom of God. He had claimed to be the Messiah (Jn. 10:24-25); through His miracles He had given Israel a foretaste of the miraculous powers by which the Messiah would usher in the theocratic kingdom (Lk. 7:19-22; Jn. 10:25; 12:37; 20:30-31; Acts 2:22; Heb. 6:5). He had preached the gospel of the kingdom: "Repent; for the kingdom of heaven is at hand" (Mt. 4:17, 23; 9:35); and He had commissioned His apostles to preach the gospel of the kingdom and to perform the miracles associated with the kingdom only to the people of Israel (Mt. 10:1-8).

In spite of Jesus' claim to be the Messiah who would set up the theocratic kingdom, and in spite of the foretaste of miraculous kingdom powers demonstrating the truthfulness of His claim, Israel was determined to reject Him and His claim (Jn. 12:37-41). This determination had become obvious before Jesus' Matthew 16 declaration that He would build His church. In Matthew 12 the religious leaders of Israel had begun to plot His death and to assert that Satan was the source of His miraculous powers. In Matthew

16:13-14, the apostles reported the people's reaction to Jesus. The Jews were saying that He was John the Baptist, Elijah, Jeremiah, or one of the prophets; but they were not acclaiming Him to be the Messiah.

In light of Israel's obvious determination, in Matthew 16 Jesus began to give His apostles several indications that things would change significantly for Him and His ministry. One indication was Jesus' shocking declaration of His death and resurrection (v. 21). Matthew's words, "From that time forth began Jesus to show unto his disciples, how he must . . . be killed, and be raised again the third day," reveal that Jesus had never clearly declared His death and resurrection to the apostles prior to that time. Peter's strong negative reaction to Jesus' declaration (v. 22) indicated that this was a shocking new concept to the apostles and that the gospel of the kingdom, which they had been proclaiming for some time, did not include the ideas of Jesus' death, burial, and resurrection. Thus, through this shocking declaration Jesus was indicating that instead of accepting Him as their Messiah, Israel would reject Him by having Him put to death.

Another indication of coming change in Matthew 16 was Jesus' charge to the apostles "that they should tell no man" that He was the Messiah (v. 20). Earlier they had proclaimed Him to be the Messiah (Jn. 1:41), but now they were forbidden to do so.

A third indication was His Matthew 16:18 declaration. Since Israel would reject Him as the Messiah who would set up the theocratic kingdom, He would not establish that kingdom in the near future. Instead, He would do something different—He would build a new "ekklesia," the church. There were other "ekklesias" or assemblies in the ancient world, such as the "ekklesia" of Israel in the wilderness during its exodus (Acts 7:38) and the "ekklesias" of citizens of cities when they gathered together for public meetings (Acts 19:32, 39, 41); but Jesus emphasized that the "ekklesia" He would build would be uniquely related to Him ("my church"). The Israel of Jesus' generation refused to be associated with Him; therefore, He would build a new assembly of people who would acknowledge and belong to Him. Later, the Apostle Paul emphasized the unique relationship of the church to Christ through the use of the relationships between the body and head (Eph. 1:22-23; 4:15-16; 5:23; Col. 1:18; 2:19) and bride and bridegroom (Rom. 7:1-4; 2 Cor. 11:2; Eph. 5:22-23).

The Seventh Line of Evidence. The church could not exist until after Christ's ascension. Two things indicate that this is so. First, in Ephesians 1:20-23 Paul taught that God gave Christ the position of head of the church in conjunction with His being seated at God's right hand after His ascension to heaven. This means that Christ was not head of the church until after His ascension. In Ephesians 4:15-16 and Colossians 2:19, Paul also taught that the church is dependent upon Christ, as its head, for growth and development. Just as the human body cannot live, function, or develop without its head, so the body of Christ, the church, cannot live, function, or develop without Christ as its head, and since Christ was not head of the church until after His ascension, the church could not have existed until after Christ's ascension.

Second, in Ephesians 4:8, 11-12, Paul indicated that in conjunction with His ascension to heaven, Christ gave spiritual gifts to people so that the body of Christ, the church, could be built. Through this teaching Paul implied that the church could not be built apart from these spiritual gifts, and the church therefore could not have existed before Christ's ascension.

Taken together, these seven lines of evidence indicate that the church did not begin historically until the Acts 2 day of Pentecost after the death and ascension of Jesus Christ.

AN EXAMINATION OF THE 70-WEEKS PROPHECY OF DANIEL 9

Near the end of Israel's Babylonian captivity, in response to the Prophet Daniel's concern about Israel's future, God sent a significant prophecy to him through the angel Gabriel. This prophecy is recorded in Daniel 9:24-27.[8] For the purpose of this present study, we must note several significant facts concerning this prophecy.

The First Significant Fact. This prophecy involved "Seventy weeks" (lit., "seventy sevens") of time (v. 24). Seventy sevens is the same as 70 times seven or 490. Thus, the prophecy involved 490 units of time. How much time would be involved in these 490 units? Would these units consist of 490 days, weeks, months, or years? We shall note later that these units of time were determined by God specifically for Israel. Seventy sevens of *years* would have been very meaningful to the people of Israel. God had divided their calendar into seven-year periods with every seventh year being a sabbatic year (Lev. 25:3-9). In addition, Israel's Babylonian captivity lasted 70 years because the people of Israel had violated 70 sabbatic years over the course of 490 years (Lev. 26:34-35; 2 Chr. 36:21). These facts, together with the fact that Daniel himself had been thinking in terms of years in the context of this 70-weeks prophecy (9:1-2), indicate that the units of time involved consist of 490 years.

The Second Significant Fact. God determined all 70 weeks or 490 years for Daniel's people and holy city (v. 25); therefore, all 70 weeks were determined specifically for Israel and Jerusalem. God did not determine the 70 weeks for the church. This is significant because, as we noted earlier in this chapter, the church is distinct from Israel.

The Third Significant Fact. Gabriel said that the time from the beginning of the 70 weeks until the Messiah, the Prince, would be 69 weeks or 483 years (v. 25). Thus, 483 years after the beginning of the 70 weeks, the Messiah would be present in the world. The fact that this prophecy gave a very specific time when the Messiah would be present indicates that a significant event would happen with regard to the Messiah at the end of the first 69 weeks. What could that event be?

The fact that Gabriel referred to the Messiah as "the Prince" implies that the event must be related significantly to the Messiah's being Israel's Prince or coming King. Zechariah 9:9 declared that Israel could identify its coming King by the fact that He would come to Jerusalem mounted on the foal of a donkey. In light of this, it would appear that the specific event that would happen at the end of the first 69 weeks or 483 years would be the Messiah's official presentation of Himself to Israel as its Prince or coming King by coming to Jerusalem mounted on the foal of a donkey.

Jesus Christ fulfilled this part of the 70-weeks prophecy when He officially presented Himself to Israel as its Messiah-Prince through His triumphal entry into Jerusalem on the foal of a donkey on Palm Sunday.[9] Several things indicate that this was the specific event that ended the first 69 weeks or 483 years of the 70-weeks prophecy. First, some of the crowd on that Palm Sunday recognized the significance of Jesus' actions on that day, for they called Him "King" (Lk. 19:37-38).

Second, as Jesus approached Jerusalem on that day, He wept over the city and said, "If thou hadst known, even thou, at least in this thy day, the things which belong unto thy peace! But now they are hidden from thine eyes." He warned Jerusalem that it would be destroyed by enemy forces "because thou knewest not the time of thy visitation" (Lk. 19:41-44). Jesus' language indicated that that particular day had been marked out by God as the time of Jerusalem's visitation by her Messiah-Prince—the day that could have brought lasting peace to that city if its people had accepted Jesus for who He was. It also indicated that the people of Israel should have recognized that that particular day was the day when the Messiah would visit Jerusalem as Prince because several centuries earlier, in Daniel 9, God had revealed the exact time when the Messiah would present Himself as Prince to Israel.

Third, the 70-weeks prophecy foretold that the Messiah would be "cut off" after the end of the first 69 weeks or 483 years (vv. 25-26). The word translated "cut off" was used for the death penalty (Lev. 7:20-21, 25, 27) and often referred to a violent death (1 Sam. 17:51; Obad. 9; Nah. 3:15).[10] In this instance, it referred to the fact that the Messiah would be condemned to suffer the death penalty and thus would experience a violent death after the end of the first 69 weeks. It is a fact of history that Jesus was condemned to death and crucified several days (less than a week) after His triumphal entry into Jerusalem on Palm Sunday (Mk. 11–15).

Fourth, the 70-weeks prophecy foretold that Jerusalem and the Temple would be destroyed after the end of the first 69 weeks (vv. 25-26). It is a fact of history that Jerusalem and the Temple were destroyed by the Romans in 70 A.D., some 30 to 40 years after Jesus' triumphal entry into Jerusalem on Palm Sunday. As we noted earlier, on that Palm Sunday Jesus warned Jerusalem concerning that destruction by enemy forces as He approached the city.

Taken together, these four items indicate that the first 69 weeks of the 70-weeks prophecy ended on the day when Jesus made His triumphal entry into Jerusalem on the foal of a donkey and officially presented Himself to Israel as its Prince or coming King.

The Fourth Significant Fact. The church did not exist during any part of the first 69 weeks or 483 years of the 70 weeks. We have just observed that the first 69 weeks ended on the day of Jesus' triumphal entry into Jerusalem. Earlier in this chapter we demonstrated that the church did not begin historically until the day of Pentecost (Acts 2), which took place nearly two months *after* the day of Jesus' triumphal entry into Jerusalem; therefore, the church did not begin historically until nearly two months *after* the end of the first 69 weeks of the 70-weeks prophecy.

We should note that God consistently kept the church out of all the first 69 weeks. Thus, it is evident that He intended the first 69 weeks of the 70-weeks prophecy to be His program specifically for Israel, but not for the church. This was consistent with the concept developed earlier in this chapter that Israel and the church are distinct entities. In addition, it was consistent with the second significant fact noted earlier concerning the 70-weeks prophecy—that God determined all 70 weeks specifically for Israel and Jerusalem, not for the church.

The Fifth Significant Fact. God temporarily interrupted His 70-weeks program for Israel at the end of the first 69 weeks or 483 years with a gap of time that is now approaching 2,000 years in duration. Thus, the 70th week or last seven years of the 490 years involved in the prophecy did not follow immediately after the end of the first 69 weeks or 483 years. This indicates that the seven-year Tribulation period has not yet begun.

There are several evidences for this gap of time between the end of the first 69 weeks and the beginning of the 70th week. First, Daniel 9:27 teaches that abomination will come with desolation *during* the 70th week, but Jesus indicated that this abomination of desolation spoken of by Daniel will come shortly before His Second Coming immediately after the Great Tribulation (Mt. 24:15-21, 29-31), meaning that the 70th week or last seven years of the prophecy must also come shortly before Jesus' Second Coming.

Second, Daniel 9 indicates that the destruction of Jerusalem and the Temple by the Romans fits within the scope of the 70 weeks or 490 years of the prophecy. Thus, this destruction was to occur before the end of the 70th week or last period of seven years. In light of this and the fact that the first 69 weeks ended with Jesus' triumphal entry, if the last seven of the 490 years had followed immediately after the end of the first 69 weeks, Jerusalem and the Temple would have been destroyed just seven years after Jesus' triumphal entry into Jerusalem in the early 30s A.D. It is a fact of history, however, that Jerusalem and the Temple were not destroyed until 70 A.D., several decades after Jesus' triumphal entry. Only if there were a gap of time between the end of the first 69 weeks and the beginning of the 70th week could this destruction have taken place so late and still be within the scope of the 70-weeks or 490-years prophecy.

Third, it is not unusual for biblical prophecies to contain gaps of time. For example, Isaiah 9:6 says, "For unto us a child is born" (referring to the Messiah's first coming), and "the government shall be upon his shoulder" (related to the Messiah's Second Coming). Zechariah 9:9-10 states, "behold, thy King cometh unto thee . . . lowly, and riding upon an ass, and upon a colt, the foal of an ass" (referring to the Messiah's triumphal entry during His first coming), and "his dominion shall be from sea even to sea, and from the river even to the ends of the earth" (related to the Messiah's Second Coming).

The Sixth Significant Fact. God started the church very shortly after He interrupted His 70-weeks program for Israel and Jerusalem with a gap of time at the end of the first 69 weeks. God brought the church into existence just 57 days after the first 69 weeks ended with Jesus' triumphal entry into Jerusalem.

A SUMMARY OF FACTS

The examination of the 70-weeks prophecy of Daniel 9 has produced several significant facts. First, the Daniel 9:24-27 prophecy involved 70 weeks or 490 years of time. Second, God determined all 70 weeks or 490 years specifically for Israel and Jerusalem, not for the church. Third, the first 69 weeks or 483 years ended with Jesus' triumphal entry into Jerusalem on the foal of a donkey on Palm Sunday. Fourth, the church did not exist during any part of the first 69 weeks or 483 years. God consistently kept the church out of this entire period of time. It is evident that He intended the first 69 weeks or 483 years to be His program specifically for Israel, not the church. Fifth, God temporarily interrupted His 70-weeks program for Israel at the end of the first 69 weeks or 483 years. Sixth, God started the church very shortly after He interrupted His 70-weeks program for Israel and Jerusalem with a gap of time at the end of the first 69 weeks.

STRONG INFERENCES

These six facts, when taken together and combined with the distinction between Israel and the church noted at the beginning of this chapter, prompt three strong inferences.

The First Strong Inference. God does not intend the church to be present on the earth for any part of the 70 weeks or 490 years He has determined specifically for Israel and Jerusalem. He intends to keep His 70-weeks program for Israel and Jerusalem and His program for the church separate and distinct from each other, just as Israel and the church are distinct entities.

This does not mean that God stopped working altogether with Israel and Jerusalem when He interrupted the 70-weeks program and started the church. Instead, it means that God temporarily stopped one specific program (the 70-weeks program) with Israel and Jerusalem while He works His program with the church in the world. There is a major difference between saying that God stopped working with Israel altogether and saying that He temporarily stopped one specific program with that nation. God worked with Israel and Jerusalem in ways other than the 70-weeks program for many centuries before He started that specific program after Daniel's time. In like manner, during the present interruption of the 70-weeks program, He works with the nation and city in ways other than that program.

The Second Strong Inference. God intends the church to be present on the earth specifically during the interrupting gap of time between the end of the first 69 weeks or 483 years and the beginning of the 70th week or last seven years. If God intended to mix any part of His 70-weeks program for Israel and Jerusalem with His program for the church, why didn't He start the church during the first 69 weeks of the 70-weeks program?

The Third Strong Inference. God will remove the church from the earth before the 70th week begins with the resumption of His 70-weeks program for Israel and Jerusalem.

CONCLUSION

A strong inference in favor of the Pretribulation Rapture of the church has been derived from this chapter's study of the 70-weeks prophecy recorded in Daniel 9:24-27. The pretribulation view is the only view of the Rapture that has the church being removed from the earth before the 70th week begins (before God resumes His 70-weeks program with Israel and Jerusalem). Thus, it is the only view of the Rapture that keeps God's specific 70-weeks program for Israel and Jerusalem separate and distinct from His program for the church.

All other views of the Rapture have the church going through at least part of the 70th week, meaning that all other views mix God's 70-weeks program for Israel and Jerusalem together with His program for the church.

ENDNOTES

1. Gerhard Delling, "arche," *Theological Dictionary of the New Testament*, Vol. I, ed. by Gerhard Kittel, trans. and ed. by Geoffrey W. Bromiley (Grand Rapids: Wm. B. Eerdmans Publishing Company, 1969), p. 479.

2. William F. Arndt and F. Wilbur Gingrich, *A Greek-English Lexicon of the New Testament*, 4th rev. ed. (Chicago: The University of Chicago Press, 1957), p. 532.

3. Johannes Behm, "kainos," *Theological Dictionary of the New Testament*, Vol. III, ed. by Gerhard Kittel, trans. and ed. by Geoffrey W. Bromiley (Grand Rapids: Wm. B. Eerdmans Publishing Company, 1965), p. 447.

4. Arndt and Gingrich, *A Greek-English Lexicon of the New Testament*, p. 655.

5. *Ibid.*, p. 356.

6. H. E. Dana and Julius R. Mantey, *A Manual Grammar of the Greek New Testament* (New York: The Macmillan Company, 1927), p. 191.

7. Otto Michel, "oikodomeo," *Theological Dictionary of the New Testament*, Vol. V., ed. by Gerhard Friedrich, trans. and ed. by Geoffrey W. Bromiley (Grand Rapids: Wm. B. Eerdmans Publishing Company, 1967), p. 139.

8. For a thorough study of the Daniel 9 70-weeks prophecy see: Renald E. Showers, *The Most High God* (Bellmawr, NJ: The Friends of Israel Gospel Ministry, 1982), pp. 111-138.

9. Sir Robert Anderson, *The Coming Prince* (Grand Rapids: Kregel Publications, 1954), pp. 125-127.

10. Edward J. Young, *The Prophecy of Daniel* (Grand Rapids: Wm. B. Eerdmans Publishing Company, 1970), p. 206.

CHAPTER THIRTEEN

REFERENCES TO THE CHURCH AND ISRAEL IN THE BOOK OF THE REVELATION

A seventh inference for the Pretribulation Rapture of the church is gained from an examination of the references to the church and Israel in the Book of the Revelation.

REFERENCES TO THE CHURCH

Twenty-four verses in the Book of the Revelation refer to the church. Nineteen of these verses refer to the church as the "church" or "churches" (*ekklesia*); two verses refer to it as the "bride" (*numphe*); two verses indicate that the church is the Lamb's "wife" (*gune*); and one verse refers to the church as both the "bride" and "wife" of the Lamb. Revelation never refers to the church as the "body" (*soma*).

Twenty of the 24 verses refer to the church in the present church age (1:4, 11, 20; 2:1, 7, 8, 11, 12, 17, 18, 23, 29; 3:1, 6, 7, 13, 14, 22; 22:16, 17). Two verses refer to the church in the marriage of the Lamb, which will take place *in heaven*, not on the earth (19:7, 8).[1] Two verses refer to the church in the future eternal state (21:2, 9).

It is important to note that there are no references to the church *on the earth* in chapters 4 through 18, the chapters relating specifically to the 70th week of Daniel 9, including the seals, trumpets, and bowls.

REFERENCES TO ISRAEL

Twenty-two verses in the Book of the Revelation refer to Israel. One of these verses refers to Israel as "the twelve tribes of the children of Israel" (21:12). Ten verses refer to the 144,000 Jewish men by several designations (7:3, 4, 5, 6, 7, 8; 14:1, 3, 4, 5). Ten verses describe Israel through various terms as the woman who is pursued by the dragon (Satan) [12:1, 2, 4, 5, 6, 13, 14, 15, 16, 17]. One verse refers to "the children of Israel" (2:14).

One of the 22 verses refers to Israel in Old Testament times (2:14). One other refers to the nation in the future eternal state (21:12). Four verses refer to Israel during the time of the first coming of Christ (12:1, 2, 4, 5). It is important to note that the remaining 16 verses refer to Israel on the earth during the 70th week (7:3, 4, 5, 6, 7, 8; 12:6, 13, 14, 15, 16, 17; 14:1, 3, 4, 5).

A SIGNIFICANT CONTRAST

More than 72% of the references to Israel in the Book of the Revelation refer to it on the earth during the 70th week. By contrast, none of the references to the church in Revelation refer to it on the earth during the 70th week.

The fact that significant parts of Revelation contain no reference to the church but make many references to Israel has been recognized by scholars who do not advocate a Pretribulation Rapture of the church. For example, the Roman Catholic scholar, C. Van Den Biesen, stated, "The Apocalypse abounds in passages which bear no specific Christian character but, on the contrary, show a decidedly Jewish complexion."[2] In addition, according to the same writer, because of this contrast in Revelation, the German scholar, Vischer, held "the Apocalypse to have been originally a purely Jewish composition, and to have been changed into a Christian work by the insertion of those sections that deal with Christian subjects."[3] The present author rejects Vischer's conclusion as being erroneous but would point out that his wrong conclusion was the result of his trying to explain the contrast of references to the church and Israel that actually exists in Revelation.

This contrast is consistent with the three strong inferences noted near the end of the previous chapter in conjunction with the 70-weeks prophecy. First, God does not intend the church to be present on the earth for any part of the 70 weeks or 490 years that He has determined specifically for Israel and Jerusalem. He intends to keep His 70-weeks program for Israel and Jerusalem and His program for the church separate and distinct from each other, just as Israel and the church are distinct entities.

Second, God intends the church to be present on the earth specifically during the interrupting gap of time between the end of the first 69 weeks or 483 years and the beginning of the 70th week or last seven years.

Third, God will remove the church from the earth before the 70th week begins (before He resumes His 70-weeks program for Israel and Jerusalem).

This contrast between the references to the church and Israel is exactly what should be found in Revelation, if all three strong inferences related to the Daniel 9 prophecy are true. The major percentage of references to Israel in Revelation should refer to that nation's being on the earth during the 70th week, since God determined all 70 weeks or 490 years of the Daniel 9 prophecy specifically for Israel and Jerusalem. By contrast, there should be no references to the church on the earth during the 70th week in Revelation because the church is distinct from Israel and God has not determined any part of the 70 weeks of the Daniel 9 prophecy for the church.

This contrast between the references to the church and Israel in Revelation is significant for two reasons. First, it supports the validity of the three strong inferences noted near the end of the previous chapter in conjunction with the 70-weeks prophecy.

Second, it serves as an inference in favor of the Pretribulation Rapture view. The fact that there are no references to the church on the earth in any of the chapters of Revelation that refer specifically to the 70th week, including the seals, trumpets, and bowls, infers that the church will be absent from the earth for the entire 70th week, including the seals, trumpets, and bowls. By contrast, every view of the Rapture except the pretribulation view has the church present on the earth for at least part of the 70th week.

SAINTS IN REVELATION

The Book of the Revelation clearly indicates that saints will be present on the earth during the 70th week. For example, Revelation teaches that the Antichrist will wage war against the saints (13:7; cp. Dan. 7:21, 25) during the 70th week and that many saints of that period will be martyred (6:9-11; 20:4).

This teaching prompts the following question: Doesn't the fact that saints will be present on the earth during the 70th week require the conclusion that the church will be present on the earth during the 70th week? The answer to that question is: The fact that saints will be present on the earth during the 70th week does not require that conclusion because not all saints are church saints.

That answer is based on two factors. First, the Bible clearly teaches that there were saints on the earth in Old Testament times. For example, Psalm 16:3 referred to "the saints who are in the earth," and Psalm 116:15 declared that the death of God's saints is precious in His sight (cp. 1 Sam. 2:9; 2 Chr. 6:41; Ps. 79:2; Hos. 11:12).

Second, the previous chapter demonstrated that the church did not begin historically until the day of Pentecost in Acts 2, after the death and ascension of Christ. Since the church did not begin until that time, the saints who lived and died before the day of Pentecost did not belong to the church; they were Old Testament saints, not church saints. Thus, there was an extensive period of history prior to the birth of the church when saints were not church saints.

The fact that saints in the Old Testament were not church saints prompts several conclusions. First, not all saints in the Bible are church saints. Second, since the Bible refers to saints who are not church saints, the fact that saints will be present on the earth during the 70th week does not require the conclusion that they will be church saints. They could be designated as 70th week or Tribulation saints. Third, since we are not required to conclude that the saints present on the earth during the 70th week are church saints, we are not required to conclude that the church will be present on the earth during the 70th week.

THE GREAT MULTITUDE OF REVELATION 7

Between the sixth and seventh seals, John saw a great multitude of redeemed people from "all nations, and kindreds, and peoples, and tongues" standing before the throne of God and before the Lamb in heaven (Rev. 7:9-17). They were clothed with white robes and held palms in their hands. One of the 24 elders in heaven declared that they "came out of the Great Tribulation, and have washed their robes, and made them white in the blood of the Lamb" (vv. 13-14).

Two Necessary Questions. Two questions must be asked concerning this great multitude. First, does the fact that they were clothed in white robes and held palms in their hands require the conclusion that they are resurrected with literal, physical resurrection bodies (cp. Lk. 24:36-43)? Second, if they are resurrected, since the Rapture of the church will involve the resurrection of church saints' bodies, is this great multitude the church, having just been raptured from the earth between the sixth and seventh seals of the 70th week? If it is the church, having just been raptured between the sixth and seventh seals, it would mean that the church will be on the earth through the first six seals of the 70th week.

The Answer to the First Question. The fact that these people were clothed with white robes and held palms in their hands does not require the conclusion that they are resurrected with literal, physical resurrection bodies. There are several reasons for this answer. First, when Christ broke the fifth seal, John saw under the altar in heaven the souls of saints who had been slain for the Word of God during the 70th week (Rev. 6:9-11). Since they had been slain, they were without physical bodies, and yet they were given white robes to wear (v. 11). Thus, in Revelation the wearing of a white robe did not require a resurrection body. Even bodiless souls could wear such a robe.

Second, when the rich man of Luke 16 died, his body was buried (v. 22), and his soul went to hell (v. 23). Even though his soul was without its body, Jesus ascribed eyes (v. 23) and a tongue (v. 24) to his bodiless soul.

Third, angels are spirit beings (Heb. 1:14; Eph. 6:12). As a result, by nature they do not have physical bodies (in Eph. 6:12 Paul put angels in a different category from those beings who have flesh and blood bodies; in Lk. 24:39 Jesus stated that a spirit does not have flesh and bones such as He had in His resurrected body). In spite of the fact that angels do not have physical bodies by nature, the Bible ascribes wings, faces, feet, and hands to them (Isa. 6:2, 6; Rev. 10:1-2, 5, 8, 10) and portrays them wearing clothing (Mt. 28:2-3; Mk. 16:5; Acts 1:10; Rev. 15:6).

Fourth, God is a Spirit (Jn. 4:24). As a result, by nature He does not have a physical body. In spite of that fact, the Bible ascribes to Him a head and hair (Dan. 7:9), eyes and a face (Jer. 16:17), an arm (Isa. 40:10), hands (Heb. 10:31), feet (Nah. 1:3), and a finger (Dt. 9:10) and portrays Him wearing clothing (Dan. 7:9).

All four of these reasons indicate the same truth: Although the Bible ascribes such things as hands, feet, faces, tongues, and the wearing of clothing to human, angelic, and divine beings, it does not mean that those beings have literal, physical bodies such as resurrected people have. Since this is true, the fact that the people of the great multitude of Revelation 7 were clothed in white robes and held palms in their hands does not require the conclusion that they are resurrected with literal, physical resurrection bodies.

The Answer to the Second Question. This answer is twofold. First, since we are not required to conclude that the people of the great multitude are resurrected people, we need not conclude that they are the church, having just been raptured from the earth between the sixth and seventh seals.

Second, several things militate against identifying the great multitude of Revelation 7 as the church, having just been raptured from the earth. First, as noted above, one of the 24 elders declared that the people of the great multitude "came out of the Great Tribulation" (v. 14). Concerning this Tribulation, William Barclay stated, "It is not tribulation in general of which he is speaking, but of the tribulation of the end time, that tribulation which the Gospels tell us that Jesus foretold" in Matthew 24:21 and Mark 13:19.[4] Thus, the elder's declaration indicated that the great multitude was limited just to those saints who lived on the earth during the Great Tribulation part of the 70th week.

Since this is true, if the great multitude is the church, having just been raptured between the sixth and seventh seals, we must conclude that this was only a partial Rapture of the church—a Rapture of only the part of the church that had lived on the earth during the Great Tribulation. This Rapture would not include all the church saints who had lived and died during all the centuries of the church's existence on the earth prior to the 70th week and who, therefore, never lived on the earth during any part of the 70th week, including the Great Tribulation. When would all those other church saints be raptured?

By way of contrast with a partial Rapture, the biblical passages that clearly present teaching concerning the Rapture of the church strongly imply that the entire church will be raptured at the same time (Jn. 14:2-3; 1 Cor. 15:51-52; 1 Th. 4:13-18).

The second thing that militates against identifying the great multitude as the church, having just been raptured, is the fact that the expression "they who came" in the elder's declaration "These are they who came out of the Great Tribulation," is a translation of a present tense participle. Concerning the use of this specific present tense participle in Revelation 7:14, A. T. Robertson wrote, "Present middle participle with the idea of continued repetition."[5]

R. H. Charles came to the same conclusion as Robertson. He asserted that the combination of this present tense participle with the two finite verbs ("washed" and "made . . . white") in the same verse (14) is a Semitic type construction giving the sense of continuous action to the participle.[6]

In light of the significance of this participle, we can conclude that the elder was indicating that the people of the great multitude were coming out of the Great Tribulation individually (one by one) and continuously through death, mainly death by martyrdom. Thus, when discussing the continuous action significance of the participle in the elder's declaration, Charles stated, "The martyrs are *still* arriving from the scene of the Great Tribulation."[7] Jeremias also concluded that the great multitude of Revelation 7 consisted of martyrs.[8]

This means, then, that the elder was not indicating that the great multitude came out of the Great Tribulation as one body all at the same time, which would have been true if it had been the church, having just been raptured.

The third thing that militates against identifying the great multitude of Revelation 7 as the church, having just been raptured, is the fact that John did not know the identity of the great multitude. In response to the elder's question, "Who are these who are arrayed in white robes? And from where did they come?" (v. 13), John replied, "Sir, thou knowest" (v. 14).

Numerous scholars assert that the force of John's language in his reply reveals that he was ignorant of the great multitude's identity. For example, Henry Swete stated that John's reply "is at once a confession of ignorance, and an appeal for information."[9]

If the great multitude were the church, it seems strange that John did not recognize it (at least those who belonged to the church in his time), in light of the fact that he was one of the church's apostles and part of its foundation (Eph. 2:20). In the same vein, J. A. Seiss wrote concerning John's inability to identify the great multitude,

> If they represent the finally complete Church, did he not know that the Church was to be thus exalted and glorified? Was he so ignorant of the character and destiny of that chosen body of which he was an apostle and a chief, as not to know it, or whence it came, upon encountering it in heaven? Would it not be a sorry impeachment of his apostolic character and enlightenment, besides very stupid and unreasonable, to proceed on such an assumption, or on anything which involves it? The manifest fact that he was perplexed

and in doubt with reference to these palm-bearers, and that the Elder interfered to solve his questionings, proves that they are not the Church proper, but . . . a body of saved ones, with a history and place peculiarly their own, and not as yet exactly understood by the apostle.[10]

Conclusion. The answers to the two questions concerning the great multitude of Revelation 7 indicate that we are not required to conclude that the great multitude is the church, having just been raptured between the sixth and seventh seals. In fact, the answers prompt the conclusion that the great multitude of Revelation 7 is not the church.

CONCLUSION

This chapter has presented evidence to the effect that none of the references to the church in Revelation refer to its being on the earth during the 70th week or Tribulation period. In addition, it has given reasons for concluding that the saints, who according to Revelation will be on the earth during the Tribulation, and the great multitude of Revelation 7 are not the church. Thus, the references to these saints and the great multitude do not contradict the evidence that none of the references to the church in Revelation refer to it on the earth during the Tribulation.

Since that evidence is not contradicted, the fact that Revelation has no references to the church on the earth during the Tribulation strongly infers that the church will not be on the earth during any part of the Tribulation or 70th week, including the seals, trumpets, and bowls. This, then, is a strong inference in favor of the Pretribulation Rapture view.

ENDNOTES

1. See Renald E. Showers, "The Marriage and Marriage Supper of the Lamb," *Israel My Glory* magazine, June/July 1991, pp. 9-12.

2. C. Van Den Biesen, "Apocalypse," *The Catholic Encyclopedia*, Vol. I (New York: The Encyclopedia Press, 1913), p. 599.

3. *Ibid.*

4. William Barclay, *The Revelation of John*, Vol. 2 (Philadelphia: The Westminister Press, 1960), p. 35.

5. A. T. Robertson, *Word Pictures in the New Testament*, Vol. VI (Nashville: Broadman Press, 1933), p. 352.

6. R. H. Charles, *The Revelation of St. John* in *The International Critical Commentary* (New York: Charles Scribner's Sons, 1920), Vol. I, p. 213.

7. *Ibid.*

8. Joachim Jeremias, "hades," *Theological Dictionary of the New Testament*, Vol. I, ed. by Gerhard Kittel, trans. and ed. by Geoffrey W. Bromiley (Grand Rapids: Wm. D. Eerdmans Publishing Company, 1964), p. 149.

9. Henry Barclay Swete, *The Apocalypse of St. John* (Grand Rapids: Wm. B. Eerdmans Publishing Company, n.d.), p. 102.

10. J. A. Seiss, *The Apocalypse* (Grand Rapids: Zondervan Publishing House, 1957), pp. 172-73.

CONCLUSION

CHAPTER FOURTEEN

SO WHAT?

THE ATTITUDES OF MANY CHRISTIANS

When confronted with the issue of when the Rapture of the church will take place, many Christians respond, "Pretrib, midtrib, posttrib! So what? What difference does it make?" Others exclaim, "If it doesn't affect my salvation, I couldn't care less about when it happens!" Still others try to dodge the issue by stating either "I'm a pro-Rapturist—I'm for it!" or "I'm a pan-Rapturist—I believe it will all pan out."

Does it really matter when Christ will come to take His bride to be with Him? Should the timing of the Rapture make any practical difference in the life of a Christian, or is the issue so insignificant that Christians shouldn't bother with it?

THE SIGNIFICANCE OF THE ISSUE

Thankfully, a person's salvation from the penalty of sin or assurance of spending eternity with the Lord is not determined by the issue of when the Rapture of the church will take place. That does not mean, however, that Christians can ignore the matter of the timing of the Rapture without consequence.

In an earlier chapter entitled "THE IMMINENT COMING OF CHRIST," we noted that the Pretribulation Rapture view is the only view of the Rapture of the church that comfortably fits the New Testament teaching of the imminent coming of Christ. It is the only view that can honestly say that Christ could return at any moment, because it alone teaches that Christ will come to rapture the church before the 70th week of Daniel 9 or the Tribulation period begins and that nothing else *must* happen before His return. All the other Rapture views teach that at least part of the 70th week *must* transpire before Christ can come to rapture the church. Those views therefore destroy the New Testament teaching of the imminent coming of Christ.

In addition, the New Testament imminency passages examined in that chapter indicate that the imminent coming of Christ should have an incredible practical effect on the lives of individual Christians and the church as a whole. The fact that the glorified, holy Son of God could step through the door of heaven at any moment is intended by God to be the most pressing, incessant motivation for holy living and aggressive ministry (including missions, evangelism, and Bible teaching) and the greatest cure for lethargy and apathy. It should make a major difference in every Christian's values, actions, priorities, and goals.

Since the imminent coming of Christ is intended to have such a tremendous practical effect on the lives of individual Christians and the church as a whole, and since all views of the Rapture except the pretribulation view destroy the New Testament teaching of the imminent coming of Christ, we can conclude that the issue of when the Rapture of the church will take place really does matter.

MARANATHA—Our Lord, Come!

ADDENDUM

CHAPTER FIFTEEN

WHAT ABOUT THE LAST TRUMP?

A POTENTIAL PROBLEM

This book has presented inferences for the Pretribulation Rapture view. A potential problem for that view is found, however, in a statement by the Apostle Paul in 1 Corinthians 15:51-52: "Behold, I show you a mystery: We shall not all sleep, but we shall all be changed, In a moment, in the twinkling of an eye, at the last trump; for the trumpet shall sound, and the dead shall be raised incorruptible, and we shall be changed."

We should note that in this passage Paul taught that a trumpet will be sounded in conjunction with the resurrection of the bodies of dead church saints and the changing of the bodies of living church saints. In 1 Thessalonians 4:16-17 Paul taught that a trumpet will be sounded in conjunction with the resurrection of the bodies of dead church saints and the rapturing of those saints, together with living church saints, from the earth to meet Christ in the air. A comparison of these two passages indicates that Paul was referring to the same event in both. Thus, we can conclude that since 1 Thessalonians 4:16-17 is a reference to the Rapture of the church, 1 Corinthians 15:51-52 is also a reference to that Rapture, and both passages refer to the same trumpet. It also means that the trumpet to be sounded in conjunction with the Rapture of the church is "the last trump" of 1 Corinthians 15:52.

The fact that it is "the last trump" that will be sounded in conjunction with the Rapture of the church seems to pose a problem for the Pretribulation Rapture view. Since that view teaches that the Rapture of the church will take place *before* the Tribulation period, it must place "the last trump" *before* the Tribulation period. But how could a trumpet *before* the Tribulation be "the last trump," in light of the fact that Revelation 8–11 indicates that seven trumpets will be sounded later during the Tribulation and Christ's teaching that another trumpet will be sounded even later in conjunction with His coming *after* the Tribulation period (Mt. 24:29-31)?

POSSIBLE IDENTIFICATIONS
OF THE LAST TRUMP

Introduction. Any approach to this potential problem must try to discern what Paul meant by "the last trump." In this attempt it is necessary to examine what he could not have meant as well as the possibilities of what he did mean.

Foundational to this attempt is the fact that Paul simply *referred* to the last trump. He did not give the Corinthians any explanation of what that designation meant. This implies that the Corinthians already knew the identification of the last trump. Apparently the last trump related to something in the portions of Scripture they already possessed or had been taught before Paul wrote 1 Corinthians; to something with which they were familiar from their own Greek background or from practices of the Roman Empire in which they lived; or to something from the beliefs and practices of Judaism of which they had knowledge as the result of contact with Jews in their community.

What Paul Could Not Have Meant. If one insists on understanding the word "last" in the expression "the last trump" to mean that it will be absolutely the final trumpet, after which there will be no more trumpets, then there are certain things that Paul could not have meant by "the last trump."

For example, he could not have meant that the seventh trumpet of Revelation 11:15 or all seven trumpets of Revelation collectively are the last trump. There is more than one reason for this conclusion. First, Jesus taught that a trumpet will be sounded in conjunction with His coming with His angels (Mt. 24:29-31), and the chronological order of Revelation indicates that that coming will take place sometime *after* all seven trumpets of Revelation have been sounded. Thus, the trumpet associated with that coming of Christ will be sounded *after* the seven trumpets.

Second, Zechariah 14:16-19 indicates that the Feast of Tabernacles will be observed each year throughout the Millennium, and the Feast of Tabernacles involves the sounding of trumpets.[1] The Millennium will begin after the seven trumpets of Revelation, meaning that the trumpets of the Feast of Tabernacles during the Millennium will take place *after* the seven trumpets of Revelation.

Third, the Book of the Revelation, which records God's revelation concerning all seven trumpets, was not written until several decades after Paul wrote 1 Corinthians with his statement about the last trump. As a result, the Corinthians would not have known about the seventh trumpet of Revelation 11:15 or all seven trumpets of Revelation. Thus, they could not have identified the last trump with any or all of those seven trumpets. By contrast, we noted earlier that the Corinthians must have already known the identification of the last trump when they received 1 Corinthians, which means that when Paul wrote about the last trump in 1 Corinthians 15:52, he could not have been referring to any or all of the seven trumpets of Revelation. In conjunction with this, J. R. Caldwell wrote, "It would have been manifestly absurd for the apostle to refer in a letter to the Corinthian church to prophecies not yet uttered, and to a book not yet written."[2]

Fourth, Paul could not have meant all seven trumpets (plural) of Revelation collectively because in 1 Corinthians 15:52 and its parallel passage, 1 Thessalonians 4:16, Paul referred to only one trumpet (singular).[3]

If we insist that the last trump of 1 Corinthians 15:52 will be the absolutely final trumpet, after which there will be no more trumpets, Paul could not have been referring to the trumpet that Christ taught will be sounded in conjunction with His coming with His angels after the Tribulation period (Mt. 24:29-31) because, as noted above, trumpets will be sounded in conjunction with the Feast of Tabernacles each year throughout the Millennium. Since Christ's coming with His angels will take place before the Millennium begins, there will be many trumpets sounded throughout the Millennium *after* the trumpet associated with that coming.

Other Possible Meanings. It could be that when Paul referred to the last trump, he did not mean that it will be the absolutely final trumpet, after which there will be no more trumpets. In conjunction with this, Henry Alford warned that the meaning of the word "last" in the expression "the last trump" should not be "pressed too closely as if there were necessarily no trump after it."[4] Several uses of trumpets in the ancient world, together with the context of Paul's statement in 1 Corinthians 15:52, make possible other meanings of the expression "the last trump."

The Background of the First Possible Meaning. To understand the first possible meaning, two uses of trumpets in the ancient world plus various things from the context of 1 Corinthians 15 must be examined. In ancient times, a trumpet was sounded when God called His people together for an assembly where He was present in a unique sense. An excellent example of this is found in Exodus 19:10-20 when a trumpet sounded to call the people of Israel together around the base of Mount Sinai to meet with God when He came down to that mountain.[5]

It is interesting to note that the Romans had a similar use of the trumpet. A trumpet sounded the *classicum*, the call that summoned citizens together for an assembly where the emperor was present. Because of its function, the *classicum* was known as "the Emperor's trumpet-call."[6]

The trumpet also was used in ancient times to terrify an enemy or issue a warning of coming danger or judgment.[7] Biblical examples of this use are found in Jeremiah 4:19-21; 6:1; Ezekiel 33:3-6; and Amos 3:6.

Concerning items from the context of 1 Corinthians 15, we should note several things. First, the primary subject of 1 Corinthians 15 is the bodily resurrection of the dead and the defeat of death.

Second, in 1 Corinthians 15 Paul referred to three "last" things: the last enemy to be destroyed or abolished (death, v. 26), the last Adam (Christ, v. 45), and the last trump (v. 52).

Third, much of 1 Corinthians 15 is characterized by contrasts. Paul contrasted corruption and incorruption, dishonor and glory, weakness and power, the natural body and the spiritual body, earthy and heavenly, mortal and immortality, and the first Adam and the last Adam. Most, if not all, of these contrasts are related to the contrast between physical death and bodily resurrection. For example, in the contrast between the first Adam and the last Adam, Paul emphasized that physical death came through the first Adam, but victory over death by means of bodily resurrection or transformation will come through the last Adam, Christ (vv. 20-22, 45, 54, 57).

Fourth, in 1 Corinthians 15:56 Paul indicated that death is caused by sin (cp. Rom. 5:12-19) and that the strength of death-causing sin was the law that God gave at Mount Sinai (cp. Rom. 4:15; 5:13, 20; 7:7-13).

Explanation of the First Possible Meaning. Earlier we noted that the trumpet of 1 Thessalonians 4:16, which will be sounded in conjunction with the Rapture of the church, is "the last trump" of 1 Corinthians 15:52. Paul called it "the trump of God" (1 Th. 4:16), indicating that the sounding of the last trump will have the same use or purpose as the sounding of "the Emperor's trumpet-call" or *classicum*. The Corinthians would have been familiar with this because, as we noted earlier, it was a practice of the Roman Empire. Just as the sounding of "the Emperor's trumpet-call" summoned citizens together for an assembly where the emperor was present, so the sounding of "the trump of God" or "the last trump" will summon church saints together by rapture for an assembly where Christ will be present in the air (1 Th. 4:16-17).

But why did Paul call the trump of God "the last trump"? In light of the fact that he drew many contrasts in 1 Corinthians 15, including the contrast between the first Adam and the last Adam, it appears that he called the trump of God "the last trump" because it is to be contrasted with the first trump of God mentioned in the Scriptures. In addition, since, as we noted earlier, most, if not all, of the contrasts in 1 Corinthians 15 are related to the contrast between physical death and bodily resurrection, it seems that the contrast between the first trump of God and the last trump of God is also related to the contrast between physical death and bodily resurrection. Finally, since the primary subject of 1 Corinthians 15 is the bodily resurrection of the dead and the defeat of death, it appears that the last trump of God has some relationship with the bodily resurrection of the dead and the defeat of death.

In light of the intended contrast between the first trump of God and the last trump of God, an examination of the use or purpose of the first trump is necessary to understand the use or purpose of the last trump. Interestingly, the first biblical reference to a trump of God, found in Exodus 19:10-20, is also the first mention of any kind of trumpet. As we noted earlier, that passage records the sounding of a trumpet for the purpose of God's calling the people of Israel together for an assembly around the base of Mount Sinai to meet with Him when He descended from heaven to that mountain. The purpose of that meeting was the establishment of the Mosaic Law Covenant relationship between God and the people of Israel through God's giving of that law (Ex. 19:3-8; 20:1-18). Thus, the first trump of God was related to the Mosaic Law of God, because it called the people of Israel together to meet God and be placed under that law.

What relationship does this first trump of God have to the contrast between physical death and bodily resurrection in 1 Corinthians 15? Earlier we observed that in 1 Corinthians 15:56 Paul declared that sin causes death and that the strength of death-causing sin was the law that God gave to Israel at Mount Sinai. When God met with Israel at that mountain to give them the law, He warned that physical death would come to people or animals if they touched that mountain while He was there (Ex. 19:12-13, 21-25). Paul stated that the law works wrath (Rom. 4:15); that the passions of sins, which are through the law, work in people to bring forth fruit unto death (Rom. 7:5, 13); and that the law kills (2 Cor. 3:6). These statements clearly indicated that the Mosaic Law of God had a definite relationship to human physical death. Indeed, the law was a ministry of death and condemnation (2 Cor. 3:7-9).

Since the first trump of God called the people of Israel together to meet with God and be placed under the law, and since the law was the strength of death-causing sin and was a ministry of death, we can conclude that the purpose of the first trump of God was to call people together to God at Mount Sinai and thereby begin that ministry of death (cp. Heb. 12:18-21).

By contrast, 1 Corinthians 15 and 1 Thessalonians 4 indicate that the purpose of the last trump of God will be to call people together to Christ in the air and thereby begin incorruptible, immortal, bodily resurrection and change. Thus, it will call people together for the opposite purpose of that to which the first trump of God called people. It thereby will signal the beginning of the end for death, the last enemy of mankind to be destroyed or abolished, and will fulfill another use of the trumpet in ancient times— that of terrifying an enemy or issuing a warning of coming danger or judgment.

Since the *first* trump of God called people to the beginning of the ministry of death, Paul called the trump of God that will call people to the beginning of incorruptible, immortal, physical life "the *last* trump." He did so, not because no other trumpets will be sounded after it, but because, just as "last" is the opposite of "first," so this trump of God, which will be sounded in conjunction with the Rapture of the church, will call people together to the opposite of that to which the first trump of God called people.

In conjunction with this first possible meaning of "the last trump," the following comments of J. R. Caldwell are significant:

> We read of "the first man" and "the last man." Here the expression "last trump" may fitly be contrasted with that former trump which heralded Jehovah's advent to Sinai, when the ministration of condemnation and death was promulgated . . . That was the heralding of condemnation and death—this the heralding of the resurrection and the life. The first trump sounded "cursed"—as its awful tones, prolonged and loud, caused Israel to quake and fear. The last trump sounds only blessing as it summons the dead to life and the living to immortality.[8]

The Second Possible Meaning. This meaning has been presented by Arnold G. Fruchtenbaum and is derived from the Jewish observance of the Feast of Trumpets.[9]

Fruchtenbaum pointed out that in 1 Corinthians, Paul demonstrated the association between New Testament truth and Israel's seven holy seasons found in Leviticus 23. For example, in 1 Corinthians 5:6-8 Paul associated Christ's death and the sinlessness of His blood offering with Israel's Passover and Feast of Unleavened Bread. In 1 Corinthians 15:20-24 he tied Christ's resurrection to the Feast of Firstfruits.[10]

Fruchtenbaum said that Paul, in 1 Corinthians 15:50-58, connected the Rapture of the church with the Feast of Trumpets. He wrote,

> The "last trump" refers to the Feast of Trumpets and the Jewish practice of blowing trumpets at this feast each year. During the ceremony, there is a series of short trumpet blasts of various lengths, concluding with the longest blast of all, called the *tekiah gedolah*: the great, or "last trump." Judaism connected this last trump with the resurrection of the dead, and so does Paul. So, Paul's point here is that the Rapture will be the fulfillment of the Feast of Trumpets.[11]

Fruchtenbaum expressed the conviction that Paul had already taught the Corinthians about the seven holy seasons of Israel before he wrote 1 Corinthians.[12] The fact that Paul referred to several of those seasons in 1 Corinthians without explaining them indicates that the Corinthians already knew about them. Thus, they would have known about this last trump of the Feast of Trumpets and its association with the bodily resurrection of the dead.

In addition to this explanation of "the last trump" in 1 Corinthians 15:52, Fruchtenbaum asserted that the fulfillment of Israel's seven holy seasons of Leviticus 23 takes place in the order in which those seasons occur. He pointed out that the Feast of Trumpets occurs before the Day of Atonement,

Israel's day of affliction of soul and national atonement. He claimed that the Day of Atonement will "be fulfilled by the seven years of Tribulation, during which Israel will suffer affliction leading to her national repentance and restoration."[13] In light of this Tribulation fulfillment of the Day of Atonement, Fruchtenbaum concluded that since the Feast of Trumpets occurs before the Day of Atonement, and since the Feast of Trumpets will be fulfilled by the Rapture of the church, the Rapture of the church will occur before the seven-year Tribulation period.[14]

The Third Possible Meaning. A number of scholars assert that the word Paul used for the trumpet in the expressions "the last trump" (1 Cor. 15:52) and "the trump of God" (1 Th. 4:16) normally refer to the war trumpet. For example, Liddell and Scott claimed that the *salpigx* was "a war trumpet."[15] G. G. Findlay wrote that "The *salpigx* was the war-trumpet, used for signals and commands (cf. *en keleusmati*, 1 Thess. 4:16)."[16] Friedrich stated that in the ancient world the *salpigx* was used mainly in the army to give signals.[17]

Friedrich indicated that in the Greek world the trumpet was used to give several different battle signals to soldiers. For example, "By means of the trumpet signals were given to prepare for battle and to attack."[18] In addition, "The trumpet was also used 'to end the battle . . . to gather the scattered . . . and for the march back to camp.'"[19] Thus, there was a last trumpet with regard to battle.

Friedrich also pointed out that, in addition to the Greeks, the trumpet played an important role in war for the Jews.[20] The book entitled *The War of the Sons of Light with the Sons of Darkness* in the Dead Sea Scrolls indicates that this was so. According to this book, the first trumpet sounded in conjunction with warfare was the trumpet of assembly. It summoned soldiers together to go forth to fight. Other war trumpets included the trumpet of the war-blast sounded over the slain, the trumpet of ambush, and the trumpet of pursuit. The last trumpet sounded was the trumpet of reassembly or return from battle.[21] Examples of such trumpets of reassembly or return are found in 2 Samuel 18:16 and 20:22. Concerning this latter passage, Friedrich wrote that the Israelite army "was dismissed and sent home by the trumpet."[22]

It is important to note that, concerning this last trumpet of war, *The War of the Sons of Light with the Sons of Darkness* declared, "they shall write on the trumpets of return 'The Gathering of God.'"[23] The fact that the Jews designated their last trumpet of warfare "The Gathering of God" is significant in light of Paul's calling "the last trump" of 1 Corinthians 15:52 "the trump of God" in the 1 Thessalonians 4:16-17 Rapture passage.

The Romans also used trumpets to communicate signals in warfare. David L. Woods wrote,

One other common method of tactical military communication is by means of trumpet and horn . . . A common Roman trumpet was the *cornu*—a large curved instrument with a fairly high tone used to pass along the signals of the *tuba*. The Roman *tuba* was a long straight instrument with a fluttering end. Its deep notes were used to signal advances or retreats.[24]

The Roman writer Renatus stated that through trumpet sounds Roman soldiers were signaled "to pursue the enemy or to retire."[25]

In light of what has been observed concerning the military use of trumpets in relationship to battle, it appears that the people of the ancient world consistently had a last battle trumpet. In contrast with the first battle trumpet, which summoned soldiers together to go forth to fight, the last trumpet signaled them to end the battle and reassemble to return to camp or home.

It should be noted that in 1 Corinthians 14:8 Paul used "the metaphor of the military trumpet."[26] There he asserted that "If the trumpet does not give a definite signal the troops will not prepare for battle."[27] This indicates that Paul had the first trumpet of battle in mind when he wrote 1 Corinthians 14. This fact makes it very probable that he was still thinking of a battle trumpet when he referred to "the last trump" in the very next chapter. In line with this, Kingsley Rendell wrote that Paul's reference to the last trump was an allusion to the use of trumpets by the Roman army.[28] Cornelius Stam stated that "The term 'the last trump,' in 1 Cor. 15:52, is a *military expression*, denoting the trumpet which is sounded . . . to call the soldiers home."[29]

This would mean, then, that "the last trump" in 1 Corinthians 15:52 was a reference, not to the absolutely last trumpet of history, but to the kind of trumpet with which the Corinthians and other people of the ancient world would have been very familiar—the last trumpet of a battle. Thus, Harry A. Ironside asserted that the expression "the last trump" in 1 Corinthians 15:52 "was very familiar to the people who lived in Paul's day. It was in common use in connection with the Roman Army."[30]

Through his use of the expression "the last trump" for the trump of God, which will be sounded in conjunction with the bodily resurrection, change, and Rapture of the church saints, Paul indicated that there is some connection between that trump of God and the last trumpet of battle.

Some background sheds light on that connection. The Scriptures teach that while the church exists in the world, it is at war against Satan and his forces. For example, Paul talked about the church saints' war and weapons of war (2 Cor. 10:3-4; 1 Tim. 1:18) and the armor of God that they are to wear during this life because of attacks by Satan and his forces (Rom. 13:12; 2 Cor. 6:7; Eph. 6:10-18; 1 Th. 5:8). Peter talked about the devil, the adversary of the church saints, who seeks to devour them (1 Pet. 5:8-9). Church history records the many battles of the church against the forces of evil and the persecutions and martyrdoms of church saints, thereby verifying the biblical teaching concerning the warfare of the church against Satan and his forces.

In addition, as we noted in an earlier chapter, church saints have their commonwealth or home in heaven and therefore should be waiting eagerly for Christ to come from heaven to take them there (Phil. 3:19-20).

In light of this background, the connection between the trump of God and the last trumpet of battle is as follows: Just as the last trumpet of battle signaled the soldiers to end the battle and reassemble to return to camp or home, so the trump of God will signal the end of the church saints' warfare against Satan and his forces and their assembly with Christ in the air to go with Him to their heavenly home. The trump of God associated with the Rapture of the church will have the same kind of function or purpose as the last trumpet of battle in the ancient world. For this reason, Paul called it "the last trump."

The Fourth Possible Meaning. It is possible that another aspect of the military use of trumpets in the ancient world may be relevant to "the last trump" of 1 Corinthians 15:52. Friedrich said, "Among the Romans the guards were summoned by trumpet to take up their posts at the time of the evening meal."[31] Further, the Roman writer Renatus stated that in the Roman army "The ordinary guards and outposts are always mounted and relieved by the sound of trumpet."[32] Just as there was always a first trumpet to start a guard's watch, so there was always a last trumpet to end a guard's watch.

In conjunction with this military use of trumpets, it is interesting to note that church saints are commanded and exhorted to watch for several things (Acts 20:31; 1 Cor. 16:13; Eph. 6:18; Col. 4:2; 1 Th. 5:6; 2 Tim. 4:5; 1 Pet. 4:7; Rev. 3:2). Some of these commands or exhortations are found in contexts containing military terminology. In light of the fact that Paul delivered most of these commands or exhortations, it may be that he had an analogy in mind when he wrote 1 Corinthians 15:52: Just as there was a last trumpet to signal the end of a Roman guard's watch, so the trump of God will signal the end of the church saints' watch in the world. The trump of God associated with the Rapture of the church will have the same kind of function or purpose as the last trumpet of a Roman guard's watch. For this reason, Paul called it "the last trump."

It could very well be that Paul had a combination of both military uses of a last trumpet (the third and fourth possible meanings presented in this chapter) in mind when he called the trump of God associated with the Rapture "the last trump."

CONCLUSION

In light of what has been observed in this chapter, we can conclude that Paul's reference to "the last trump" in 1 Corinthians 15:52 does not require the view that the trump of God associated with the Rapture of the church will be the absolutely final trumpet of history, after which no other trumpets will be sounded. Several other views, which refer to uses of trumpets familiar to the Corinthians and which fit the context of Paul's 1 Corinthians 15:52 statement, are both possible and plausible. As a result, Paul's reference to "the last trump" does not require rejection of the Pretribulation Rapture of the church.

ENDNOTES

1. *Mishnagoth*, Succah 4:9, Vol. II, *Order Moed* (London: Mishna Press Ltd., 1952), p. 339.

2. J. R. Caldwell, *The Charter of the Church*, Vol. 2 (London: Pickering & Inglis, n.d.), pp. 256-57.

3. Heinrich August Wilhelm Meyer, *Critical and Exegetical Hand-Book to the Epistles to the Corinthians*, trans. by Douglas Bannerman (New York: Funk & Wagnalls Company, 1884), p. 387.

4. Henry Alford, *The First Epistle to the Corinthians* in *Alford's Greek Testament*, Vol. II (Chicago: Moody Press, 1958), p. 620.

5. Gerhard Friedrich, "salpigx," *Theological Dictionary of the New Testament*, Vol. VII, ed. by Gerhard Friedrich, trans. and ed. by Geoffrey W. Bromiley (Grand Rapids: Wm. B. Eerdmans Publishing Company, 1971), p. 80.

6. Sir Ian Richmond, *Trajan's Army on Trajan's Column* (London: The British School at Rome, 1982), pp. 12-13.

7. Friedrich, *Theological Dictionary of the New Testament*, Vol. VII, pp. 74, 78, 80.

8. Caldwell, *The Charter of the Church*, Vol. 2, pp. 256-57.

9. Arnold G. Fruchtenbaum, "A Review of *The Pre-Wrath Rapture of the Church*" (Tustin, CA: Ariel Ministries), p. 58.

10. *Ibid.*

11. *Ibid.*

12. *Ibid.*

13. *Ibid.*

14. *Ibid.*, pp. 58-59.

15. Liddel and Scott, *An Intermediate Greek-English Lexicon* (Oxford: The Clarendon Press, 1900), p. 723.

16. G. G. Findlay, *The First Epistle of Paul to the Corinthians* in *The Expositor's Greek Testament*, Vol. II (Grand Rapids: Wm. B. Eerdmans Publishing Company, n.d.), p. 941.

17. Friedrich, *Theological Dictionary of the New Testament*, Vol. VII, p. 73.

18. *Ibid.*, p. 74.

19. *Ibid.*

20. *Ibid.*, p. 78.

21. Millar Burrows, "Selections from The War of the Sons of Light with the Sons of Darkness" in *The Dead Sea Scrolls* in *Burrows on the Dead Sea Scrolls* (Grand Rapids: Baker Book House, 1978), p. 392.

22. Friedrich, *Theological Dictionary of the New Testament*, Vol. VII, p. 79.

23. Burrows, *Burrows on the Dead Sea Scrolls*, p. 392.

24. David L. Woods, *A History of Tactical Communication Techniques* (Orlando, FL: Martin Company, Martin-Marietta Corporation, 1965), p. 2.

25. Flavius Vegetius Renatus, *The Military Institutions of the Romans*, ed. by Brig.-Gen. Thomas R. Phillips, trans. by Lieutenant John Clark (Harrisburg, PA: Stackpole Books, 1960), p. 56.

26. Friedrich, *Theological Dictionary of the New Testament*, Vol. VII, p. 85.

27. *Ibid.*

28. Kingsley G. Rendell, *Expository Outlines from 1 and 2 Corinthians* (Grand Rapids: Baker Book House, 1970), p. 70.

29. Cornelius R. Stam, *Commentary on the First Epistle of Paul to the Corinthians* (Chicago: Berean Bible Society, 1988), p. 273.

30. H. A. Ironside, *Addresses on the First Epistle to the Corinthians* (New York: Loizeaux Brothers, 1955), p. 529.

31. Friedrich, *Theological Dictionary of the New Testament*, Vol. VII, p. 74.

32. Renatus, *The Military Institutions of the Romans*, p. 56.

INDEX OF SUBJECTS AND AUTHORS

INDEX OF SCRIPTURE REFERENCES